GREED & GRIEVANCE

 *A project of the International Peace Academy*

GREED & GRIEVANCE

Economic Agendas in Civil Wars

EDITED BY

Mats Berdal
David M. Malone

LYNNE RIENNER PUBLISHERS

BOULDER & LONDON

INTERNATIONAL DEVELOPMENT RESEARCH CENTRE

OTTAWA • CAIRO • DAKAR • JOHANNESBURG • MONTEVIDEO • NAIROBI • NEW DELHI • SINGAPORE

Published in the United States of America in 2000 by
Lynne Rienner Publishers, Inc.
1800 30th Street, Boulder, Colorado 80301
www.rienner.com

and in the United Kingdom by
Lynne Rienner Publishers, Inc.
3 Henrietta Street, Covent Garden, London WC2E 8LU

Paperback edition published in Canada by the
International Development Research Centre
PO Box 8500, Ottawa, Ontario, KIG 3H9 Canada
www.idrc.ca/booktique

Library of Congress Cataloging-in-Publication Data
Greed and grievance : economic agendas in civil wars / edited by
  Mats Berdal and David M. Malone.
    p. cm.
  Includes bibliographical references and index.
  ISBN 1-55587-892-X (hardcover : alk. paper)
  ISBN 1-55587-868-7 (pbk. : alk. paper)
    1. Civil war—Economic aspects. 2. War—Economic aspects.
3. Profiteering. I. Berdal, Mats R., 1965–   II. Malone, David M.
HB195.G72   2000
330.9—dc21   99-086829

Canadian Cataloguing in Publication Data
Berdal, Mats
Greed and grievance : economic agendas in civil wars
  Includes bibliographical references and an index.
  ISBN 0-88936-915-1
    1. Civil war—Economic aspects. 2. War—Economic aspects.
3. Political violence—Economic aspects. 4. Social conflicts—
Economic aspects. I. Malone, David, 1954– . II. International Development
Research Centre (Canada). III. Title. IV. Title: Economic agendas in civil wars.
HC79.D4B47   2000   303.6'4   C00-980099-9

British Cataloguing in Publication Data
A Cataloguing in Publication record for this book
is available from the British Library.

Printed and bound in the United States of America

     The paper used in this publication meets the requirements
  ∞ of the American National Standard for Permanence of
     Paper for Printed Library Materials Z39.48-1984.

  5 4 3 2 1

Contents

Acknowledgments

This volume had its genesis in the conference "Economic Agendas in Civil Wars" held in Canada House, London, in April 1999. We would like to express our deep appreciation to the cosponsors of the conference: the Department of Foreign Affairs and International Trade of Canada, the Foreign and Commonwealth Office and the Department for International Development of the United Kingdom, the International Bank for Reconstruction and Development, the Centre for International Studies at Oxford University, and the International Peace Academy. The Ford Foundation and the governments of Sweden and Norway generously funded Oxford's significant contribution to the success of the conference. We would also like to extend our thanks to Michael Small for his successful efforts to coordinate the sponsorship for this event and his contribution to shaping the agenda, and to Ben Rowswell for his dedication to making the logistics a success.

We are deeply grateful to the International Development Research Centre for its financial support for the dissemination of this volume. We would also like to acknowledge the excellence, professionalism, and enthusiasm of our authors. It has been a most agreeable and enriching education for us to work with them in shaping the chapters that follow. Lucy Mair and Charlie Cater provided superb research and editorial assistance at the International Peace Academy. To them, warmest thanks. We are also grateful to our publisher, Lynne Rienner, and to her dedicated, efficient, and friendly team.

The Editors

1

Introduction

Mats Berdal and David M. Malone

The presence of economic motives and commercial agendas in wars is not so much a new phenomenon as a familiar theme in the history of warfare. In the war-ravaged and politically fragmented German lands of the Thirty Years War, war itself became a vast "private and profit-making enterprise," with Wallenstein's imperial army at one point "the greatest business enterprise of the age."[1] In a later and apparently more heroic age, many of Napoleon's more celebrated marshals—Massena, Soult, and Brune—displayed as much skill in the art of private plundering and the accumulation of personal wealth as they did in the art of war. In much more recent times, as contributors to this volume show, the licensing of economically motivated violence in such places as Sierra Leone and Liberia has resembled, in terms of its *functional* utility, both medieval and early modern patterns of warfare. To historians and social scientists, the importance of economic factors to the understanding of any particular conflict will always be a source of dispute. Yet, the need to incorporate, at some level and in some form, the "economic dimension" in order to better understand the causes and the persistence of conflict is uncontroversial.

In spite of this, in the recent literature on conflict and, even more so, in the practice of international and nongovernmental organizations, comparatively little *systematic* attention has been given to the precise role of economically motivated actions and processes in generating and sustaining contemporary civil conflicts. This volume is intended to improve our understanding in

1

this area. Specifically, it explores how economic considerations often shape the calculations and behavior of the parties to a conflict, giving rise to a particular *war economy* and a distinctive dynamic of conflict. As several of the contributors note, the nature of these war economies challenge many of the core assumptions that have informed thinking and guided policy with respect to civil wars and internal conflict in the 1990s. Indeed, in some of the cases examined, what is usually considered to be the most basic of military objectives in war—that is, defeating the enemy in battle—has been replaced by economically driven interests in continued fighting and the institutionalization of violence at what is for some clearly a profitable level of intensity. The extent to which the economic agendas of belligerents actually shape the course of a conflict undoubtedly varies from case to case. Yet, even where military and political objectives appear to provide the obvious rationale for fighting, conflicts are still likely to be influenced by economic motives and opportunities, especially at the local level. Moreover, as David Keen notes in Chapter 2, the experiences of the 1990s show that civil wars are not static but have often "mutated into wars where immediate agendas assume an increasingly important role." These agendas, in turn, may "significantly prolong civil wars: Not only do they constitute a vested interest in continued conflict, they also tend to create widespread destitution, which itself may feed into economically motivated violence."

It is this complex web of motives and interactions that allows us to speak of the *political economy* of civil wars. In one sense, of course, to speak of "civil wars" is misleading since, as Charles King has noted elsewhere, such wars are never entirely *internal* in character.[2] Indeed, a recurring theme in this book is that the persistence of conflict and, in particular, the crystallization of war economies within "weak" states can only be understood within a broader global context. A narrow state-centric approach to assessing these conflicts is, therefore, both of limited analytical value and policy relevance. Yet, the notion of "civil war," though imprecise in certain respects, remains justified in the sense that the wars considered here do differ sharply from "classic" interstate conflict, do take place predominantly within "weak" states, and do all impact very directly on the civilian population and society at large.

Although this volume does not aim to provide any kind of consensus on the variety of issues and cases it covers (let alone add up to a claim that contemporary civil wars can all be reduced to "economic" explanations), contributors and participants at the London conference agreed upon the importance of the subject. In particular, they focused on the need to address critically the three overall aims of the conference:

- to improve our understanding of the political economy of civil wars through a focused analysis of the economic agendas of competing factions in civil wars.
- to examine how "globalization" creates new opportunities for the elites of competing factions to pursue their economic agendas through trade, investment, and migration ties, both legal and illegal, to neighboring states and to more distant, industrialized economies.
- to examine the possible policy responses available to external actors, including governments, international organizations, nongovernmental organizations (NGOs), and private sector firms, to shift the economic agendas of elites in civil wars from war toward peace.

These aims also provide the background to these chapters, and each of them therefore merits some further comment.

Economic Agendas and the Study of Civil Wars

Much of the writing and policy debate relating to civil wars in the 1990s has tended, not unreasonably, to emphasize the *costs* of conflict. The staggering number of deaths and the widespread destruction associated with these wars have naturally reinforced a tendency to view them as an unmitigated calamity for all concerned. In this view, the outbreak of war and its persistence represent the breakdown of "normal" or "peacetime" patterns of social, economic, and political intercourse within society. It is a view that rests on a conception of "peace" and "war" as separate and distinct categories, a dichotomy that has a long tradition in Western thinking about war.

This dichotomy is also implicit in what Mark Duffield identifies in Chapter 4 as three of the more influential, partly competing approaches to the study of the causes and persistence of civil wars in the 1990s. The first of these, often found in reports by NGOs and UN agencies, tends to view conflict and wars as a temporary "interruption" to an ongoing process of development; conflict is seen as a form of "developmental malaise." A second approach, associated primarily with peace and conflict studies, has emphasized the role played by misperceptions and failures of "communications" in explaining the incidence and persistence of civil conflict. The third approach, which has received the greatest amount of popular attention (as well as most of the academic criticism), has focused on the supposed reemergence, in heightened and more virulent forms, of "ancient hatreds" and long-suppressed animosities. In all these cases, the resort to violence and the initiation of war are seen as signaling the collapse of a process or a particular order and are, for this very reason, both "irrational" and dysfunctional.

As the empirical evidence presented in this book shows, however, to view civil wars as no more than costly disruptions from "normal peacetime" conditions conceals the degree to which organized violence, especially within politically fragmented and economically weak states, may also serve a range of different purposes. The fact is that much of the violence with which bodies such as the UN have been concerned in the post–Cold War era has been driven not by a Clausewitzian logic of forwarding a set of political aims, but rather by powerful economic motives and agendas. Indeed, important and stimulating statistical investigations by Paul Collier, which are presented in Chapter 5 and cover much of the Cold War period, suggest that economic agendas are "central to understanding why civil wars get going" and shed considerable light on factors predisposing countries to internal conflicts. In some cases, as William Reno argues in Chapter 3 with reference to the ongoing conflict in Central Africa, warfare is better understood as "an instrument of enterprise and violence as a mode of accumulation." In such circumstances, the continuation of war represents not so much the collapse of one system as the emergence of a new one; one that benefits certain groups—government officials, traders, combatants, and international actors who stand to gain from dealing with local actors—while further impoverishing other sections of the community. Evidence of this can be found in a number of the wars that have raged in the 1990s, and some of the more striking examples of the "benefits of war" have, by now, become fairly well documented. Others are explored and documented more fully in this volume.

In Liberia, Charles Taylor is estimated to have made more than U.S.$400 million per year from the war in the years between 1992 and 1996. In Chapter 7, Musifiky Mwanasali points out how the ongoing war in the Democratic Republic of the Congo (DRC) has enabled neighboring countries such as Rwanda and Uganda to become major exporters of raw materials, including gold or cobalt, which they do not naturally possess. He notes how "timber, palm oil, coffee, elephant tusks, and precious minerals," which have been looted from the former Zaire and exported through the black market, "have now become a main source of foreign exchange for Zaire's resource-deprived neighbors." In Angola, the National Union for the Total Independence of Angola (UNITA) has since 1992 controlled some 70 percent of the country's diamond production, which has allowed it to continue the war while creating the conditions for local traders, middlemen, and regional commanders to accumulate considerable fortunes. On the government side, the Popular Movement for the Liberation of Angola (MPLA) "business elite" has also benefited from Angola's war economy by selectively granting attractive foreign exchange and import licenses, as well as by the selling of weapons to UNITA (see Chapter 8). This kind of collusion between supposedly opposing parties is certainly not unique to the case of Angola. Between 1993 and 1997, many Khmer Rouge commanders, Cambodian government officials, and Thai army officers were more concerned about enriching themselves through illegal logging activity and trading in gems than they were about bringing war to an end. Stephen Ellis, in his carefully researched study of the Liberian civil war between 1989 and mid-1997, observes that "as far as possible, factions avoided fighting other armed groups," and that "simulated attacks, designed solely to facilitate looting, were a common tactic, particularly in front line areas where tensions ran high."[3] Likewise, during the brutal war in Bosnia between 1992 and 1995, unlikely alliances emerged on the ground that were not exclusively motivated by the desire to defeat the main enemy. At certain critical moments during the war in Bosnia, the war effort of the Bosnian Serb Army was heavily dependent on the supply of fuel from Croat forces. The willingness to provide this fuel, a practice that continued after the signing of the Federation agreement between Bosnian Muslims and Bosnian Croats in early 1994, not only served to prolong the war but also offered rich earnings for "petrol barons" and various middlemen throughout the war zone.[4] In many of these cases, the benefits of war are closely linked to the presence of and access to natural resources in the area of conflict. The precise relationship between mineral wealth and conflict is explored more fully in this volume by Indra de Soysa (Chapter 6), who using quantitative analysis argues that "an abundance of mineral wealth is positively and significantly related to armed conflict."

In addition to the economic opportunities generated by war itself, the growing involvement of international agencies in efforts to contain and alleviate the worst effects of civil conflict has created another set of economic opportunities for local actors. As David Shearer shows in Chapter 10, relief aid made available during conflicts in order to mitigate the humanitarian consequences of fighting has often been diverted, stolen, and taxed by warring parties (Shearer is careful, however, to add that the degree to which aid has actually prolonged conflict and fueled further violence is probably exaggerated.)

The wider point here should be obvious: Understanding the sources of violence requires an understanding of "the economics underpinning it." As David Keen has noted elsewhere:

> Conflict can create war economies, often in the regions controlled by rebels or warlords and linked to international trading networks; members of armed gangs can benefit from looting; and regimes can use violence to deflect opposition, reward supporters or maintain their access to resources. Under these circumstances, ending civil wars becomes difficult. Winning may not be desirable: the point of war may be precisely the legitimacy which it confers on actions that in peacetime would be punishable as crimes.[5]

"Globalization" and Modern War Economies

It was argued at the outset that the attempt to benefit materially from war, through looting or other forms of violent accumulation, is hardly a new phenomenon. Some scholars, also rejecting any claim to novelty, have suggested that many civil wars are best understood as the inescapable phase of ongoing processes of "state building." In this view, similar processes have long since been completed in places such as Western Europe but were delayed, partly by the effects of the Cold War, in much of the developing world. In the words of Mohammed Ayoob, "state making and what we now call 'internal war' are two sides of the same coin."[6] The extent to which there is, in fact, anything fundamentally new about the kinds of war economies described above is another central theme of this book. It is a theme discussed under the rather ill-defined, overused notion of "globalization."

The term *globalization* is notoriously imprecise and as such it is undoubtedly, as Jean Marie Guehenno suggests, a "symptom of the conceptual uncertainties of our time."[7] Yet, as Andrew Hurrell has also noted, the term "has become a very powerful *metaphor* for the sense that a number of universal processes are at work generating increased interconnection and interdependence between states and between societies."[8] Arguably the most influential, essentially liberal, and largely optimistic view of globalization has tended to stress the "integrating and homogenising influence of market forces" and the conflict-mitigating potential inherent in the "increased flows of values, knowledge and ideas" across borders.[9] In the long run, it is argued, the cumulative impact of these processes will be to weaken exclusive loyalties and to hasten the emergence of a "world society."

In the present book, globalization refers primarily to the transformations taking place within the international economic and financial system. In this more limited sense, globalization refers to the increasing ease with which capital and services now flow within the world economy, a process initially encouraged by financial deregulation and now continuously stimulated by rapid technological change. This in turn has aided other related forms of economic globalization, notably the "internationalization of production" as reflected in the growth of foreign direct investment and the increasingly important role for transnational corporations in the world economy. In this more restricted view of globalization, some of the evidence presented in the book points to a more complex relationship between globalizing trends in the world economy and violent conflicts in areas and within states at the margin of that economy. The findings would, at the very least, qualify the more optimistic readings of the effects of globalization alluded to above and that have been influential in much of the Western thinking about international affairs after the Cold War.

William Reno, building on his earlier and important work on African conflicts, argues in Chapter 3 that "internal warfare in some very weak states represents neither dissolution of political order itself nor the initiation of state building projects with parallels to the process as it occurred in early modern Europe." He instead seeks to explain internal warfare in terms of "economic motivations that are specifically related to the intensification of transnational commerce in recent decades and to the political economy of violence inside a particular category of states." Other contributors also emphasize that modern war economies are "rarely self-sufficient or autarkic" and that though warring parties and political actors may control local assets, they remain heavily dependent on external support and supplies. In particular, as Mark Duffield writes in Chapter 4, the "marketing of local resources and procurement of arms and supplies" rely on relatively easy access to global networks and markets. To the extent that such access has become easier it has also increased the prospects for local elites to benefit economically from continued violence and conflict. This in turn has adversely affected the balance of incentives in favor of peace and provides part of the explanation for the seemingly intractable nature of many contemporary conflicts. In short, it is the highly "transnational and networked characteristics" of modern war economies that allows us to talk of a fundamentally new context in which to study and approach civil wars.

Support for this argument can be found in several of the specific cases referred to above: Members of the Cambodian government, Khmer Rouge, and the Thai military encountered few difficulties exporting gems and high-grade tropical timber, and in Sierra Leone the sale of diamonds and gold on the world market has kept the war going and generated wealth for officials, commanders, and various international companies and businesses. In Liberia, as Ellis has shown, from the "beginning to the end of the war, each Liberian warlord of any substance had alliances with foreign businessmen and at least one foreign government."[10] Virginia Gamba and Richard Cornwell in Chapter 8 provide perhaps the most detailed example of the sinister linkages between the war economy inside one country, Angola, and the global economy. In particular, they show how

UNITA, once heavily reliant on Cold War patronage, has been able not only to survive but to become a more resilient and formidable military force through its diamond trade (now apparently channeled through South Africa, Belgium, and Israel) as well as by building up a "substantial investment portfolio abroad to supplement" revenues from diamond trading.

Policy Implications for Governments and International Organizations

The insights gained into the economics underpinning contemporary civil wars are clearly of more than academic interest. There is now much evidence to suggest that the failure to account for the presence of economic agendas in conflicts has, at times, seriously undermined international efforts to consolidate fragile peace agreements. In particular, the tendency among donors and within international organizations to treat "conflict" and "postconflict" as separate categories and distinct phases in a quest for "lasting peace" has carried with it the expectation (and planning assumption) that the formal end of armed hostilities also marks a definitive break with past patterns of violence. In fact, and as this book amply confirms, even in the best of circumstances this is rarely the case. Grievances and conflicts of interest usually persist after the end of hostilities and, in turn, affect the "peace building" activities initiated and sponsored by international organizations, NGOs, and donor countries. As an earlier study into the impact of economic agendas on some of these activities suggested, "Transitions from war to peace . . . are more usefully seen as involving a realignment of political interests and a readjustment of economic strategies rather than a clean break from violence to consent, from theft to production, or from repression to democracy."[11]

It would, of course, be deeply misleading to suggest that all of those concerned with making and implementing policy in this area have been entirely unaware of the economic dimensions of the conflicts with which they have been dealing. Yet, there is a deeper problem faced by policymakers and intergovernmental bodies attempting to address civil wars, and it is one that is brought into stark relief when the focus of inquiry is shifted to the kind of economically motivated *substate* violence examined in this book. The problem arises out of the state-centric framework within which donor countries and international organizations, especially the UN and its agencies, necessarily operate. This framework has clearly not prevented donors and organizations from engaging in civil war–type situations, but it has placed constraints both on the manner of their involvement and the official debate about the nature and challenges of operating in such complex environments. At the London conference where the contributions to this volume were first presented, participants from the policymaking community stressed the difficulty of addressing phenomena such as "shadow states," warlordism, and substate violence within existing institutional and policy frameworks. The limitations of the state-centric framework that such observations reflect should not tempt us to embrace glib and empirically unsustainable assertions about the "withering away of the state" and "end of sovereignty." Yet, as indicated above, a narrow state-centric approach—one that focuses on *formal* state structures alone, ignores the realities of "factual sovereignty," and underestimates the degree to which transnational and other processes have in many places eroded the substantive content of statehood—is certain to provide a very incomplete picture of the dynamics that sustain civil wars.

There is a further reason, however, why the kinds of issues examined in this book have been difficult to address within existing institutional settings, and it is particularly evident in the case of the UN and its agencies. The fact is that a number of countries, especially those in the developing world, continue to view with suspicion "Western" debates about the need to "move beyond sovereignty." To many countries, notably India and China, there is still a very real tension between the activism of the UN with regard to internal conflicts in the 1990s and the cardinal principle of international society: the sovereign equality of states and its corollary that there is a duty of nonintervention by states in the internal affairs of other states.[12]

It is against this background that the real value of the research findings collected and presented in this book should be seen. A better understanding of the political economy of civil wars, the subject of Part 1, is contained within the wider challenge of how best to ensure that the international community can effectively assist transitions from protracted conflict to more durable peace. How the international community goes about providing that assistance—how it deals with the challenge of criminal and economically motivated violence in civil wars—is examined in Part 2. In addition to evaluating the role of policy instruments such as financial sanctions and international legal instruments (as done by Samuel Porteous and Tom Farer, respectively), the section considers some of the dilemmas faced by those charged with implementing aid policy in civil-war settings (examined by David Shearer).

Though the range of issues covered is wide, this book should properly be seen as introducing a subject that deserves further attention from both academic analysts and policymakers. As such, the book and the London conference have provided some useful directions for future research.

The Future Research Agenda

Several dogs either did not bark or merely whimpered at the London conference, in spite of strenuous efforts by those designing the meeting to stimulate discussion on the broadest possible range of topics in the general subject area.

Although the role of the private sector in shaping and furthering economic agendas in civil wars was widely accepted as key, only local trading networks were addressed in any depth. The interaction between shadow states and international corporations was discussed, but little light was shed on the motivations and strategies of these companies. Nevertheless, in seeking to come to grips with means for international actors to influence belligerents, the corporate factor looms large in the equation. Preexisting and entirely legitimate operations of international companies are often engulfed by civil war, forcing on them strategies of survival they do not necessarily welcome. Both the risks and the opportunities they face on the fluid terrain of civil wars for them doubtless shape their strategies. These strategies and their relative weight within overall corporate life need to be better understood.

Parallel to the legitimate and well-established international private sector exist criminal networks ideally placed to interact with belligerents in civil wars. Narcotics trafficking is but the most obvious source of rapid personal enrichment and of funding for weapons, munitions, and other supplies to keep war efforts running. However, the relationship between belligerents and large international crime networks is not well enough understood for points of vulnerability to be readily identified and exploited by international actors seeking to cut off such commerce.

Belligerents in civil wars have long been reputed to stash abroad large sums of money skimmed from their war chests. The fruits of wider corruption have notoriously enriched many national leaders and their immediate supporters. Not only have international actors (the international financial institutions [IFIs], commercial banks often benefiting handsomely from the corresponding deposits, and donor governments) done little to counteract this syndrome, they have never been consistent, coddling favored tyrants while criticizing others, and have not, to date, favored a systemic attack on this scourge. Nevertheless, a regime (either established by treaty or under administrative arrangements agreed on at a high level) designed systematically to combat this noxious form of white-collar crime is urgently needed. With the Statute of an International Criminal Court agreed on in Rome in 1998, should parallel arrangements be far behind to address the financial rape and ruination of whole countries, often those at war?

Finally, the conference fell short on one of its stated goals— to identify incentives and disincentives that could help turn parties to (and potential belligerents in) civil strife from war to peace. Some of the incentives required relate to the gaps identified immediately above. However, attention is required more broadly on the policy tools for international actors in this area.

The research community is beginning to turn its attention more systematically to this subject area, and several recent volumes have explored aspects of it.[13] The discussions at London suggested several clusters of issues for further policy-relevant research not yet fully addressed by others:

- The *role of the international private sector,* particularly that of extractive industries (petroleum, mining), is key. Whereas leading firms have mostly adopted a studiously "neutral" stance on civil strife, disclaiming any political agenda at all, their actions on the ground and in global markets inevitably tend to favor some parties over others. The situation of Shell Oil Company in southeastern Nigeria and De Beers vis-à-vis Angola makes this clear. For research on this topic to make headway, it would be necessary to engage meaningfully with a range of international firms, inter alia in the extractive and service (e.g., banking) fields, to establish how they view their own roles in civil war situations and what factors might influence them to support actively the settlement of civil wars. This would be a delicate undertaking and would probably require more discretion and off-the-record exchange than would normally be desirable in research activities.

- The absence of an *international legal regime to deal with "white collar crime"* taking advantage of the disruptions created by civil unrest and strife can be construed as a strong incentive for parasitic elite economic agendas. A major issue raised during the London conference was the need to distinguish between money sheltered internationally for tax reasons and caches of money secluded from detection because of its reprehensible origins. The recent relaxation of bank secrecy in Switzerland and a greater disposition there (and in some other financial centers) to freeze such accounts obscure the issue of whether governments in the industrialized world are prepared to take a lead on stigmatizing and sequestering ill-gotten gains not narrowly tied to the narcotics trade and other abhorrent forms of trafficking by leaders and their followers in conflict situations. The negotiation of an international agreement on the subject seems far off but need not be viewed as utopian. (Talk of an international criminal court seemed utopian only a very few years ago.)
- Though economic activities at the local level that are illegal under international agreements and domestic law will inevitably occur in the struggle for survival that attends most civil wars (and may not warrant much international concern), funding for war efforts based on *large-scale criminal activity* deserves further attention. For example, the activities of Arkan and other Balkan warlords are widely reported to have been largely directed toward (and otherwise funded by) drug trafficking. The

impact of such predatory warlords on civil wars is so over-whelmingly negative that the international community should better equip itself to combat their fund-raising activities. Building on existing norms and agreements, such efforts should focus on practical measures to combat large-scale and high-level criminality of this type.

- *Incentives and disincentives* for peace available to international actors attempting to influence economic agendas in civil wars fall into several categories: the coercive (e.g., UN Security Council–mandated sanctions, intergovernmental agreements on money-laundering, etc.); the exemplary (often focusing on basic human needs of civilian populations, such as food and health, e.g., corridors of peace negotiated for specific purposes); the financial (multilateral and bilateral assistance and potential funding from certain key private-sector actors); and the rhetorical. Little comprehensive work has been done to catalogue and assess what these measures are and how effective they have proved in the past. In particular, are efforts aimed at addressing basic human needs in countries afflicted by civil strife effective in shaming or inspiring leaders to better care for those dependent on them, or do they merely in practice serve to absolve them from their responsibilities to local populations? Here, regional differences may be significant.

Several of the authors of ensuing chapters have argued, directly or indirectly, that in a world awash with weapons—many of them produced in countries with few other viable exports—the best means of choking off arms supplies to belligerents is to turn off the financial spigot. This volume illustrates how difficult this will be. Policy instruments could certainly be crafted to do so, but this prospect seems still distant, because knowledge is as yet scant, the motivations of key international actors conflict, the governments of major powers have often displayed a mercantilist bent even where conflict threatens or rages, and, there is understandable although excessive reluctance by leading governments to focus on the role of multinational companies in the drama.[14] Further research may encourage governments and others to act sooner rather than later. We hope that this volume may represent a modest step in this direction.

Notes

1. M. S. Anderson, *War and Society in Europe of the Old Regime, 1618–1789* (London: Fontana Press, 1988), 48.

2. Charles King, "Ending Civil Wars," *Adelphi Paper* 308 (Oxford: Oxford University Press for the International Institute for Strategic Studies, 1997).

3. Stephen Ellis, *The Mask of Anarchy* (London: Hurst and Company, 1999), 145.

4. Tim Judah, *The Serbs: History, Myth, and the Destruction of Yugoslavia,* pp. 247–255 (New Haven: Yale University Press, 1997).

5. David Keen, "The Economic Functions of Violence in Civil Wars," *Adelphi Paper* 320 (Oxford: Oxford University Press for the International Institute for Strategic Studies, 1998).

6. Mohammed Ayoob, "Subaltern Realism: International Relations Theory Meets the Third World," in Stephanie Neuman (ed.), *International Relations Theory and the Third World* (New York: St. Martin's Press, 1998), 42.

7. Jean-Marie Guehenno, "Globalisation and Its Impact on International Strategy," paper presented at the Fortieth IISS Annual Conference, Oxford, September 1998, 1.

8. Andrew Hurrell, "Explaining the Resurgence of Regionalism in World Politics," *Review of International Studies,* 21, no. 4 (1995): 345. For a sophisticated discussion of the liberal view of globalization see also Andrew Hurrell and Ngaire Woods, "Globalisation and Inequality," *Millennium: Journal of International Studies,* 24, no. 3 (1995): 447–470.

9. Hurrell, "Explaining the Resurgence of Regionalism," 345.

10. Stephen Ellis, *The Mask of Anarchy,* 164.

11. For an attempt to substantiate this assertion with respect to two particular areas of external support—the disarmament, demobilization, and reintegration of combatants after conflict, and the restructuring of the "security sector," see Mats Berdal and David Keen, "Violence and Economic Agendas in Civil Wars: Some Policy Implications," *Millennium: Journal of International Studies,* 26, no. 3 (1997).

12. The debate sparked at the UN following Kofi Annan's advocacy, in a September 1999 speech to the General Assembly of greater international willingness to intervene in support of humanitarian goals, demonstrates how lively and serious the issue remains.

13. For example, see Jackie Cilliers and Peggy Mason (eds.), *Peace, Profit or Plunder: The Privatisation of Security in War-Torn African Societies* (Johannesburg: Institute for Security Studies, 1999); and R. T. Naylor, *Patriots & Profiteers: On Economic Warfare, Embargo Busting and State-Sponsored Crime* (Toronto: McClelland & Stewart, 1999).

14. Recent action by Canada somewhat breaks the mold. Its permanent representative to the UN, Robert Fowler, who chairs the UN Security Council's Angola sanctions committee, in May 1999 traveled to Africa and other venues relevant to the diamond trade in order to engage with those active in this trade and encourage better compliance with the sanctions regime against UNITA. Academic and NGO research played a significant role in influencing Canadian thinking on sanctions. On Angola, a cautious but damning study, *A Rough Trade: The Role of Companies and Governments in the Angola Conflict,* produced by Global Witness (a London-based NGO) in 1999, was particularly useful.

PART ONE

Approaches to the Political Economy of Civil Wars

2

Incentives and Disincentives for Violence

David Keen

Those who wish to facilitate peace will be well advised to understand the nature of war. Yet the label *war* is one that often conceals as much as it reveals. We think we know what a war is, but this in itself is a source of difficulty: Throwing a label at the problem of conflict may further obscure its origins and functions; and the label, moreover, may be very useful for those who wish to promote certain kinds of violence. The idea of war can confer a kind of legitimacy upon certain types of violence, given the widespread belief that certain kinds of war are just and legitimate. This chapter attempts to throw some light on the nature of contemporary warfare by looking closely at some of its functions—notably, the economic functions, which are often partially obscured. The chapter challenges two common notions: that war is a contest between two sides, with each trying to win; and that war represents only a *breakdown* or *collapse* rather than the creation of an alternative system of profit, power, and protection. A number of economic functions of warfare are outlined, and attention is given to the *interaction* of political and economic agendas.

Conflict as "Breakdown"

Partly in reaction to the perceived inappropriateness of the traditional model of warfare as a contest between two disciplined teams, analysts in recent years have often portrayed war as a kind of *breakdown*. Conflicts have frequently been explained as the result of intractable ethnic hatreds or a descent into tribal violence and anarchy. In some ways, this view of conflict as breakdown has been reinforced by a media/NGO discourse that stresses the economic, physical, and human destruction wrought by war.

Although the demise of the Cold War has apparently facilitated progress toward peace in some areas like Central America, it has not significantly stemmed the tide of civil conflicts across the world. Some conflicts have been born precisely from the demise of Communist regimes in Yugoslavia and the Soviet Union. Others—such as those in Angola, Burma, and Sudan— have simply refused to go away. Even the apparent "success stories" of conflict resolution—such as El Salvador, Mozambique, and most especially Cambodia—have shown signs that they may yet be mired in intractable conflicts.

In these circumstances, one of the most urgent tasks is to gain a better understanding of the internal dynamics that appear to be generating and sustaining a range of contemporary civil conflicts. Such an understanding will be necessary for anyone thinking of "policy prescriptions" that might facilitate a lasting peace: A good doctor will need to get some idea of the nature of the disease before rushing to the medicine cabinet to pull out a remedy.

Discussion of internal dynamics tended to be minimal and unsophisticated during the Cold War, and unfortunately it has often remained so in the post–Cold War era. Many analysts have stressed the irrationality and unpredictability of contemporary civil warfare, portraying it as evil, medieval, or both. Contemporary civil conflicts often give the appearance of mindless and senseless violence, with a proliferation of militias, chains of command breaking down, and repeated brutal attacks on civilians.

In 1994, Robert Kaplan famously claimed to have detected a "coming anarchy" in West Africa and beyond, a descent into mindless violence propelled by a kind of "witches' brew" of overpopulation, tribalism, drugs, and environmental decline. Kaplan is only one of a number of analysts who have pointed to an apparent resurgence in "tribalism." A common argument has been that a variety of Cold War regimes kept the lid on long-standing tribal, ethnic, and national rivalries, and that these "ancient enmities" have now resurfaced in the absence of strong regimes. This was a major theme in Kaplan's *Balkan Ghosts,* sometimes seen as influential in persuading the Clinton administration that little could be done to resolve hostilities in the former Yugoslavia. The need to ensure peace between competing "tribes" or ethnic groups has also been an enduring theme in British policy—in both the colonial and postcolonial eras.

Another strand of the literature on contemporary civil wars, which we might call the "development" literature, emphasizes the negative consequences (especially economic) of war. Not unnaturally, war is portrayed as disrupting the economy, an interruption in a process of development that is seen as largely benevolent. From those adhering to this apparently common-sense perspective (including many UN agencies and NGOs), it is common to hear appeals for a speedy transition from wartime "relief" back to "development," a transition that is sometimes urged even while conflict is still raging. In the aftermath of a conflict, homage is habitually paid to a set of goals that appears to be self-evidently desirable. Significantly, these usually begin with the prefix "re": for example, rehabilitation, reconstruction, repatriation, and resettlement.

Such interpretations should not be too readily dismissed. The economic devastation wrought by wars is all too evident and has been well documented. The importance of ethnic tensions is also clear in many countries.

However, the emphasis on war as irrational anarchy or as a dramatic setback to development tends to give a dangerous and in many ways misleading impression that war (and perhaps particularly civil war) is a disaster for almost everyone concerned. The resulting temptation is to turn away from warfare as quickly as possible, to put the madness of war into the past, and to get back to "normal" with the greatest possible haste. Of course, it is quite possible to put forward a number of causes of the apparent futility of war, whether these are religious, political, ethnic, or whatever. But the habitual (and natural) emphasis on war as a negative phenomenon, the idea of war as breakdown, may ultimately induce in the observer a sense of puzzlement: How is it that a phenomenon so universally disastrous could be allowed, and indeed made, so frequently to happen—and very often to persist over years or decades? And there is a further problem: One is likely to gain little sense, in the habitual enthusiasm to restore the prewar economy, of the way that war was generated by precisely this *status quo ante.*

Those who point to "ancient ethnic hatreds" as a root cause of civil conflicts will need to explain why a variety of "hostile" peoples have been able to live peacefully alongside each other for long periods, or why, for example, the Baggara pastoralists of western Sudan have raided their fellow Arabs among the neighboring Fur and their coreligionists among the Nuba. As David Turton[1] and David Campbell[2] have argued, the "ethnic hatreds" school has often failed to recognize that ethnicity— and the importance attached to it—is shaped by conflict rather than simply shaping it. More worrisome, those who are ready to use easy labels and to accept the *inevitability* of ethnic violence may actually play into the hands of local actors seeking to bolster their own power and privileges by forcing politics along ethnic lines and by presenting themselves internationally and domestically as the leaders of "ethnic groups." An emphasis on the inevitability of ethnic hatreds can be profoundly disabling and demoralizing.

The rigidity sometimes visible in academic disciplines has sometimes further muddied the waters. Disciplines like economics and political science usually focus on a restricted area that is ordered and predictable; and when messy phenomena like contemporary civil wars do not fall easily within the orbit of these systems of analysis, the temptation to wheel out the label of chaos is very great. Moreover, at both the national and international levels, there may be vested interests not only in chaos and ethnic strife but in the *depiction* of chaos and ethnic strife.

Rather than portraying war as irrational or as an aberration or interruption in development, I want to stress the importance of investigating how violence is generated by particular political economies, which it in turn modifies (but does not destroy). Part of the problem with much existing analysis is that conflict continues to be regarded as simply a breakdown in a particular system rather than as the emergence of an alternative system of profit, power, and even protection. Yet the problem of war should also be put in more positive terms. What use is war? What functions does it perform?

The Functions of Violence

The functions of violence in civil wars can be divided into two broad categories. First, violence may be oriented toward changing (or retaining) the laws and administrative procedures of a society. In a sense, this is political violence. Of course, much of this political violence centers on the long-term distribution of economic resources: For example, violence may be used to protect (or undermine) economic privileges (such as landownership) that are cemented through control of the state. Second, violence may be aimed at circumnavigating the law—not so much changing the law as ignoring it. This covers a range of functions that, rather than being concerned with rewriting the rules at the national level, are local and immediate.

The local and immediate functions of violence are of three main types: economic, security, and psychological. All of them suggest limitations in *state-centric* analysis.[3] War may be profitable for a range of groups. It may be safer to be in an armed band than outside one, particularly when the majority of attacks are being directed against civilians. And violence may provide a range of psychological payoffs, including an immediate reversal of relationships of dominance and humiliation that have sometimes prevailed in peacetime. Participation in armed groups may also offer excitement and a chance to revenge past wrongdoings. Even acts of revenge, vandalism, and ritual humiliation (which appear to serve no economic, military, or political purpose) should not always be seen as "mindless" or "senseless." Such violence will have been generated by a particular political economy: It may be fueled by fear and anger, which themselves reflect political and economic processes in the immediate or distant past.

Where civil wars have not simply been dismissed as a form of madness or irrationality, they have traditionally been viewed as a political insurrection that is met with a counterinsurgency. This model appeared particularly applicable from the 1950s to the early 1980s, when anticolonial wars often ran alongside (and sometimes gave way to) a variety of revolutionary struggles. Of course, traditional revolutionary and political struggles (such as the struggle for land reform in Latin America) have not simply gone away just because the Cold War era has drawn to a close. However, two characteristics have set many recent conflicts apart from this "revolutionary" model. First, much of the violence has been initiated not so much by revolutionaries seeking to transform the state as by a range of elites seeking to deflect political threats by inciting violence, often along ethnic lines. Many of these elites have been those who gained ascendancy in postcolonial states, and many others enjoyed privileges under Communist regimes. Pressure for democratization (often internal and international) has constituted a threat to such elites, and sometimes this pressure for democratization has been combined with outright rebellion. These threats, often combined with conditions of economic austerity, have created conditions for major "elite backlashes." The 1994 Rwandan genocide is the most notable example, but the catastrophe in Kosovo also bears many of these imprints.

Although elites have often amassed considerable personal wealth, they have frequently presided over states that lack the means for effective and disciplined counterinsurgency (not least because available revenues have been siphoned into private pockets). In these circumstances, and particularly in Africa, we have seen elites repeatedly recruiting civilians into unpaid or underpaid armies or militias. Such recruitment has typically, but not always, been along ethnic lines. Very often, some combination of fear, need, and greed has created a willingness to be mobilized for violence among this civilian population.

This brings us to the second deviation from the traditional conception of civil war: the fact that for many of those implementing violence (and indeed for many of those orchestrating it), the violence has often served more immediate functions, often economic in nature. Conflicts have seen the emergence of war economies (often centered in particular regions controlled by rebels or warlords and linked to international trading networks). Members of armed gangs have profited from looting and other forms of violent economic activity. And chains of command have become notably weak in a number of countries, including Somalia, Sierra Leone, and Liberia. These developments add to the difficulties of bringing violence to an end, both because many may have a vested interest in prolonging violence and because "leaders" may be unable to control their followers.

Civil wars are not static over time. A growing proportion of civil wars appear to have started with the aim of taking over or

retaining the reins of the state or of breaking away in a seces-
sionist revolt and appear to have subsequently mutated (often
very quickly) into wars where immediate agendas assume an increasingly important role. These immediate agendas (notably
economic agendas) may significantly prolong civil wars: Not
only do they constitute a vested interest in continued conflict,
they also tend to create widespread destitution, which itself may
feed into economically motivated violence.[4]

Top-Down and Bottom-Up Violence

It is helpful to distinguish between "top-down" violence and
"bottom-up" violence. Top-down violence refers to violence that
is mobilized by political leaders and entrepreneurs—whether
for political or economic reasons. The existence of powerful
groups mobilizing violence from the top will be sufficient to
create large-scale violence where major coercion is used to get
recruits. However, in practice violence has often been actively
embraced by a variety of ordinary people (either civilians or
low-ranking soldiers) as a solution to problems of their own.
This can be called bottom-up violence. Getting involved in violence may serve a range of psychological and even security
functions as well as economic functions. Often, a regressive,
top-down political function will combine with more local and
immediate aims on the part of those at the bottom.

In order to move toward more lasting solutions for the
problem of mass violence, we may need to understand and acknowledge that for significant groups this violence represents
not a problem but a solution. We need to think of modifying
the structure of incentives that are encouraging people to orchestrate, fund, or perpetrate acts of violence.

The idea that violence may offer a *solution*—whether for
some of those "at the top" or for some of those "at the bottom"—tends to get missed in human rights discussions. Here,
the emphasis is often on condemnation rather than explanation, and violence may be labeled as inhumane or even inhuman, as if it were not human beings (with all their diverse motivations of need, greed, fear, lust, resentment, and, indeed,
altruism) that were carrying out these acts. Although violence
is often projected as outside the normal human experience or

as invading a country like an enemy virus, violence may also be actively generated by particular cultures, societies, and economies. The Oklahoma City bombing was perhaps a particularly startling example of a violence that was initially blamed on external factors—with local suspicions falling initially on Muslims in the area—but that was soon found to have sprung from the ideology of white extremists, a term that is more appropriate than we might think since followers had taken to an extreme certain elements of American culture, including a hostility to central government and a desire to defend the possession of guns.

If contemporary civil wars have been widely labeled as mindless, mad, and senseless, in some ways nineteenth- and twentieth-century Western notions of war may be closer to madness. When war is seen as an occasion for risking death in the name of the nation state and with little prospect of financial gain, it may take months of brainwashing and ritual humiliation to convince new recruits of the notion. A war where one avoids battles, picks on unarmed civilians, and makes money may make more sense.

More to War Than Winning: Conflict in a Weak State

Part of the allure of labels such as "ethnic hatred," "mindless violence," and "chaos" is that many contemporary civil wars have been seen to depart from the traditional model of two competing professional teams with civilians as bystanders.

However, a better reaction to problems with this traditional model would be to think again about the aims of warfare. A common assumption has been that parties to a civil war are only concerned with gaining or retaining control of the state. Another has been that the aim in a war is to win it. Yet both are open to question.

Civil wars have usually been presented as a contest between government and rebel groups, with each seeking to "win the war" and "defeat the enemy." Diplomats and journalists have tended to operate within this conceptual framework. However, the image of war as a contest has sometimes come to serve as a smokescreen for the emergence of a wartime political economy from which rebels and even the government (and government-affiliated groups) may be benefiting. As a result of these benefits, some parties may be more anxious to prolong a war than to win it.

Civil wars have often, rather misleadingly, been discussed as if both government and rebel forces were homogenous: The tale, very often, is of rebel advances and government fightbacks (or vice versa), as if these were two rival armies in World War II. A more sophisticated kind of analysis considers how the success of either side is influenced by its ability to garner support from a variety of groups in civil society. This aspect of the problem was highlighted by Mao's famous analysis of the fishes and the sea, and it was to some extent taken on board by governments seeking to resist revolutionary movements (as in U.S. attempts to "win hearts and minds" in Vietnam and Central America). However, an analysis emphasizing the need to garner support may not go far enough: In some circumstances, the most revealing question may not be which groups support a rebellion or counterinsurgency campaign but which groups seek to *take advantage of* a rebellion or a counterinsurgency campaign and for which kinds of purposes of their own. Just as this question can usefully be applied to those in a position to orchestrate violence from the top, it can usefully be applied to ordinary civilians.

The military historian von Clausewitz saw war as overwhelmingly waged by states, which were envisaged as possessing a monopoly on the means of violence. He famously said that war was a continuation of politics by other means. But states may not have a monopoly on the means of violence, and rebel groups may also find it hard to direct or control violence within their areas of operation. Particularly where chains of command are weak, war may be a continuation of *economics* by other means.

In the course of a political struggle over the state, it may be necessary to harness the energies, violence, and grievances of groups who are not fully in your pay or your control—particularly in a weak state—that is, a state that is unable to extend security or basic services, including the rule of law, to its population. This may have the effect of privatizing violence, with economic agendas assuming considerable importance. Elites are likely to try to harness economic agendas within civil society in order to fight civil wars on the cheap: Violent private accumulation at the local level can serve as a substitute for supplies from the center. In addition, in weak states elites are likely to try to mobilize violence to carve out private profits from civil conflict. For rebels, the incentive to take over the state may not be all that great in circumstances where the state is unable either to monopolize violence or to tax economic activity.

In certain respects, the licensing of economically motivated violence represents a return to the past. In medieval Europe and well into the eighteenth century, before strong states had been established, conflict was funded to a large extent through plundering civilians, which compensated for inadequate provisioning and for pay that was generally low, late, or nonexistent. Particularly in a context where some states have come close to collapsing, the assessment of warfare in medieval Europe made by Contamine would appear to be relevant today. He noted that warfare could be deliberately spread from the top through a decision by official authorities or it could rise from below. Medieval conflicts were also characterized by a tendency to avoid pitched battles. Dangerous new elements have been added, however. The value of particular minerals, crops, and areas of land has been boosted by demand from abroad. The state has often been intentionally run down by international financial institutions. And the availability of cheap automatic weapons has risen sharply.

Whereas medieval patterns of warfare were eroded by the rise of modern, bureaucratic states in Europe, such states have still not been properly established in many parts of the world, and in Eastern Europe there has been something of a retreat from them. The weakness of states in many countries has reflected their weak economies (often based primarily on agricultural production and the export of primary products) as well as the limited ability of governments to capture this economic activity. This difficulty in raising revenue typically reflects the low pay of state officials (which makes them susceptible to corruption) and a shortage of capital (which allows foreign investors to drive a tough bargain on the distribution of profits from primary production in particular). If the institutions of the state (such as schools, social security, police, and the army) are eroded by international pressures for austerity or by economic crisis more generally, this state will find it hard to address the needs that may otherwise be met through a resort to violence. Government counterinsurgency and policing functions can all too easily break down into economic violence, in turn encouraging a surge in sympathy for the rebels that governments purport to be opposing.

The way that pursuit of local and immediate solutions to economic and psychological grievances can count against military success has been shown in Sierra Leone, where rebel Revolutionary United Front (RUF) atrocities against, and exploitation of, civilians have alienated civilians from their cause. (The same can also be said of the abusive and exploitative counterinsurgency in Sierra Leone, especially in the period 1991–1995). These "counterproductive" actions have often continued even beyond the point when it becomes clear they are inhibiting military and political goals, underlining the point that the aim of war is not necessarily to win it.

Abuses against civilians have usually been portrayed as an unfortunate deviation from the laws of war or as a means to a military end. However, such abuses may confer benefits that have little or nothing to do with winning the war (and may actively impede this endeavor). The "point" of war may lie precisely in the legitimacy it confers on these abuses—in other words, the legitimacy it confers on actions that in peacetime would be punishable as crimes. Whereas analysts have tended to assume that war is the "end" and abuses the "means," it is important to consider the opposite possibility: that the "end" is to engage in abuses or crimes that bring immediate rewards, whereas the "means" is war and the perpetuation of war.

Various groups—including government officials, traders, and soldiers—may take advantage of conflict and conflict-related scarcities.

Many short-term economic functions of violence do not depend on control of the reins of state. One subcategory is pillage. The fruits of pillage have often been used to supplement—or even to replace—the wages and salaries of soldiers or other officials, a standard practice in medieval warfare that found echoes in former Yugoslavia and Zaire, to give just two examples among many.

A second immediate economic function of warfare is securing protection money from those who are spared from having violence (or confinement) inflicted upon them.

A third immediate economic function is the (monopolistic) control of trade. War—like famine—may lead to price movements that are very profitable for some. And in the context of a war, it may be particularly easy to subject trading rivals to a variety of threats and constraints. Wartime trading restrictions imposed by governments may be very profitable for officials who allow breaches of these restrictions. Alternatively, a partial breakdown in state control may facilitate previously prohibited trade, for example in drugs. In general, the distribution of resources may be governed less by market forces than by "forced markets." Control of trade has been an important factor in conflicts in a wide range of contemporary conflicts from Sudan, Somalia, Angola, and Sierra Leone in Africa to Peru and Colombia in Latin America and Afghanistan, Cambodia, and Burma in Asia. In northern Somalia, in the 1980s, war was used by clans associated with Siad Barre as a means of divesting members of the Isaak clan of their property, jobs, and businesses. One specialized but particularly profitable aspect of trade may be in the procurement of arms.

A fourth short-term function of conflict is that it may facilitate the exploitation of labor. Threatening violence against an individual or group may be used to force the individual or group to work cheaply or for free. In extreme cases, such as in Burma and Sudan, conflict has facilitated the reemergence of forms of slavery.

A fifth short-term economic function of conflict—not quite immediate, but still relying on direct action rather than control of the state—is the prospect of staking a direct claim to land. Conflict may lead to the partial or near total depopulation of tracts of land, allowing new groups to stake a claim to land, water, and mineral resources. These were some of the important economic benefits promised (and to some extent delivered) by warfare and related famine in Sudan in the late 1980s.

A sixth short-term economic function of conflict may lie in the benefits extracted from aid that is sent during the conflict. In some circumstances, the prospect of appropriating relief appears to have encouraged raiding, since raiding can create predictable suffering and a predictable windfall of aid. Violence may serve a purpose, first, in precipitating relief and, second, in gaining access to this relief once it arrives.

A final set of short-term economic benefits that may arise from conflict are those institutionalized benefits accruing to the military. These may be greater where there exists a conflict to justify a sizable military and/or a role of the military in the government itself.

Many of these processes may have a defensive component. In the case of pillage and gaining forcible access to labor and land, some persons may resort to violence as a way of protecting themselves from such forced transfers. The need to defend oneself against economically motivated violence is one of the factors underpinning the growing role of private security firms during civil conflict.[5]

Falling Below the Law:
The Interaction of Greed and Grievance

To some extent, both rebel groups and groups allied with the government may expropriate food, "taxes," and labor for the purpose of making war—in other words, they may exploit civilians in order to fight a war. But they may also fight a war in order to exploit civilians: A situation of "war" may provide, in effect, a license to take advantage of particular groups of civilians.

Civil conflicts have typically seen the emergence of groups (often ethnic groups) who can safely and, in a sense, legitimately be subjected to extreme exploitation, violence, and famine. Some groups fall below the law, and some are elevated above it. This process may take place in peacetime as well as wartime, and it can precipitate, as well as shape, outright conflict. Particular communities may experience a process of falling below the law and of losing the law's protection, eventually prompting outright rebellion—the experience of the Nuba and southern Sudanese is a good example.

Paul Collier has emphasized the importance of greed rather than grievance in driving civil wars. My own work gives a good deal of importance to economic motivations. However, this process of falling below the law underlines the continuing importance of grievances and not greed in contemporary conflicts. Indeed, we need to understand how the two interact.

Rather than a traditional model of conflict as a contest between two sides trying to win, or a model that suggests political
agendas have been replaced by economic agendas, I urge the
importance of investigating how it is that particular groups can
come to fall at least partially outside the physical and economic
protection of the state, the exploitation or expropriation of
these groups by those having superior access to the state (sometimes in alliance with international capital), the generation of
a sense of grievance and of rebellion among these exploited
groups, and the hyperexploitation and hyperexpropriation of
"rebel suspects" that typically take place under the cover of an
outright conflict.

Or, to put it another way, we need to investigate how greed
generates grievances and rebellion, legitimizing further greed.
The first part of this dialectic is frequently labeled "peace," and
the second, "war."

Abuses against civilians frequently create their own justification—in Sudan, for example, abuses have stimulated support
for the other side that was previously weak or absent. The concept of war provides a convenient cover both for greed and for
the suppression and division of political opposition that is designed to remedy grievances. Labeling political opponents as
rebels is one convenient way of limiting political opposition. In
wartime—as Burma, Sierra Leone, and Sudan attest—it can be
a relatively easy matter to accuse unarmed civilians of collaboration with one side or another, and to use such accusations as
legitimacy for widespread exploitation. Another way of weakening political opposition is by deflecting the discontent of one
ethnic group by turning their frustrations against another ethnic group. A third way to limit political opposition is to prolong
the war, which legitimizes its suppression.

Undemocratic or "exclusive" regimes have often sought to
protect the economic interests of their supporters by portraying certain kinds of political opposition (including trade
unions) as manifestations of rebel activity or as the work of
enemy sympathizers. This can provide cover for moves against
the opposition, and the concept of a rebel or an enemy may be
kept conveniently fluid. A continuation of conflict may serve to
stifle political opposition through the preservation of a military
regime—the declaration and prolongation of "states of emergency" that accord special powers to repressive governments or

the military—and through restrictions on freedom of speech that are justified as part of a "war effort." Prolonging conflict may also offer the significant advantage that it may be very difficult, from a practical point of view, to hold elections. This may be particularly good news for those whose previous violence and exploitation might lay them open to prosecution under a more democratic regime.

One of the main reasons for the apparently pointless dispute between Ethiopia and Eritrea over a small tract of borderland may lie in the deflecting of domestic resentments (perhaps particularly resentments in Ethiopia at perceived economic privileges for Eritrea) and defusing political opposition by means of nationalism. In Cambodia, opponents of government corruption have been repeatedly tarred with the brush of "rebel sympathizer": Those who voice dissent have often been attacked by the government as supporting the Khmer Rouge.

In circumstances where conflict is functional, threatening someone—a Milosevic or a Saddam Hussein—with war may be more like a promise than a threat. This is particularly likely when an international aversion to committing ground troops means that conflict can take place at two levels (an international conflict involving one-sided airstrikes, and a domestic conflict involving largely one-sided attacks on the ground, against Kosovan Albanians in the south of the Federal Republic of Yugoslavia or Shi'ite Muslims in the south of Iraq). In a sense, these simultaneous one-sided conflicts are hardly adequately described with the label *war*.[6] Without the committal of ground troops, this could be interpreted as a kind of system in which it is understood by both "sides" that the lives of some ethnic groups are relatively expendable (Kosovan Albanians in Yugoslavia, Shi'ite Muslims in Iraq) whereas those of others (American and British soldiers, etc., Serbian civilians) will not be lost on any substantial scale. At the same time, each one-sided attack is in some sense both legitimated and encouraged by the other (so that two "wars" fought alongside each other can be presented domestically as legitimate). This adds further to the possibility that these are better interpreted as "systems" than as "wars." One can argue that in the case of Iraq and the Federal Republic of Yugoslavia, as in Sierra Leone, Liberia, Cambodia, Algeria, and a number of other countries, military conflict has been limited in the interests of both warring parties while aggression against particular groups of civilians has been subject to far fewer limits.

There are reasons to believe that Milosevic has seen conflict as inherently useful. First (at least for most of the NATO bombing campaign), conflict helped rally political support behind him. This was partly because of the historical importance of Kosovo, partly because of Milosevic's control of the media, and partly because bombing brought people together against a common enemy. Second, conflict provided an excuse to suppress the media and elements of the opposition. Though he was elected, Milosevic faced powerful opposition protests in the winter of 1996/97 as well as a potential challenge from the reformist presidency of Milo Djukanovic in Serbia's sister republic, Montenegro.[7] Third, conflict appeared to weaken the ability of the Montenegrin leadership to resist Milosevic once Montenegro was being hit by NATO bombs.

Second, conflict may offer—in particular through looting and through control of trade—a crude form of payment for the very substantial security forces that the Serb authorities, whether Bosnian Serb authorities or those in Belgrade, have sometimes struggled to pay and to control. Although Milosevic has boosted the police as a key buttress of his power, elements of the army have been restive, and even the police need continuing economic benefits if loyalty is to be assured. Under conditions of continuing international sanctions, control of illicit trade has been extremely profitable for a small elite around Milosevic (including the notorious warlord Arkan) and for many in the security services; this has been true also for a privileged few in Iraq. Behavior that perpetuates sanctions, including the fomenting of conflict, may help to perpetuate these profits. Particularly in the context of economic depression induced, in large part, by these international sanctions, it would be politically risky for Milosevic, as well as economically risky for the cabal around him, to embrace a policy of peace and demobilization rather than a policy of permanent conflict and predation. In other words, this would appear to be a predatory political formation that requires permanent, or at least intermittent, conflict.[8] In a sense, Milosevic has been able to move the focus of his aggression from one geographic area to another, using his leverage as a "peacemaker" at Dayton to protect himself from prosecution and to provide a springboard for aggression in Kosovo. Whereas Milosevic is routinely presented in the Western media as all-powerful and, more or less, evil, it may be precisely the vulnerability of his position—notably in relation to the security services, in relation to Montenegro and in relation to an often-nationalist political opposition—that has encouraged him to pursue a policy of violence and ethnic destruction.

The international community has repeatedly allowed itself to be bamboozled by the term *war,* so that in Sudan the government has been able to disguise its manipulation of ethnic divisions and its greed for land and oil as a religious war. In the mid-1990s forces associated with the Sierra Leonean counterinsurgency were able to exploit civilians under the guise of fighting a rebel war, and the Rwandan government was able to pursue its genocide in 1994 while large sections of the international community called for a cease-fire in the war with the Rwandan Patriotic Front (RPF) when it was the RPF's advance that eventually stopped the genocide.

A Case in Point: The Civil War in Sierra Leone

The civil war in Sierra Leone cannot really be understood without comprehending the deep sense of anger at lack of good government and educational opportunities (the significance of the latter suggesting a problem with taking lack of education as a proxy for greed rather than grievance). In this overall context of grievance, greed has undoubtedly played a role. The failure of the state to provide economic security was matched by a failure to provide physical security.

Conflict in Sierra Leone has involved bizarre forms of collaboration between government and rebel Revolutionary United Front forces, including coordinated movements to rob civilians, transfer of arms from one side to the other, the avoidance of pitched battles, government soldiers posing as rebels and deserting to the rebels, and, finally, in May 1997, a joint coup by the RUF and elements of the military. Both sides have exploited diamond resources and cash crops at the expense of civilians, with youth—as Collier would predict—playing a key role in the violence. Such strange, collaborative behavior has been labeled by some Sierra Leoneans as "sell-game"—akin to a fixed football match.

Particularly in the period 1991–1995, the emergence of an exploitative political economy in which armed groups preyed on and taxed civilians was to a large extent concealed under a veil of silence both at national and international levels. Aid appears to have played a significant part in sustaining this silence. Insofar as the international community was anxious to be seen to be "doing something," humanitarian operations served as a substitute for more vigorous action on the diplomatic front, including an honest discussion of the government's role in the violence. Meanwhile, helped by international aid and loans, the military government of the National Provisional Ruling Council (NPRC) (1991–1996) was remarkably successful in promoting itself as a model student of financial orthodoxy, which in turn brought forth more aid and loans. In effect, the NPRC was able to present a facade of moral and financial probity in Freetown while tolerating and participating in increasingly violent forms of extortion elsewhere. When in 1996 and 1997 democracy and peace came to pose too great a threat to the system of economic exploitation that had evolved under the cover of war, the RUF combined with disgruntled government soldiers in the May 1997 coup to oust the democratic government of Tejan Kabbah and to launch a coordinated assault on the civil defense fighters, or *kamajors,* who had stood up to the twin threat of government soldiers and rebels.

Conclusion: Peace and Policy

When looking at conflict and possible solutions, a useful comparison can be made once again with disease, and specifically with infectious disease, which clearly serves important functions for the germs that flourish (perhaps temporarily) even as the patient falls sick. When it was recognized that disease had beneficiaries and that disease was often a complicated process of struggle between competing organisms rather than simply a set of symptoms, major medical advances in the treatment of disease were facilitated.

The diverse aims of those involved in warfare (and in crimes during war) should be taken into account by those who

are seeking to intervene in some way, whether such intervention takes the form of emergency aid, attempts to broker a
peace, or rehabilitation efforts.

The functions of violence—and by extension, the functions
of famine—have important implications for humanitarian relief. There is a pressing need to take account of the interests of
those who are trying to promote suffering when doing needs-
assessment or planning the delivery and distribution of aid. Insofar as the relief process centers on adding up the numbers of
displaced, measuring how thin they are, and shipping out relief
(the pattern, for example, in Sudan in the late 1980s), it will be
very difficult to address the root causes of a famine. As in
Sierra Leone, international donors hushed up the abuses by
forces associated with the counterinsurgency, particularly in the
late 1980s.

At the same time, the positive potential of aid in relation to
violence should be recognized.

Aid may reduce the need for civilians to turn to violence in
pursuit of sustenance. In Sudan, the *absence* of effective relief to
the west in the 1983–1985 drought-famine helped produce an
impoverishment of the cattle-herding Baggara, and elements of
the Baggara were soon seeking to reverse this impoverishment
by raiding southerners and inducing famine in the south. Even
aid that is stolen can help reduce market prices and prevent
people from turning to violence in order to sustain themselves,
as De Waal and Omaar have shown in relation to Somalia. In
the absence of effective relief in much of Sierra Leone, those
fleeing this violence have often faced the stark choice between
joining the ranks of the destitute and starving, or joining an
armed band (perhaps the rebels or the government forces).[9]

Rather than simply concentrating on negotiations between
the "two sides" in a war, it may be helpful to try to map the benefits and costs of violence for a variety of parties and to seek to
influence the calculations they make. This means creating disincentives for violence and positive incentives for peace.[10] It
could include attempts to reduce the economic benefits of violence (for example, through sanctions such as freezing bank
accounts), to increase the economic benefits of peaceable activities (for example, through the provision of employment and
forms of development), and to reduce the legal (and moral) impunity that may be enjoyed by a variety of groups (for example,

by publicizing abuses, initiating international judicial proceedings, and making aid explicitly conditional on human rights observance). We need to investigate what international interventions (aid, diplomacy, publicity, investment, trade) are doing to accelerate or retard the processes by which people fall below the protection of the law. "Intervention" is not simply something that the West or the international community does to remedy humanitarian disasters once they occur; it is something, more often than not, that occurs prior to the disaster, perhaps helping to precipitate it—witness, for example, the international support for abusive and unrepresentative governments like those of Barre in Somalia, Doe in Liberia, and Habyarimana in Rwanda. When evidence of abuses emerges, quick and explicit international action is needed to limit impunity. Despite the periodic massacres of Tutsis in the run-up to the Rwandan genocide of 1994, international donors did not reduce aid with specific reference to human rights violations (although the Belgians threatened to do so). As in Sudan in the late 1980s, the donors' emphasis was on encouraging structural adjustment and fiscal reform.[11] In fact, the case of Rwanda suggests rather clearly that there are dangers in pursuing the kinds of ends—growth, democracy—that statistics may show are positively correlated with a lack of conflict without adequately considering the possibility of violence by those threatened by these processes. In theory, human rights are protected by a plethora of international and national laws. But providing practical economic and physical protection on the ground will involve a more variegated and realistic appraisal of which groups can be given *an interest in contributing to the enforcement of these rights,* whether these are articulated at the national or international level. This means proper pay and conditions for security services alongside a democratic transition that ensures these security services are accountable.

Everyone favors peace, at least ostensibly. But it is important to ask what kind of peace one is working toward. The existence of peace begs the questions, Whose peace? Peace on what terms? Peace in whose interests? And peace negotiated by which individuals or groups?

Even when a peace agreement has been reached, a transition from war to peace is likely to represent a realignment of political interests and a readjustment of economic strategies rather than a clean break from violence to consent, from theft to production, or from repression to democracy. In his analysis of Somalia after the 1991–1992 famine, Alex De Waal points to the shared interest of many landlord-elders in a particular kind of peace, one that has excluded politically marginalized agriculturalists from land they used to cultivate before it was taken away by quasilegal means or simply by force.[12] Menkaus and Prendergast (1995) have pointed to the shared interest of Somali warlords in a version of an "armed peace" that preserves their control of trade within respective areas of interest while limiting outright conflict and attracting increased international aid. The boundaries between war and peace, as between war and crime, may be quite blurred.

In a sense, for an effective peace agreement you need two things: First, an agreement between leaders; second, legitimate leaders who can maintain a following that includes all important sectors of the population and who, moreover, do not sacrifice a significant part of this following by the very act of making a peace agreement. One immediately thinks of the nascent Palestinian state and the split between Arafat and those who would wish to see a more far-reaching solution to the Palestine/Israel problem. Peace may institutionalize all manner of exploitation and violence that can feed into war. Indeed, it is difficult to imagine how civil wars would occur at all unless this were the case. A lasting solution to civil war depends not simply on creating incentives for the acceptance of peace, irrespective of how exploitative it may be, but on the creation of a peace that takes account of the desires and the grievances that drove people to war in the first place. This means being ready to *listen* to grievances. Though Collier is right to suggest that rebels may be reluctant to acknowledge the degree to which they are driven by greed, there are equal dangers in suggesting that the expression of grievances tells us nothing about their real motivation. Indeed, if we do not ask people why they are resorting to violence or listen to their own accounts of why this might be, we are lost. Creating a peace that takes account of grievances is a profoundly political endeavor. It means going beyond the mere reconstruction of a peacetime political economy that *generated* war. It also means guarding against the processes of highly uneven development and inequitable growth that may, if we are not careful, continue to be supported by the World

Bank and International Monetary Fund (IMF). It means avoiding those kinds of privatization that as in Sierra Leone ended up putting much of the economy in a few oligopolistic hands and deepening a popular sense of grievance. It also means checking the proliferation of small arms.

Paul Richards has noted that "young people, modernized by education and life in the diamond districts, are reluctant to revert to this semi-subsistence way of life; many treat it only as a last stand-by."[13] And Joanna Skelt has underlined the point that peace is not to everyone's taste:

> The greatest challenge for peace education is to create the conditions (or empower people to create the conditions) in which the young can find employment, recognition, security, belonging and a sense of control over their lives so that they do not become the victims of peace, so they feel an ownership of the peace process and benefit from a Sierra Leone of their own making. Unfortunately, the peace movement still finds itself sheltering in safety surrounded by language and ideals that resonate with 'femininity'. Without an adequate perception of 'masculine' psychology, and without incorporating this into peace education, glory will never be situated in peace.[14]

"Employment, recognition, security, belonging and a sense of control"—an economic agenda is implied there, but also something much more than that. Rehabilitation should be more than an attempt to turn the clock back to a rural idyll that never actually existed.

Notes

This chapter represents a development in the argument in "The Economic Functions of Violence in Civil Wars," *Adelphi Paper* 320 (Oxford: Oxford University Press for the International Institute of Strategic Studies), 1998.

1. David Turton (ed.), *War and Ethnicity: Global Connections and Local Violence* (New York: University of Rochester Press, 1997).

2. David Campbell, *National Deconstruction: Violence, Identity and Justice in Bosnia* (Minneapolis: University of Minnesota Press, 1998).

3. Mark Duffield, "Post-modern Conflict: Warlords, Post-adjustment States and Private Protection," *Civil Wars*, 1, no. 1 (Spring 1998); P. Chabal and J.-P. Daloz, *Africa Works: Disorder as a Political Instrument* (Oxford: James Currey, 1999).

4. Human Rights Watch, *Somalia—A Government at War with Its Own People: Testimonies About the Killings and the Conflict in the North* (New York/Washington/London: Human Rights Watch, January 1990).

5. David Shearer, *Sierra Leone Situation Analysis: A Report for the International Crisis Group* (London: International Crisis Group, April 1997).

6. Nicholas Zurbrugge (ed.), *Jean Bruillard, Art and Artefact* (London: Sage, 1997).

7. Robert Thomas, *Serbia Under Milosevic: Politics in the 1990's* (London: Hurst and Company, 1999).

8. Mary Kaldor, *New and Old Wars: Organized Violence in a Global Era* (Cambridge: Polity Press, 1999); Duffield, "Post-modern Conflict: Warlords, Post-Adjustment States and Private Protection."

9. J. D. Kandeh, "What Does the 'Militariat' Do When It Rules? Military Regimes: The Gambia, Sierra Leone and Liberia," *Review of African Political Economy*, no. 69 (1996).

10. See, for example, Mats Berdal and David Keen, "Violence and Economic Agendas in Civil Wars: Considerations for Policymakers," *Millennium* 26, no. 3, (1997); and Mats Berdal, "Disarmament and Demobilisation After Civil Wars: Arms, Soldiers and the Termination of Armed Conflict," *Adelphi Paper* 303 (Oxford: Oxford University Press for the International Institute for Stategic Studies, 1996).

11. Howard Adelman and Astri Suhrke, *The International Response to Conflict and Genocide: Lessons from the Rwanda Experience* (Copenhagen: Joint Evaluation of Emergency Assistance to Rwanda, March 1996).

12. Alex de Waal, "Land Tenure, the Creation of Famine, and the Prospects for Peace in Somalia," in M. Mohamed Salih and L. Wohlgemuth (eds.), "Crisis Management and the Politics of Reconciliation in Somalia: Statements from the Uppsala Forum," 17–19 January 1994.

13. Paul Richards, *Fighting for the Rainforest: War, Youth, and Resources in Sierra Leone* (London: James Currey, 1996), 51.

14. Joanna Skelt, *Rethinking Peace Education in War-Torn Societies: A Theoretical and Empirical Investigation with Special Reference to Sierra Leone* (Cambridge: International Extension College, 1997).

3

Shadow States and the Political Economy of Civil Wars

William Reno

Mining and logging activities were actively going on in NPFL [National Patriotic Front of Liberia] territory. . . . All these businesses were operated by the rebels. For them to talk of opening the roads or uniting with the Monrovia-based government only remained an illusion because their business was at stake if that happened.[1]

By one measure, the old Soviet bloc and postcolonial states hosted 37 major internal wars (where death tolls exceeded 1,000) in 1997, compared to 12 in 1989, the end of the Cold War.[2] Some see the destruction of political order in these wars, as well as the "increasing erosion of nation-states and international borders, and the empowerment of private armies, security firms, and international drug cartels."[3] Analysts Alvin and Heidi Toeffler extend this vision of disorder, identifying "a new dark age of tribal hate, planetary desolation, and wars multiplied by wars."[4] A French observer warns that this "new dark age" in broken-down postcolonial states will generate massive refugee flows that will swamp Europe.[5]

On the other hand, these developments appear to turn toward universal conditions of state-building that Charles Tilly describes, of "a portrait of war makers and state makers as coercive and self-seeking entrepreneurs."[6] This view would interpret the Cold War as an unusual opportunity for rulers to count on aid from superpower patrons, which enabled these rulers to bypass bargaining with subjects. Ignoring citizens' claims on state power, rulers abjured large-scale, efficient, but politically obstreperous internal administrations.[7] But the end of the Cold War should force these rulers to heed the model of state-building elsewhere, which has often taken the path of plunder and banditry.[8] For troubled, weak states, this internal disorganization will be resolved by war. "In particular, weak states—not in the military sense," notes Kalevi Holsti, "but in terms of legitimacy and efficacy, are and will be the locales of wars. To the extent that those issues might be settled once and for all . . . it will be by armed combat."[9] Likewise, Mohammed Ayoob states that "state making and what we now call 'internal war' are two sides of the same coin."[10]

Here, I explain how internal warfare in some very weak states represents neither dissolution of political order itself nor the initiation of state-building projects with parallels to the process as it occurred in early modern Europe. I explain internal warfare instead with reference to economic motivations that are specifically related to the intensification of transnational commerce in recent decades, and to the political economy of violence inside a particular category of states. This is not to say that economic gain motivates all individuals at all times in internal warfare in weak states. Fighters in civil wars may pursue diverse objectives simultaneously.[11] I argue that some internal warfare, and the rise of so-called warlords and other armed factions, develops out of a particular Cold War–era relationship between private power, commerce, and state institutions in weak states. It is this dynamic that shapes and guides the pursuit of interests and that enhances the salience of economic interests in this equation.

I use the term *shadow state* to explain the relationship between economic and political organizations, which I explore in greater detail elsewhere.[12] I explain why and how some state officials choose to exercise political control through market channels, rather than pursuing politically risky and materially costly projects of building effective state institutions. I then consider external threats to this strategy that appeared with the end of the Cold War, conditions that some observers associate with a forced reversion to conventional state-building strategies. This process, however, does not mark a turn toward more rigid distinctions between spheres of state authority and private enterprise, a key element in most theories of state-building. Intensified transnational market transactions in the context of shadow state relationships of internal authority and markets can lay the groundwork for further integration of markets and political control. Rulers boost their direct, personal interventions into markets, both formally and clandestinely, to bolster their personal power and private wealth. These developments reinforce incentives for challengers to pursue more exclusively economic agendas. This development underlies the primacy of economic motives in shaping the participation of key actors in civil wars in shadow states.

Shadow States in Theory

Shadow state is a concept that explains the relationship between corruption and politics. The shadow state is the product of personal rule, usually constructed behind the facade of de jure state sovereignty. Nearly all governments recognize shadow states as interlocutors in global society and conform to the practice of extending sovereignty by right to former colonies. This principle even applies in cases where formal state capacity is practically nil. For example, Somalia holds a seat in the United Nations, exists as an entry in World Bank tables, and presumably has access to foreign aid, provided an organization there can convince outsiders that it is the rightful heir to Somalia's existing sovereignty. Somalia's northern region, Somaliland, has a functioning administration. To date, however, its leaders have received no outside recognition of their own claims of sovereignty, complicating their efforts to attain creditworthiness or access to the array of diplomatic resources that are available to Somalia. Jackson observed that this leads to external support for de jure sovereignty of states with very weak internal administrations, relieving rulers of the need to strengthen institutions to protect productive groups in society, from which regimes could extract income.[13] In other words, rulers adopted a shortened political horizon, gathering critical resources either from superpower patrons or from investors willing to invest in enclave operations, rather than nurturing taxable autonomous groups of internal producers.

Income acquired independently of the enterprise of the country's population gave rulers the option of imposing heavy demands for resources from their own population, even if these demands drastically reduced societal productivity and wealth. This tendency has been especially pronounced in instances where regimes control concentrated, valuable resources that attract foreign enclave investment; that is, foreign firm operations confined to a small piece of territory containing portable, valuable resources, an issue that I will explore further below.[14] In these circumstances, rulers had little prospect of attracting popular legitimacy, or even compliance with their directives. Thus, many rulers preferred to conserve resources that otherwise would be spent for services, devoting them instead to payouts to key strongmen in return for obedience and support. Payouts could be material, as in providing subsidies or preferred access to state assets, or discretionary exercises of power, as in not prosecuting wrongdoings, or other selective exemptions from regulations. This distinction in the nature of payouts is an important element that helps shape the organization of power and incentives for members, as we will see below.

These private uses of state assets and prerogatives created a framework of rule outside formal state institutions, a shadow of state bureaucratic agencies based on personal ties. Max Weber made the key observation of similarly constituted patrimonial regimes: "The patrimonial office lacks above all the bureaucratic separation of the 'private' and the 'official' sphere. For the political administration is treated as a purely personal affair of the ruler, and political power is considered part of his personal property which can be exploited by means of contributions and fees."[15] Illustrating the blurring of public and private, state and markets, in 1992, Zaire's president Mobutu (1965–1997) reportedly controlled a fortune of $6 billion, exceeding the recorded annual economic output of his country.[16] Malawi's president Banda managed much of the country's commercial activity through family trusts.[17] Illustrating very close ties between state agents and illicit markets, Albanian officials in the early 1990s turned their state into an entrepôt for trade in arms, drugs, and stolen goods.[18] After a decade in power, Liberia's president Samuel Doe accumulated a fortune equivalent to half of Liberia's annual domestic income, and he distributed commercial opportunities to bind associates to his personal favor.[19]

To make patronage work as a means of political control, the ruler must prevent all individuals from gaining unregulated access to markets. A shadow state ruler thus logically seeks to make life *less secure* and *more materially impoverished* for subjects. That is, a shadow state ruler will minimize his provision of public goods to a population. Removing public goods, like security or economic stability, that are otherwise enjoyed by all, irrespective of their economic or political station, is done to encourage individuals to seek the ruler's personal favor to secure exemption from these conditions.[20] These informal connections, in the sense of not being legally sanctioned or even officially acknowledged, are the networks of the shadow state. It is thus proper to conceive of "state collapse" as predating the end of the Cold War, insofar as one identifies the destruction of formal state bureaucratic institutions at the hands of the shadow state ruler and his associates as the indicator of collapse. A semblance of public order is compatible with this collapse, but such order is coincidental with the private interests of a shadow state elite. This elite, however, is not dependent upon public order to secure private benefits, as we will see shortly.

Taken to extremes, there are no shadow state–supplied public goods, in the sense of an authority providing nonexclusionary benefits. In fact, the reverse is usually the case, since the ruler seeks to impose negative externalities—that is, costs or hindrances on subjects—while distributing relief from these burdens on the basis of personal discretion in return for compliance or loyalty. Thus there can be no civil rights because there is no rule of law in the shadow state, since relations with authorities are subordinate to the personal discretion of those authorities. Personal security, protection of property, and economic opportunity (in lieu of public services or security) are subject to the personal discretion of a superior, rather than as a consequence of impersonal institutions. Therefore, the "ideal" shadow state fails to fulfill Robert Nozick's minimalist definition of a state in a classic Hobbesean sense; a monopoly over the control of force in a territory sufficient to protect everyone, whether they like it or not.[21] The shadow state as an analytical "ideal" in fact describes the opposite of this classic definition of state. I write elsewhere that some shadow states that enjoy global recognition as sovereign states are better understood as private commercial syndicates, though I use the term *warlord politics*.[22] This elucidation of shadow states that focuses on the conversion of organizational resources and goals to private, noncollective benefits leads to two key propositions useful for analyzing some motives of warfare in potential or actual shadow states.

Proposition 1. A shadow state ruler who fails to control free-riding risks losing the loyalty of followers who comply in return for payouts. This is a common starting point for civil wars in shadow states.

This logical tendency of shadow state rulers to ignore or abjure tasks and institutions commonly associated with governments appears in simple matters such as postal services. The U.S. Postal Service will not accept mail for a number of shadow states because they lack postal services. But the point is not only that rulers save scarce resources. The shadow state ruler's interests include ensuring that other groups (including shadow state agents) do not provide subjects with this service, or any other public good, lest these activities overshadow lesser attractions of accommodation with the shadow state. From the ruler's perspective, officials or local organizers (it does not matter which) who appropriate resources and tasks nominally allocated to a state could curtail the ruler's power. Thus rulers of places that lack postal services also usually act to prevent the appearance of "self-help" or even local private providers. They prefer to incorporate entrepreneurs into their shadow state networks, and farm out postal duties to politically neutral foreign firms such as DHL or UPS, which service elite needs while posing no threat of building autonomous power bases in exchange for services.

This also suggests that creditors and donors who insist on bureaucratic retrenchment in return for giving resources to a regime can hasten transitions to shadow state conditions. Sierra Leone's rulers, for example, trimmed one-third of state employment in the mid-1990s while fighting a rebel war that absorbed up to 75 percent of official state expenditures.[23] Targets of austerity included health care workers and teachers, both of whom largely went without pay by 1995. Regimes may mobilize "self-help" that begins as spontaneous community activity. This happened in Sierra Leone. Latching on to community efforts, "Government declared the last Saturday of each month as 'Cleaning Day' throughout Sierra Leone. Cleaning exercises are being undertaken with zeal and enthusiasm and we are clearly winning the war against filth."[24] Such initially grassroots efforts in the context of a shadow state, however, may eventually resemble colonial forced labor, where cash-strapped state officials argue that essential community projects cannot be carried out in any other way, and justify compulsion as for the good of those forced to labor.

Creditor proposals to contract out revenue collection to foreign firms may have a similar anti-bureaucratic impact. Foreign customs collection agencies and fisheries monitors can free rulers from dangerous tasks of building indigenous revenue agencies, and of having to trust (or coerce) their agents to hand over resources. These strategies have the added virtue of pleasing creditors, who prefer less corrupt, more transparent collection methods which heighten prospects for repayment. Rulers appreciate the opportunity to centralize and pare down a patronage network. In Nigeria, "privatization" has gone even further, with the replacement of state agencies with "tax consultants." Loyal to a particular faction, "consultants" may use violent means to extract "tax" from businesses and individuals, particularly those who consort with the political opposition.[25] This strategy, however, poses dangers, since "tax consultants" may freelance or remain loyal to a faction after its removal from power (as has in fact occurred in Nigeria) as civilian leaders encounter this problem. Armed "consultants" thus could become another vector for the violent fragmentation of a shadow state.

In this deeply anti-bureaucratic vein, a key shadow state ruler technique is to foster conflicts within local communities and among factions in the shadow state itself. This encourages local strongmen to appeal to the personal favor of the ruler to settle disputes that in the past were settled amongst themselves. Zaire's Mobutu, for example, skillfully manipulated conflicts by siding with one faction, then another, to force all sides in the conflict to seek presidential favors to settle scores.[26] Kenya's presidential "strategy of tension" divided opposition communities along ethnic lines to assure Moi's continued control after foreign creditors forced him to hold elections.[27] As we will see below, this technique, which was also a central strategy of the rule of Nigeria's Abacha (1993–1998), generates divisions that uphold the shadow state, which then become fault lines of warfare once the shadow state fails.

This elite strategy of control also puts weapons into the hands of agents who obey no bureaucratic rules, which encourages these subordinates to invade economic activities of other people, especially those who have little to offer the shadow state beyond existing as targets for direct exploitation. Financially pressed rulers in Sierra Leone, for example, directed armed soldiers to engage in "Operation Pay Yourself" in lieu of any state capacity to actually pay them. As a consequence, "there developed," writes Arthur Abraham, "an extraordinary identity of interests between NPRC [regime] and RUF [rebels]." These coinciding interests incorporated a variety of agendas. Senior officers used the turmoil and increased spending during wartime to help themselves to state assets. Less privileged soldiers found ways to help themselves too. "This," continues Abraham perceptively, "was partly responsible for the rise of the *sobel* phenomenon, i.e. government soldiers by day become rebels by night."[28] This buttresses Abraham's very important observation that the Sierra Leone army's and rebels' looting operations gave each incentives to see that the war would continue.

Recalling that civil wars may reflect multiple agendas of fighters, ruling through provoking insecurity and then selling private protection are likely to intensify societal frictions. Lacking much in the way of formal military or civil institutions, Mobutu incited enmity in eastern Zaire against "newcomers" (of two centuries' standing). He incorporated local officials and armed bands into a coalition to loot the targeted population.[29] Similar techniques have appeared in the Niger Delta area of Nigeria. Quasi-official "task forces," often raised by a local faction or politician, have used alliances with powerful national figures to settle local political disputes and share clandestine commercial gains with patrons.[30] Liberia's president Doe (1980–1990) deliberately used his uneven protection of unpopular ethnic minority businessmen to extract income and commercial opportunities from them.[31]

Challenges by counterelites in shadow states also tend to mix enterprise and violence. In Nigeria, it is possible that opposition figure and former governor under military rule Ken Saro-wiwa attempted to use local muscle to force his way back into the governor's office under a proposed transition to civilian rule.[32] This member of the Nigerian political class discovered that he could tap into environmental rhetoric (and real griev-ances) of people in oil-producing regions of Nigeria. This gave Saro-wiwa the possibility of mobilizing outside nonstate actors to pressure Nigeria's military government to give more re-sources to his region (and the local government that Saro-wiwa perhaps wished to head), and of using local grassroots activism to force the government to deal directly with him to control this activism. Foreign oil producers also might be forced to hand over more resources. Local activists saw opportunities to help themselves to the prerogatives of the shadow state too. No doubt some fought against the environmental degradation of their oil-producing communities. Others probably envisioned accountable government along the procedural lines of elec-toral democracy. Revenge against the dreaded Rivers State In-ternal Security Task Force possibly motivated others, especially young fighters. It is also likely that many envisioned a world where "everyone would become a millionaire, and own a Mer-cedes Benz car." The 200,000-strong Ogbia community, for ex-ample, demanded $50 billion in compensation.[33]

Nor is this strategy confined to the Niger Delta. Groups that identify themselves as promoters of Yoruba culture and politi-cal fortunes, such as the Oodua People's Congress (OPC), may recruit violent "area boys" to battle their political opponents and the police. In the face of government counterattacks, this strategy usually has the effect of marginalizing nonviolent fac-tions within these organizations, as has appeared to happen in the OPC.

A ruler's protection of favored factions against others cre-ates costs for most people, including even those who receive ex-clusive protection. Officials manipulated violence in the Saro-wiwa case to create clear winners and losers and to assure that local organization would fragment along these lines. Armed groups like the Rivers State Internal Security Task Force mobi-lized others who had grievances with Saro-wiwa's Ogoni back-ers. For the prize of the federal government's adjudication of boundary disputes, informal elevation of local factions, and the creation of new local government units, Ogonis clashed with Andonis, Okrika fought Ogonis, and Ogonis and Ijaws battled each other.[34]

Nor will protection permit those so favored to develop significant independent means to provide for needs of their communities, as shifts in the ruler's support demonstrate to all that his favor shifts, and must be cultivated all the more strenuously. Thus benefits of the ruler's protection are not likely to become generalized, since protection is sold as a private good and must remain a private good to force supplicants to seek the ruler's personal favor. Recipients of this protection have greater incentives to pursue purely private gains for themselves to recoup expenses. Recipients of this protection are also more likely to treat others in an exploitative fashion, since they recognize that the ruler's favor is temporary and that the ruler will punish widely popular associates in any case. Many Nigerians have become accustomed to the tendency for popular officials to suffer mysterious fatal traffic accidents or fall afoul of highway bandits. "Road safety" thus became a concern for many opposition members during the Abacha regime.

In Nigeria (as elsewhere), assistance from foreign firms helps sustain shadow states. Returning to the Ogoni case, a local subsidiary of a large oil company helped arm and train a local paramilitary. This was justified as "industrial security" and eased by the presence of third parties willing to help circumvent external restrictions governing arms transactions with Nigeria.[35] For foreign firms with enclave operations, their only need is for a secure local environment. They are not trying to create markets where they operate, so they, like their shadow state partners, need not trouble themselves with the social requirements of a local market or state administration. They need only manage their immediate economic environment.

In these places, state officials risk losing control over ethnic and regionally based armed groups as their centrality as personal patrons diminishes. In some places, presidential associates mobilize to defend ethnic communities, as among Liberia's former presidential secretary and information minister, and among several Somali faction leaders. The more enterprising rely more heavily on mobilizing commercial connections that they inherited from their old shadow state positions. A similar fragmentation of state (and shadow state) control over violence appears in Colombia. In Armenia, officials attempting to respond to earthquake damage in January 1999 found that local paramilitaries rebuffed central-government efforts to reassert control. These paramilitaries, many involved in drug trafficking, were those that government officials earlier used as proxies in a war against leftist insurgents.

A key reason that shadow state rulers prefer weak formal and informal institutions, not only in the sense of straying from rule-based principles but also from the provision of public goods, lies in their fear that enterprising rivals could use control over successful institutions to challenge their rulers. Administrators who provide popular services, such as security amidst chaos created by other officials and their allies, would gain support from grateful beneficiaries of this public good.[36] This fear reflects the dangers that coups and other violent actions on the part of subordinates pose to the physical security of rulers. John Wiseman, for example, found that 60 percent of Africa's rulers from 1960 to 1992 left office either for prison, exile, or a premature grave.[37] The security of African rulers has not improved during the 1990s. Nigeria boasts a civilian president prevented from assuming office by an incumbent military ruler (1993), a palace coup (1993), and the suspicious nocturnal demise of a military ruler (1998). Burundi experienced a coup (1996) as did Gambia (1994) and Comoros (1999). Niger experienced two (1996, 1999). Sierra Leone suffered not only two coups (1992, 1996) but also two rebel advances that caused a civilian president to flee (1997, 1999). A rival politician's militia removed the president of Congo-Brazzaville (1997), and Central African Republic's president survived three military uprisings over two years (1996–1998) only with the help of French paratroopers. Congo-Kinshasa has since 1996 been the focus of a war involving eleven states.

This reinforces the point that a ruler's failure to suppress public goods (or in his view, free-riding) is likely to lead to his removal from power, and possibly, death. It is unlikely to lead to state-building, at least not immediately. This is because the shadow state strategy of rule through informal networks destroys the institutional raw materials to organize groups for the provision of public goods. Collapse of the shadow state is more likely to leave the field to fragments of the shadow state— groups of entrenched elites who will seek to protect their own private privilege. As Mancur Olson observed, "The larger the group, the farther it will fall short of providing an optimal amount of a collective good."[38] This is especially true of the collapsing shadow state, as well-placed individuals will continue to have incentives to forgo contributing to a common goal, especially if they can appropriate elements of a shadow state to provide their own benefits by force, if necessary. This is especially true where a shared, credible set of rules or recent experience with state-level, rule-based behavior is not present for a counterelite challenger to easily exploit, or for societal opposition to restore.

The Political Economy of Violence in Shadow States

This nonbureaucratic use of violence and the threat that violence poses to rulers impart a distinctive dynamic on armed struggles in collapsing shadow states that distinguishes them from cases of nonstate violence in more bureaucratized state authorities that are able (or willing) to maintain clearer boundaries between public and private spheres. This lies in the tendency for entrepreneurs, both faction leaders from within collapsing shadow states and their challengers from the broader society, to pursue enterprise in a strikingly violent manner. Some Liberians, for example, speak of a "Kalashnikov lifestyle" as a culture of war and as a means of accumulation. During that country's civil war, individuals such as General Butt Naked, General Jesus, and Major Trouble used automatic weapons as tools in their businesses in looting, logging, and trafficking of illicit substances.[39] In Sierra Leone, RUF (Revolutionary United Front) fighters reportedly enslaved captives.[40] Nigerian paramilitary units have organized as armed bandits, committing bank robberies in Lagos, the country's commercial capital, and even ambushing commercial aircraft taxiing on the runway of Murtala Mohammed airport![41] It is probable that this violent mode of enterprise gives a comparative advantage to sociopaths, who as in the case of one individual in Liberia, rose to his station by virtue of his efficiency in killing regime opponents before Doe's demise in 1990. From these observations, I offer another proposition that highlights a basic element of shadow states and their political economy of violence.

Proposition 2. In shadow states, where no authority exists that is willing or capable of providing a public good, entrepreneurs manage their own economic environments through means of violence.

A comparison of violent enterprises in shadow states to violent enterprises in other states illuminates several reasons why violent acts play such a key role in the collapse of shadow states. Organized crime syndicates in states that come close to an ideal of monopolizing violence in order to provide security for subjects profit from finding ways to circumvent that monopoly. As Diego Gambetta observes, to do so they maintain an organizational structure that pursues interests distinct from those of the state. Italian mafia activities, he notes, consist primarily of selling protection to clients.[42] Likewise, most Russian organized crime syndicates derive the bulk of their profits from protection rackets, control of wholesale and retail trades, and manipulation of financial markets.[43] Even those who offer dire predictions that syndicates will undermine state authority report that these operations dominate their activities.[44] In contrast to shadow state enterprises, these operations depend upon a state provision of a public order, in the sense that even criminals cannot be easily excluded from the benefits of that order.

Though these syndicates logically seek to subvert the loyalties and commitments of individual state agents, their interests are not served in subverting the state's provision of order overall. It is state-provided order that keeps their clients in business; it is the state capacity to define legality that enables syndicates to sell protection to illegal operators. Accordingly, Gambetta observes that customers of the organized crime syndicate are likely to include other criminals. Thus mafia essentially free-ride on state provision of rules and order. Gambetta further notes that the optimal Italian and American mafia strategy lies in exercising no violence at all and only maintaining the appearance of a tough reputation. Occasionally syndicates that attempt to limit their overhead through neglecting violent enforcement are caught out when clients actually need their protection services.[45]

In contrast, the shadow state's agents, and those who challenge them, each find powerful incentives to consistently maximize their use of violence. This is because they find that they must manage their own economic environments in lieu of state provision of a public order. Once the shadow state collapses, they still fear cooperating to provide a public order (lest one among them use necessary institutions to elevate himself over the others). Groups thus challenge each other, rather than co-operate, even where opportunities for mutual gain could be exploited more efficiently through a joint monopoly of violence and the threat of violence. Mutual competition confirms Olson's classic observation that it takes the external provision of resources and rule enforcement to impose incentives to mobilize larger groups for collective action.[46] Their behavior undermines Frederic Lane's assertion that protection rackets tend toward natural monopolies and diminishing applications of violence.[47] This is especially true in the collapsed shadow state, since, as proposition 2 explains, the short-term risks of building bureaucratic institutions outweigh long-term benefits for the builder. This situation enhances the attractions of using direct control over people and economically valuable territory to accumulate resources for the private benefit of the organization's members.

These strategies can be used against external opponents too. Liberia's Charles Taylor reportedly boasted that he would "do a RENAMO" (for Mozambique National Resistance) against the regime of Sierra Leone president Joseph Momoh (1985–1992) after Momoh rejected Taylor's entreaties for assistance.[48] What Taylor meant was that he would encourage fighters to enter Sierra Leone, loot its people, destroy its infrastructure, and create a refugee burden for the country's government. Taylor was alleged to still support such a strategy in 1998.[49] The success of Taylor's aims in the Sierra Leone case, and Taylor's overall strategy's contribution to his personal wealth, highlights the special role that natural resources play in facilitating violent entrepreneurial strategies and the positive aspects of warfare for shadow state elites.

Natural Resources and the Shadow State

Retreat from the productive potential of populations increases the attraction to shadow state syndicates of foreign investment in enclave economies, since the rent-seeking nature of the source of income lessens the marginal cost of applying violence to commercial operations yet does not require cooperation with other existing indigenous armed groups. The local population merely needs to be fenced off, or chased off, so that the expense of forcing their compliance can be avoided. These incentives and constraints effectively preclude a long-term focus on the productivity of "victims" to tax them and instead promote a short-term focus on extracting benefits as quickly and as thoroughly as possible. This strategy works well if foreign investors are willing to provide their own security forces and fence off concession areas, as in fact appears to be a virtual requirement for investment in Angola's diamond mining sector, estimated to be worth $1 billion annually.[50] Foreign firms, with their own industrial security guards, thus fill in for feeble, unreliable, or absent formal state-organized militaries.

For Angola's regime, this strategy has several advantages. Private security forces may exclude "garimpeiro [illicit mining] generals" who use their position to mine diamonds, sometimes in collaboration with rebels. Antwerp diamond buyers report that Angolan military officers have sold diamonds on the behalf of rebels.[51] Revenues and participation in joint ventures with foreigners are distributed to secure the loyalty of other generals. Companies such as Tricorn, which operates with a foreign mining firm, are connected to the Angolan army's chief of staff.[52] This man's brother heads Alpha 5, a mine protection service that reportedly worked for a Canadian firm. Other generals own stakes in security companies. The director-general of the state-run oil company bought into the (now-defunct) private South African military firm Executive Outcomes, then established Teleservices with South Africa's Gray Security Services.[53]

One finds similar motives—personal enrichment, the use of security as a more exclusively private good, and the selective reward of associates—in other shadow state wars, especially where valuable natural resources are at stake. Conflict in central Africa illustrates conditions of warfare as an instrument of enterprise and violence as a mode of accumulation. For example, Congo's regime uses payments in kind to buy weapons and military assistance against rebel attack. It has appointed a white Zimbabwean, Billy Rautenbach, as head of the state-owned mining firm, Gécamines. One of Gécamines' joint partners in copper-mining ventures is Rautenbach's Ridgepoint, a firm that includes among its officials Zimbabwe's justice minister and treasurer of the ruling party, and a nephew of the president.[54] Not surprisingly, the Congo regime receives assistance from the Zimbabwe Defense Force, creating various new opportunities for presidential family members and favored generals who receive contracts to supply the intervention force.[55]

The absence of agencies that can enforce an autonomous notion of legality also generates opportunities for politicians to use more innovative means to control natural resources and translate them into political tools. Liberia's president Taylor, for example, does business with a Florida-based "missionary" group that solicits donations and investors in the United States. In the United States, the group offers participants biblical promises of large profits in mining and trading operations. In Liberia, the group received a "concession" to "monitor and verify all donations and funding raised for humanitarian purposes." Whatever its business is in Liberia, whether it is real or "virtual" minerals, the group also counted among its associates a South African businessman who had earlier been involved in a fraudulent operation with Liberian officials.[56]

Antiregime rebels in Congo exhibit intriguing links, from the point of view of analyzing the relationship between warfare and shadow states. The Rwandan vice president, whose national army assists Congo rebels, reportedly has interests in five companies operating in eastern Congo. Likewise with Ugandan officials who aid Congo's rebels: The Ugandan president's brother is reported to be a part owner of Saracen Uganda, a private-security joint venture with South African and Anglo-Canadian ties. A high-ranking Ugandan military official was shot down and killed allegedly while flying to eastern Congo to check on his business interests. Other officials reportedly have interests in exotic firms that undertake private recruitment and training of Ugandan military experts.[57]

These violent strategies, and the relation of enterprise to violence, defy Douglass North's basic observation that it is property holders who insist on state protections of both their rights to property and from predation of the state itself.[58] Among officials in Zimbabwe, Uganda, and Rwanda, one sees the melding of rule, profit, and war in ways that cut out the interests of local property holders. In Zimbabwe, this occurs in spite of a vigorous private business community that has not been dependent on ties to government officials for survival, at least until now. It is, however, a politically emasculated group, with many white members inherited from Rhodesian rule. Reinforcing the lack of a sense of collective purpose, Zimbabwe's president Mugabe mirrors Soyinka's portrayal of the late President Abacha of Nigeria: "Beyond the reality of a fiefdom that has dutifully nursed his insatiable greed and transformed him into a creature of enormous wealth . . . Abacha has no *notion* of Nigeria."[59] This contrasts with Tilly's expectation that "state makers develop a durable interest in promoting the accumulation of capital," at least in their own state and through the activities of local producers.[60]

Yet, Ugandan and Rwandan officials—not disregarding personal profit, to be sure—seem far more willing and capable of addressing the security needs of large groups in their own societies. Their activities have had a less negative impact on public finances and overall economic conditions, in contrast to the predatory Zimbabwe regime and the country's rapid economic decline. Both places offer the classic rent-seeking businesses—mining, transit trades, and now, a fair measure of U.S. backing—that have supported shadow state regimes elsewhere. Surely Uganda's small coffee producers do not rein in their rulers, nor compel them to heed their macroeconomic interests. Rwanda's farmers hardly appear to be an organized barrier to despoilment of the country's economy.

Likewise, in the former Soviet Union, and in other formerly socialist states, the collapse of central control did not transfer property rights to a new class of autonomous owners who could assert rights against states. Small farmers in Russia, for example, face difficulties even securing clear legal title to land. They face urban marketing channels that are dominated by organized crime, often in conjunction with agents of the state. Business demands for state protection go unmet. It would seem that the best strategy for entrepreneurs in the former East Bloc would be to make deals with organized crime. In fact, many do. Does this mean that feeble state bureaucracies and wavering official commitment to a public good there signal the same kind of collapse of a shadow state, and thus, civil war shaped by violent entrepreneurship? Or is it the case that state building is not a demand-driven process in some instances; that some places with vigorous "civil societies" get real states that defend their interests, but others do not; some places without these groups end up with states anyway?

Pursuing this analysis of the political economy of violence beyond clear examples of shadow states and collapsing shadow states reveals further information about the centrality of violence and enterprise in shadow states. This has much to do with how violence is organized, about who becomes a partner in the direct exercise of power and who gets managed into becoming business firms, an issue of critical concern for building a state.

States, Shadow States, and the Organization of Violence

Significantly, Russian state agencies exercise a substantial degree of autonomy, at least in the eyes of many Russians. Public opinion surveys indicate that many Russians believe that state agencies exert a meaningful level of control over force and pursue some degree of public interests. But ominously, from the point of view of Nigerian, Sierra Leonean, or Zimbabwean experience, a 1998 survey reveals that 80 percent of Russians polled believed that "criminal structures" exercise "significant influence" in Russia.[61] In another survey, 51 percent affirm the proposition that "real power in Russia belongs to criminal structures and the mafia." Yet 46 percent believe that Russia's judicial system is fair "now and then." Sixty-eight percent report that they would seek help from police, courts, and security agents if their legal rights were violated.[62] Help from these quarters in Nigeria would be a dubious prospect at best. In another Russian survey, only 16.1 percent responded that their main complaint about government was that "its actions primarily benefit shadow-economy and mafia capital."[63]

Unfortunately, opinion polls are not common in Africa. Other indicators of public opinion are available, however. Nigeria's first 1998 local elections attracted about 5 percent of eligible voters.[64] As noted above, Sierra Leoneans refer to some government troops as "sobels," or soldier-rebels, reflecting the predatory nature of these armed men. A West African commentator complains of "uniformed buzzards," soldiers who are "grossly ignorant of their own basic purpose in society."[65]

Indices of public order provide further evidence of the nature of violence. Moscow's 1997 homicide rate of 18.1 murders per 100,000 residents (well short of Washington, D.C., at 69.3 per 100,000) fell well below an estimated 250 per 100,000 in Lagos.[66] Figures do not tell the whole story; where violence comes from is also important. Russia has seen its share of high-profile political assassinations, including the December 1998 murder of Galina Starovoitova, a military police officer from St. Petersburg, and the attempt on the life of Moscow Deputy Mayor Yuri Shantsev. Though serious, these pale beside Nigeria under Abacha, where paramilitary units assassinated opponents in the military and made an attempt on the life of the military's second in command in 1997. Opponents retaliated with a bombing campaign against military aircraft, bringing down a troop transport, and in another incident killed the president's son. As noted above, military units in Nigeria rob banks and loot airplanes. Other units based in Lagos have fought occasional battles with a special security task force assigned to control them. Some local politicians incite "task forces" to murder political opponents. In 1997, Federal Aviation Authority security agents fought an armed battle with the Air Force Presidential Task Force. Quasi-official "tax consultants" extort money from businesses. Even with murders of police officers, politicians, and businesspeople, Russia's authorities exercise more control over violence and provide people there with a greater level of personal security than enjoyed in significant portions of Africa.

These comparisons point to the critical fact that the fragmentation of the Soviet nomenclatura does not include the fragmentation of Russia's military along the same lines. Some organized crime syndicates become militarized, but they do not exercise the same systematic and widespread control over violence such that they can (or need to) directly manage their own economic environment and directly exploit people and natural resources. In lieu of Tilly's or North's "demand side" entrepreneurs seeking mutually advantageous protection for property in return for revenues, security in Russia is "supply side" in terms of following from the actions of an existing military and political elite that exhibit a distinct organizational identity and interest. This in turn creates a state structure in which Russian organized crime syndicates behave as free-riders, also benefiting from (as they selectively subvert) that interest.

Much of this difference lies in the fact that Russia appears to have an army and police in the Weberian sense of exercising something closer to a monopoly on violence on behalf of a broader state interest. Accordingly, and in spite of events in 1991 and 1993, Russia's rulers appear to fear coups much less than do their African counterparts. This reflects the low level of urgency on the part of Soviet rulers from Brezhnev onward to create new militarized shadow state networks to protect themselves from disloyal military units. This is not to say that Soviet rulers had no idea of personal interests, as the epic scale of the Uzbek cotton scheme in the early 1980s shows.[67] Nor does it preclude significant collaboration between agents of the state and business interests against public and state interests.[68]

This is still a marked contrast (to take one example) to Nigeria, where rulers, no matter how reform minded, contend with a National Security Organization, State Security Service, Defense Intelligence Agency, National Intelligence Agency, National Guard, Operation Sweep, Rivers State Security Task Force, and Airforce Presidential Task Force, to name a few, and logically fear coups. To the extent that these agencies serve the interests of particular factions, it is more likely that they become agents of militarized enterprise on their own behalf, and on behalf of factional allies.

To become a shadow state force, Russia's military would require localism in terms of linking elements of the military to entrepreneurial political structures. Russia is not devoid of moves in this direction. For example, Moscow's mayor Luzhkov provided apartments and food to soldiers of the Moscow Military District. This, however, may reflect a prophylactic posture on the mayor's part to keep local units uninvolved in capital politics. More striking has been the link between the Fourteenth Battalion and Russian ethnic separatists in Moldova's "Transdniesteria," where a counterelite political group, criminals, and military units work together. Separatist Chechen and Dagestani authorities have a hard time paying soldiers, and organized crime figures recruit fighters.[69] These more extreme instances of fragmented control over violence take place in areas that are either outside Russia proper or are peripheral to its core area of control, allowing Russian authorities to "externalize" this problem to a certain extent. Indeed, General Lebed, a key figure in limiting the power of units in Moldova and Chechnya, enjoys a measure of popularity, arguably because of his military background and his reputation for professionalism.

Furthermore, Russia's regime maintains a capacity to withhold and allocate military expenditures. The Ministry of Finance demonstrates an ability to control funding releases and specify the use of resources, for example.[70] This degree of budgetary control—and the capacity to limit military resources both in terms of state expenditures and military freelancing—has eluded Nigeria's rulers for decades.[71]

Uganda's and Rwanda's armies, the products of prolonged insurgencies that sought to reform states that they conquered, possibly impart greater unity of interest and distinct organizational identity than is the case with many other African armies. The legitimacy of the conquest of state power in both cases was based upon the insurgents' promises to at least a portion of the population to control violence, provide public security, and contrast themselves with the prior regime's incapacity or unwillingness to do so. In Uganda's Luganda language, for example, "democracy" is translated as *eddembe ery'obuntu*. That is, it is freedom to do something without interference, and civility in group and individual conduct. Applied more broadly, this concept means freedom from disorder and the destructive consequences of the Obote and Amin regimes of 1962 to 1985.[72] In Zimbabwe, where a previous regime fell to insurgents, the resulting political leadership was not drawn from combat ranks. The underlying legitimization of the regime, as with most other postcolonial successor governments in Africa, lay in Africanizing an inherited state administration, not in removing self-interested predators.

Of course legacies do not determine outcomes; Ugandan officers and politicians may see routes to quick riches in warfare, and Zimbabwean officers may lament the purposes to which they have been put. But a set of conditions may make protection of a public good, and attendant long-term benefits that accrue to rulers, a more attractive option in one case. Different conditions put a premium on short-term shadow state strategies and the entrepreneurial use of violence.

No doubt global attention to Russia's problems, in contrast to African developments, further enhances regime efforts to exercise control over violence. Russia received over U.S.$200 billion from multilateral, official, and private creditors in the decade from 1989. Critics argue that Russian politicians fritter away massive amounts of money, often through insider manipulation of economic policies. Even so, external resources and pressure to institute legal protections for property at least lay the groundwork for greater distinction between public and private boundaries. At the very least, this increases incentives for Russia's violent entrepreneurs to behave as free-riders on a state-provided order, rather than managing their own economic environment directly. This external variable remains salient in Russia, despite Western criticism of Yeltsin's policies. German politicians, for example, essentially ignored $50 billion in debts and promised more aid in 1999. This is because disorder, state collapse, and prospective shadow state behavior in Russia have far more capacity to threaten Germany's security than do comparable developments in Africa. This also shows that the internal organization of violence plays a key role in determining whether external aid helps bolster autonomous state capacity or underwrites the opposite.

Conclusion

Those who focus on state-building tend to see peace and war as separate categories, with the latter viewed as serving a specific institutional function. Alternately, contemporary concerns about creeping anarchy tend to view warfare as dysfunctional and "irrational." In fact, as the political economy of violence in the context of shadow states shows, violence may actually be integral to the exercise of power in a society. This and other interests in violence may persist, especially when it is not in the short-term interest or capability of authorities to provide basic public goods. Experiences in Sierra Leone, Liberia, Sudan, Somalia, El Salvador, Chechnya, and Cambodia show that the economic interests of belligerents may be a powerful barrier to the termination of conflict. They may use war to control land and commerce, exploit labor, milk charitable agencies, and ensure the continuity of assets and privileges to a group. It follows that key actors in conflicts have vested interests in the continuation of conflicts, as Abraham observed so acutely in the Sierra Leone war. The implication of the observations in this chapter is that purposeful action has predictable outcomes. Outcomes may take unexpected directions, however, if these economic motives and their connection to power are not factored into one's analysis.

Notes

1. Bayo Ogunleye, *Behind Rebel Line* (Enugu: Delta Publishers, 1995), 139.

2. PRS Group, *Political Risk Yearbook* (East Syracuse: PRS Group, 1998).

3. Robert Kaplan, "The Coming Anarchy," *Atlantic Monthly* (February 1994): 45.

4. Alvin and Heidi Toeffler, *War and Anti-War: Survival at the Dawn of the 21st Century* (Boston: Little, Brown), 3.

5. Alain Minc, *Le Nouveau moyen age* (Paris: Gallimard, 1993).

6. Charles Tilly, "War Making and State Making as Organized Crime," in Peter Evans, Dietrich Rueschemeyer, and Theda Skocpol (eds.), *Bringing the State Back In* (New York: Cambridge University Press, 1985), 169.

7. Charles Tilly, *Coercion, Capital, and European States, A.D. 990–1990* (New York: Basil Blackwell, 1990), 193–225; Robert Jackson, *Quasi-states: Sovereignty, International Relations and the Third World* (New York: Cambridge University Press, 1990).

8. William Hoskins, *The Age of Plunder: The England of Henry VIII, 1500–1547* (New York: Longman, 1976); Karen Barkey, *Bandits and Bureaucrats: The Ottoman Route to State Centralization* (Ithaca: Cornell University Press, 1994).

9. Kalevi Holsti, *The State, War, and the State of War* (New York: Cambridge University Press, 1996), 40.

10. Mohammed Ayoob, "Subaltern Realism: International Relations Theory Meets the Third World" in Stephanie Neuman (ed.), *International Relations Theory and the Third World* (New York: St. Martin's, 1998), 42.

11. Paul Collier, "On the Economic Consequences of Civil War," *Oxford Economic Papers* 51, no. 1 (January 1999): 168–183.

12. William Reno, *Corruption and State Politics in Sierra Leone* (New York: Cambridge University Press, 1995).

13. Robert Jackson, *Quasi-states: Sovereignty, International Relations and the Third World* (New York: Cambridge University Press, 1990).

14. Terry Lynn Karl, *The Paradox of Plenty* (Berkeley: University of California Press, 1998).

15. Max Weber, *Economy and Society* (Berkeley: University of California Press, 1978), 1028–1029.

16. Steve Askin and Carol Collins, "External Collusion with Kleptocracy: Can Zaire Recapture Its Stolen Wealth?" *Review of African Political Economy* 57 (1993) 72–85.

17. Caroline Alexander, "An Ideal State," *New Yorker* (December 16, 1991): 53–88.

18. *La Dépêche Internationale des Drogues*, "Les 'familles' parrainent l'Etat," September 1994.

19. Gus Kowenhoven, accountant's personal correspondence with his client—President Samuel K. Doe, January 7, 1989.

20. See Jacqueline Coolidge and Susan Rose-Ackerman, "High-Level Rent-Seeking and Corruption in African Regimes," Private Sector Development

Program Policy Research Working Paper 1780 (Washington: World Bank, 1997).

21. Robert Nozick, *Anarchy, State and Utopia* (Oxford: Basil Blackwell, 1974).

22. William Reno, *Warlord Politics and African States* (Boulder: Lynne Rienner Publishers, 1998).

23. John Karimu, *Government Budget and Economic and Financial Policies for the Fiscal Year 1995/1996* (Freetown: Government Printer, 1995); Economist Intelligence Unit, *Sierra Leone*, first quarter (London: Economist Intelligence Unit, 1995), 26.

24. H. E. Valentine Strasser, *Fifth Anniversary of the April 29 Revolution* (Freetown: Government Printer, April 29, 1993), 3.

25. Segun Olarewaju, "Protests Against Private Taxmen," *P.M. News* [Lagos], November 9, 1998.

26. Michael Schatzberg, *The Dialectics of Oppression in Zaire* (Bloomington: Indiana University Press, 1988).

27. Africa Watch, *Divide and Rule: Sponsored Ethnic Violence in Kenya* (New York: Human Rights Watch, 1993).

28. Arthur Abraham, "War and Transition to Peace: A Study of State Conspiracy in Perpetrating Armed Conflict," *Africa Development* 22, no. 3–4 (1997): 103.

29. Colette Braeckman, "Le Zaire de Mobutu," in André Guichaoua (ed.), *Les Crises politiques au Burundi et au Rwanda (1993–1994)* (Paris: Karthala, 1995), 387–394.

30. Cyril Obi, "Global, State and Local Intersections: A Study of Power, Authority and Conflict in the Niger Delta Oil Communities," paper presented at Workshop on Local Governance and International Intervention in Africa, European University, Florence, March 1998; Oyeleye Oyediran, "The Reorganization of Local Government," in Larry Diamond, Anthony Kirk Greene, and Odeleye Oyediran (eds.), *Transition Without End: Nigerian Politics and Civil Society Under Babangida* (Boulder: Lynne Rienner, 1997), 193–212.

31. Stephen Ellis, *The Mask of Anarchy: The Roots of Liberia's War* (New York: New York University Press, 1999).

32. Ralph Egbu, "The Ogoniland Massacre," *The Sentinel* [Kaduna], June 6, 1994, p. 10.

33. Cyril Ukpevo, "PH Boils as Ogoni, Okrika Burn, Kill," *Sunray* [Port Harcourt], December 15, 1993, p. 1.

34. Civil Liberties Organization, *Ogoni Trials and Travails* (Lagos: Civil Liberties Organization, 1996).

35. Unpublished internal correspondence of foreign oil firms and Nigerian security agencies, 1993–1995.

36. Joel Migdal, *Strong Societies and Weak States* (Princeton: Princeton University Press, 1988).

37. John Wiseman, "Leadership and Personal Danger in African Politics," *Journal of Modern African Studies* 31, no. 4 (December 1993): 657–660.

38. Mancur Olson, *The Logic of Collective Action* (Cambridge: Harvard University Press, 1965).

39. Stephen Ellis, *The Mask of Anarchy: The Roots of Liberia's War* (New York: New York University Press, 1999); Mark Husband, *The Liberian Civil War* (London: Frank Cass, 1998).

40. United Nations, "First Progress Report of the Secretary-General on the United Nations Observer Mission in Sierra Leone," S/1998/750, August 12, 1998.

41. "Kenya Airways Jet Ambushed in Lagos," *Nation* [Nairobi], January 6, 1999, p. 1.

42. Diego Gambetta, *The Sicilian Mafia: The Business of Private Protection* (Cambridge: Harvard University Press, 1993).

43. Joseph Albini et al., "Russia Organized Crime: Its History, Structure, and Function," in Patrick Ryan and George Rush (eds.), *Understanding Organized Crime in Global Perspective* (London: Sage, 1997), 153–173.

44. Stephen Handelman, *Comrade Criminal: Russia's New Mafiya* (New Haven: Yale University Press, 1995).

45. Diego Gambetta, *The Sicilian Mafia: The Business of Private Protection* (Cambridge: Harvard University Press, 1993), 45–46.

46. Mancur Olson, *The Logic of Collective Action* (Cambridge: Harvard University Press, 1965).

47. Frederic Lane, "Economic Consequences of Organized Violence," *Journal of Economic History* 18, no. 4 (December 1958): 699–715.

48. Ibrahim Abdullah, "Bush Path to Destruction: The Origin and Character of the Revolutionary United Front (RUF/SL)," *Africa Development* 22, no. 3–4 (1997): 39–54.

49. U.S. Department of State, "Statement by James P. Rubin, Sierra Leone: Rebel Atrocities Against Civilians," May 12, 1998.

50. Global Witness, *A Rough Trade: The Role of Companies and Governments in the Angolan Conflict* (London: Global Witness, December 1998).

51. "Diamonds: No Way to Stifle UNITA," *Africa Energy & Mining*, September 9, 1998, p. 1.

52. "Angola: The State Is Sick," *Africa Confidential*, June 7, 1996, pp. 1–3.

53. "Protection," *Africa Confidential*, June 12, 1998, p. 8.

54. "Billy Rautenbach," *Indian Ocean Newsletter*, November 7, 1998, p. 8.

55. "Zimbabwe/DRC: Two Armies Go into Business," *Indian Ocean Newsletter*, September 25, 1999, p. 5.

56. Michael Fechter, "Greater Ministries Defends Its Mining," *Tampa Tribune*, December 22, 1998, p. 1. Supplemented with discussions between author and Michael Fechter.

57. "Uganda: UPDF Settles Down in DRC," *Indian Ocean Newsletter*, October 3, 1998, p. 1.

58. Douglass North and Robert Thomas, *The Rise of the Western World* (New York: Cambridge University Press, 1974), 17.

59. Wole Soyinka, *The Open Sore of a Continent* (New York: Oxford University Press, 1996), 15.

60. Charles Tilly, "War Making and State Making as Organized Crime," in Peter Evans, Dietrich Rueschemeyer, and Theda Skocpol (eds.), *Bringing the State Back In* (New York: Cambridge University Press, 1985), 172.

61. Leonid Sedov, "The People Don't Consider the Authorities Legitimate," *Obshchaya gazeta*, July 23, 1998, p. 5.

62. Nugzan Betaneli, "The People, as Always, Are Smarter Than the Politicians," *Izvestia*, January 23, 1998, p. 5.

63. "Ratings as They Really Are," *Moskovsky Komsomolets*, April 15, 1998 [from *Current Digest of the Post Soviet Press*].

64. Lekan Sani, "Polls Questioned," *Guardian* [Lagos], August 18, 1998, p. 3.

65. George Ayittey, *Africa Betrayed* (New York: St. Martin's, 1992), 139.

66. For further information, see www.fbi.gov/ucr/prelim98.pdf.

67. Stephen Handelman, *Comrade Criminal*, 94–95.

68. Joel Hellman, "Winners Take All: The Politics of Reform in the Post-Communist World," *World Politics* 50, no. 2 (January 1998), 203–234.

69. "Major Armed Forces and Private Armies in Chechnya," unpublished report by expert in Chechen security.

70. Mark Galeotti, "Decline and Fall—The Right Climate for Reform?" *Jane's Intelligence Review* 11, no. 1 (January 1999): 8–10.

71. Jimi Peters, *The Nigerian Military and the State* (London: I. B. Tauris Publishers, 1997).

72. Mikael Karlstrom, "Imagining Democracy: Political Culture and Democratisation in Buganda," *Africa* 66, no. 4 (1996): 485–505.

4

Globalization, Transborder Trade, and War Economies

Mark Duffield

This chapter is concerned with the relation between globalization and the development of protracted internal and regionalized forms of conflict in the South. In particular, it analyzes what can be called *war economies* in terms of them being adaptive structures based on networked forms of parallel and transborder trade. Although globalization has not caused war economies, market liberalization has encouraged the deepening and expansion of all forms of transborder activity. The extralegal mercantilist basis of most war economies gives them a number of shared characteristics. Apart from illiberalism, these include a dependence on external markets for realizing local assets and, importantly, as a source for all forms of essential nonlocal supplies and services. This dependence raises the prospect of developing new forms of market regulation as a structural means of conflict resolution. So far, this remains a relatively underdeveloped area of inquiry.

Globalization and Durable Disorder

Despite liberal assumptions that market reform and deregulation will promote international growth and order, we are daily confronted with setbacks and evidence of serial instability and growing regional and national wealth disparities. In this respect, the term *globalization* has a number of different and conflicting meanings. Among free-market economists, for example, globalization often was represented in terms of a worldwide economic and political convergence around liberal market principles and the increasing real-time integration of business, technological, and financial systems.[1] Based on an expansion and deepening of market competition, globalization is synonymous with an irresistible process of economic, political, and cultural change that is sweeping all national boundaries and protectionist tendencies before it. Indeed, for a country to remain outside this process is now tantamount to marginalization and failure. This pervasive neoliberal view has been critically dubbed "hyperglobalization."[2] However, while accepting that the current phase of globalization does represent a new departure in world history, the optimism that usually accompanies its free-market interpretation is challenged by a position stemming from political economy. That is, in the encounter with other social systems and political projects, the forces of globalization are producing unexpected and often unwanted outcomes. In addition to the anticipated virtuous circles of growth, prosperity, and stability, globalization can also encourage new and durable forms of disparity, instability, and complexity.[3] Indeed, such aberrant and often violent developments are capable of undermining the basis of global prosperity on which the neoliberal project depends.[4] This can be called the "durable disorder" interpretation of globalization.

As a way of framing the challenge that now faces the development and security communities, this chapter is a short exploration within the durable disorder thesis. As a point of departure, the significance of globalization for the changing competence of the nation-state is first briefly examined. This process is affecting both the North and the South.[5] Since the 1970s, nation-state capacity has been increasingly qualified by the emergence of new supranational, international, and local actors.[6] These new actors have appropriated state authority from "above" and "below." The power of the international financial institutions to override national economic planning, for example, is well known. The same is true of international NGOs, intergovernmental organizations, and multinational companies in terms of the social and development policies of the countries in which they operate.[7] At the same time, within countries, local organizations together with newly privatized agencies and other commercial actors have taken on a wide range of roles formally associated with nation-states and the public domain.

Regarding the location of power, the changing competence of the nation-state is reflected in the shift from hierarchical patterns of *government* to the wider and more polyarchical networks, contracts, and partnerships of *governance.* Although sovereignty continues to be important in national and international relations, the expansion of governance networks means that states are now part of much wider and sometimes ill-defined structures of authority. Not only has decisionmaking become more extenuating and equivocal, problems of accountability and the democratic deficit associated with governance networks have come to the fore. Though globalization has similarly affected the North and the South, the response of their respective ruling networks has been different. In the North, a trend toward the formation of regional alliances based on country and regional comparative advantage has emerged. At the same time, within states, under the rubric of the New Public Policy, privatization and marketization strategies have gained ascendancy. In the South, however, such opportunities do not properly exist. Indeed, as the prevalence of internal and regionalized forms of conflict would signify, rather than regional integration there remains a strong and contrary tendency toward regional schism and destabilizing political assertiveness. The deepening of the European Union (EU) while simultaneously on its borders, Yugoslavia collapsed into a number of ethnically defined successor states, is a clear example of this contrast.[8] At the same time, despite other donor and U.S. government efforts in support of regionalization, the reemergence of conflict between Ethiopia and Eritrea and the descent of Central Africa into a regionwide conflict are further examples of a contrary global dynamism.

Though it glosses over the reawakening of economic polarization and its effects, the hyperglobalization thesis has a passing resemblance to some of the processes in the core areas of the North. In a similar fashion, durable disorder would appear more representative of the South. One way of approaching this loose distinction is to suggest that while globalization may have a similar effect in terms of qualifying nation-state competence in both regions, the actual global economy is engaging and reworking the networks of Northern and Southern governance in very different ways. In the South, changing nation-state competence has been associated in many parts of Africa and the European East with a parceling out of state sovereignty to new international and subnational actors and, as a consequence, an often radical process of nation-state deconstruction.[9] This has assumed many different forms and attracted numerous descriptions—for example, warlordism, collapsed states, weak states, ethnocentric and fundamentalist states, and so on. As in the North, globalization has encouraged a process of political decentralization and the emergence of new, multiple, and overlapping centers of authority in relation to increasingly qualified and contested forms of central sovereignty and legitimacy. In the North, in the face of market deregulation, such emerging networks of governance have sought international stability and protection through regulatory, regionalist, and integrationist strategies. In the South, however, rather than integrationism, economic liberalization has provided the new actors within the emerging political complexes with the opportunity to engage in a more direct, individualistic, and competitive fashion with the global economy. At the same time, freed from much of the regulatory requirements of Northern commercial zones, multinational companies have a high degree of flexibility to pursue advantageous arrangements in relation to such governance networks.

A central thesis of this chapter is that globalization has helped many emerging governance complexes in the South to pursue new forms of political and economic advantage. Political actors have been able to control local economies and realize their worth through the ability to forge new and flexible relations with liberalized global markets. Manuel Castells, for example, has argued that deregulation has prompted the emergence of a globalized criminal economy.[10] This economy is internationally networked, expansive, and supremely adaptive. Indeed, it has most of the characteristics but few of the responsibilities of the advanced sections of the informational economy. The drug trade is a leading example of a global criminal network. Such networks often overlap or complement what this chapter describes as globalized war economies. Though having different aims and effects, they are often interconnected and share the same networked, adaptive, and expansive character. Market deregulation and declining nation-state competence have not only allowed the politics of violence and profit to merge, but also underpin the regional trend toward protracted instability, schism, and political assertiveness in the South.

War Economies

The term *war economies* is used here with some reservation. "War" and "peace" are state-centered terms. They relate to a time when nation-states could legally start and end wars. In these circumstances, regarding war and peace as distinct and absolute conditions was justified. The war economies described in this chapter, however, not only have similar transnational and networked characteristics to the conventional global economy, at a national level, they have a good deal in common with the relations and structures that constitute the peace economies of the regions in which they operate. In many areas, war and peace have become relative concepts. That is, there has been either a speeding up or slowing down of essentially similar internal structures and relations to the external world.

It is now commonplace to cite that most conflicts and protracted political crises today do not occur between sovereign states but are of an internal or regionalized type. Moreover, compared to conventional inter-state wars, these conflicts are often characterized by their longevity and socially divisive nature. Though the exact number of such conflicts at any one time is subject to empirical argument, long-term evidence suggests that their numbers have been increasing for the past several decades.[11] While important, the question of numbers is less significant than the far-reaching changes introduced by the end of the Cold War. Internal forms of conflict, often termed *national liberation struggles* and geared to a process of state formation, existed during the Cold War. Superpower rivalry and, especially, the need to create or maintain political alliances meant that many warring parties attracted external patronage. In some cases, this was substantial. The ending of the Cold War changed this situation and has had a big impact on the strategies of existing violent actors and those that have emerged subsequently.[12] Lacking external patronage, warring parties have been forced to develop their own means of economic sustainability. Reflecting the logic of globalization, this has often meant moving beyond the state in the pursuit of wider alternative economic networks. To the extent that this has been successful, contemporary conflict has assumed a protracted nature. At the same time, state formation, at least in terms of attempting to reproduce traditional and inclusive forms of nation-state competence, has declined as a political project. Free from superpower patronage, the main consequence for the North is that the international community has found it harder to control or manage autonomous warring parties and political actors. This independence goes to the heart of the current security dilemma.

Although globalization and liberalization have not caused these new forms of instability, they have made it easier for warring parties to establish the parallel and transborder economic linkages necessary for survival. In terms of reflecting this transformation, Savimbi's National Union for the Total Independence of Angola (UNITA) is instructive. During the 1980s, it was based near the southern border with Namibia and relied on Cold War–sponsored cross-border support from South Africa. Today, it controls diamond fields in the center and north of Angola and has developed a ferocious independence based upon a shifting pattern of regional transborder and international commercial linkages.[13] This independence has enabled the conflict in Angola to reach levels of destruction far in excess of that during the Cold War. If Savimbi were chairman of a multinational company, overseeing such a transformation— apart from earning a huge bonus award—would have won international acclaim. Many emerging political complexes (the so-called weak, failed, or ethnocentric states of conventional wisdom) have followed similar adaptive trajectories.

In order to situate modern war economies, the idea of post–nation-state conflict is useful.[14] Such a concept is needed to help overcome the limitations of mainstream conflict analysis—that is, the predominance of images of conflict as temporary (*resulting from a developmental malaise*), irrational (*arising from misunderstanding and communication breakdown*), and backward (*the reappearance of ancient hatreds*). There is also a difficulty in going beyond state-centric thinking that finds expression in the extensive use of such terms as *internal, intra-state,* or *civil* war; and hence an inability to incorporate the effects of globalization and liberalization. Post–nation-state conflict suggests the appearance of nonstate or qualified state political projects that no longer find it necessary to project power through juridical or bureaucratic forms of control. Indeed, they may not even require a fixed territory in which to operate. Authority, moreover, does not necessarily require consent for it to be exercised. In relation to such emerging political complexes, post–nation-state conflict implies a move away from the inclusive or universalistic forms of social and welfare competence formally associated with nation-states. This capacity reached its apogee in the West during the 1970s. Qualified state structures have divested themselves of much of the social inclusiveness and public utility associated with nation-states and have often used the symbolic language of privatization to externalize this competence.[15]

Contemporary patterns and modalities of instability not only occur within states but across states and regions. These wider connections reflect the characteristics of modern-day war economies. They are rarely self-sufficient or autarkic after the fashion of traditional nation-state–based war economies. On the contrary, though controlling local assets, they are heavily reliant on all forms of external support and supplies. Maintaining the political entities associated with post–nation-state conflict usually requires transregional linkages. At the same time, the marketing of local resources and procurement of arms and supplies are based on access to global markets and, very often, transcontinental smuggling or gray commercial networks. In many respects, contemporary war economies reproduce the networked structures associated with globalization more generally.

The analysis of post–nation-state conflict sits awkwardly with ideas of conflict as abnormal or transitory. Contemporary war economies reflect and are embedded in what constitutes the normal social relations of the regions concerned. In this respect, their study can gain much from the work that is already being done on parallel or transborder trade. In global terms, the majority of this trade is unconnected with instability. However, in terms of its social characteristics and the impact of globalization upon it, its examination is useful.

Transborder Trade and Illiberalism

In relation to transborder trade, there is an important problem regarding terminology. Following Kate Meagher's analysis, the term *transborder trade* is seen as wider than conventional ideas of parallel or informal economic activity.[16] Parallel trade is commonly understood as illegal or unofficial trade in goods that are themselves legal; for example, the informal importation of cheap East Asian textiles and manufactured goods and their incorporation within regional parallel trade circuits. Transborder trade implies large-scale transnational trading operations that, although they also use extralegal or unofficial means, can involve illegal as well as legal goods. Illegal goods can include arms, drugs, proscribed wildlife products, raw material obtained with proper agreement, looted household equipment, stolen vehicles, and so on. Trade in such goods can generally be regarded as a prohibited activity. Whereas legal goods tend to predominate in transborder trade, the inclusion of illegal goods and services is important. It makes it possible, for example, to bring together for comparative purposes such diverse activities as the Nigerian-based Hausa-Fulani transcontinental parallel trade networks with, for example, the criminalized transborder trade controlled by Bosnia's ethnic elites. Though there are differences—for example, the Hausa-Fulani networks largely trade in legal goods—it can be argued that organizationally they are similar. In many respects, the legality of the commodities involved in transborder trade is a relative rather than an absolute difference. At the same time, globalization, structural adjustment, and the changing competence of the nation-state have encouraged the growth of parallel and transborder activity of all types.

Over the past couple of decades, the perception of transborder trade has undergone several shifts in terms of how it has been perceived by the aid community.[17] In Africa, for example, in the early 1980s, transborder trade was seen as a threat to the free market project. Price distortions following independence had given rise to the hemorrhaging of foreign exchange from many countries. Such activity was regarded as a justification for robust market reform and adjustment measures.[18] By the end of the 1980s, with growing governmental and popular resistance in the South to adjustment, the groups involved in transborder trade were represented as a surrogate constituency regarded as supportive of liberalization. From being a threat, parallel activity was seen as a popular form of resistance to arbitrary colonial borders, patrimonial corruption, and state inefficiency.[19] The informal economy was reinterpreted as an authentic grassroots response to the development challenge. During the course of the 1990s, however, the view of transborder trade has returned to one of concern. There are a number of reasons for this. An example is the growing evidence of the strong centripetal influence of transborder activity in the collapse of the former Yugoslavia[20] together with similar effects in other parts of the European East.[21] In Africa, there has been a growing frustration with the ability of transborder operators to exploit the differential implementation of adjustment policies. This has been coupled with concerns that the weakening of the state as a result of globalization is leading to patterns of conflict associated with such things as corruption, the plunder of natural resources, and illegal drug trafficking.[22]

In relation to trade in legal goods, evidence suggests that globalization and structural adjustment have increased the volume of transborder trade and deepened its regional penetration and transcontinental character. In relation to West Africa, where work on parallel activity is relatively extensive, the differential application of adjustment policies within the region, the liberalization of currency markets, the upheaval in national economies as a result of adjustment, the decline in living standards, and the cutting of costs through all forms of fiscal evasion have contributed to a marked growth in transborder trade since the 1980s.[23] This growth has also witnessed fundamental changes in the character of transborder trade. In particular, trade in local agricultural and manufactured products between ecological zones has declined. It has been replaced by the parallel export of primary products and the import of manufactured goods from the world market, thereby reproducing the dependency structure of international trade. As will be described below, although this pattern of integration within the global economy describes the situation with regard to parallel trade in legal goods, the relations and linkages involved are broadly replicated in contemporary war economies.

The neoliberal hyperglobalization position holds that the world's economies are converging and becoming increasingly interconnected. If true, such a view would seem only applicable to the core areas of the global economy. Within the Northern regional blocs, the economy is based on a production-finance complex. Within and across such core areas, economic liberalization and growing regional and transregional linkages are the means through which this arrangement has deepened.[24] Transborder trade in the South, however, is different. As its name suggests, it is primarily based on trade and not production-finance. At the same time, of the trillions of dollars that daily circulate within the global financial markets, only a small fraction is concerned with the real economy. The bulk is engaged in speculative activities. For transborder trade the reverse is true. Unlike the virtual economy of finance, almost all its resources are concerned with the real economy. Moreover, transborder trade is essentially a mercantilist activity and, in the main, is not reliant on manufacturing or long-term production-investment. It is more involved with controlling and trading existing goods, services, and resources. Profit depends upon being able to maintain, control, and exploit all forms of difference: price, access, availability, quality, and so on.[25] Transborder activity can be as much a matter of enforcement as trade. Such factors give transborder trade several distinct characteristics compared to the dominant production-finance economy:

- As an extralegal activity, the circuits involved lend themselves to different forms of socially structured control. There are normally few formal qualifications for transborder trade. Or, if there are, they are likely to be subordinate to overriding ethnic, local, kinship, religious, political, or diaspora considerations.
- Rather than promote integration, the interests of the social and political elites that control transborder trade are generally opposed to economic regionalism. Profit depends on maintaining differences and discrete forms of control.
- Rather than supporting free-market liberalism, the dynamics of transborder trade are more likely to encourage and variously enforce informal protectionism.

These characteristics arise because parallel and transborder trade is not just an unofficial mechanism for uniting disjointed official economies or a grassroots response to corruption and state decay. They reflect the tactics and strategies of elite commercial groups that have consciously made transborder trade the basis of their means of accumulation. As such, transborder trade is part of a "struggle for advantage in which the official development strategies of countries within the same region are pitted against each other, and vested interests are intrinsically opposed to economic rationalization."[26]

The literature on Africa and the European East contains many examples of the illiberal and quasifeudal tendencies associated with transborder trade. Regarding West Africa, for example, whereas Gambia's liberal import policy is highly profitable for its commercial elite, owing to extensive import smuggling, it is markedly less so for Senegal. This Gambian advantage led to its foot-dragging in negotiations concerning confederation and economic integration with Senegal. Ultimately, the confederation project collapsed in 1989.[27] Regarding the former Yugoslavia, by the end of the 1980s, several years before the outbreak of fighting, the increasing dominance of transborder trade within the republics and their attempts to link directly to the global market had propelled their economies to adopt increasingly autarkic behavior, even to the extent of unofficial and irrational customs and border controls that discouraged interrepublic trade.[28] Regarding Romania, in a deliberate mocking of the conventional envisioning of a transition to liberal democracy, Katherine Verdery shows that the evidence is far more compelling if one considers that Romania is returning to feudalism.[29]

The Relativization of War and Peace

Given the general characteristics of transborder trade, it is possible to argue that there is a similarity between peace economies and war economies. In transitional or developing countries, the differences between these conditions are relative rather than absolute. Apart from the existence of open violence in war economies, their points of similarity are greater than their points of difference. Affinities include:

- High levels of unemployment and underemployment
- Fragmented and degraded forms of public administration
- A high degree of autonomy among political actors
- Large areas of parallel, transborder, or criminalized activity within the economy

- A high degree of dependence on all forms of external
  support ranging from finance and hard currency to manufactured goods, spare parts, energy, medical supplies,
  developmental assistance, and food aid.

Given the similarity between war and peace economies, why
some countries or regions should suffer open conflict while
others do not is a question for further research. In some countries or regions, violence sustained by transborder trade does
provide a means through which some elites can forge a
politico-economic alternative. At the same time, however, it is
important to not reify open violence and turn it into an abstract thing-in-itself. Even when violence is not visible, similar
processes of exclusion and oppression can be in operation but
at a lower key. In Yugoslavia and its successor states, for example, ethnic cleansing was and is a feature of the prewar, war,
and postwar situations. It has simply varied in terms of severity
and visibility. War and peace are relative rather than absolute
conditions.

It should be reiterated that the bulk of all transborder trade
is in legal goods and, despite its informal or extralegal nature,
it is not usually associated with instability or conflict. It has
grown in response to the uncertainties and opportunities
wrought by political change and globalization. However, the
same forces of globalization that have encouraged parallel
trade have also made it easier for types of economic activity
that produce instability to expand. In this respect, the distinction between production-finance and mercantile trade-based
economies offers an interesting comment on the contrasting
regional dynamics that one can observe in the global economy—that is, as argued above, the tendency toward greater integration in its core areas while outside these regions integration remains contested and problematic. The above analysis
suggests one hypothesis to explain this situation: Though liberalism and integrationist tendencies may characterize the core
regions, through a combination of economic crisis, political
change, and liberalization, assertive and illiberal transborder
circuits have grown in importance in the periphery. As
Meagher has pointed out, however, although there may be a
structural similarity between transborder trade in legal and illegal goods, it is rare to find a social group initially associated with

the former gravitating to the latter.[30] Criminalized and conflict-prone transborder activity is usually connected with the emergence of new social and political elites.

In some places, the control and manipulation of transborder trade have been crucial in defining alternative elite politico-economic strategies in the post–Cold War period. This includes fundamentalist,[31] ethnonationalist,[32] and resource-based alternatives.[33] The anti–free market and quasifeudal tendencies associated with transborder trade find their most violent expression in contemporary forms of post–nation-state conflict. In this respect, conflict does place extra demands on transborder networks. For example, most modern war economies are highly dependent on all forms of external support and trade networks—that is, for the marketing of resources or services in order to secure arms, fuel, equipment, spare parts, munitions, clothing, food aid, funding, and so on. In order to support such external networks, some war economies involve the control and export of high-value commodities, such as diamonds, hardwoods, arms, or narcotics. In other places, traffic in more mundane items, such as household goods, furniture, vehicles, farm equipment, livestock, building materials, and economic migrants, is more common. In this respect, arising from the necessary maintenance of political patronage and support for new internal client regimes, patterns of conflict and trade are often inseparable from such things as forcible asset transfer between ethnic groups[34] or social cleansing.[35] Hence, post–nation-state war economies often involve campaigns of immiseration and violent population displacement as an essential precondition of asset realization. Such developments therefore are not an unfortunate but indirect consequence of conflict; they are usually its intended outcomes.

Not only is it misleading to see internal war as abnormal or radically different from peace, but conventional perceptions about the functions of conflict can also be challenged. In a well-known maxim, the military theorist Clausewitz characterized traditional nation-state–based warfare as the continuation of politics by other means. Conflict linked to transborder trade is different. Such wars are not necessarily about winning or securing a comprehensive settlement. Indeed, the suspension of legality due to insecurity is often a necessary precondition of asset realization through parallel and transborder means. For many violent groups, long-term suspension can confer a distinct advantage. In a wide-ranging review of the many different economic opportunities that contemporary conflict offers elite and sometimes even subordinate groups, Keen has concluded that internal forms of war are now better understood as the continuation of *economics* by other means.[36] Though political agendas remain and are sometimes cogently expounded, these are often of a sectarian or exclusive nature. In the meantime, conflict and instability provide the dynamism through which such agendas and elite fortunes are maintained.

The Privatization of Violence

Deregulation coupled with the qualification of nation-state competence is helping war economies to expand. Rather than globalization fostering development, poverty reduction, and stability, one can expect the current pattern of overt political instability outside the core areas of the global economy to continue. The violence associated with post–nation-state conflict is not a harking back to a developmental malaise or the reappearance of ancient tribal hatreds but is based on contemporary structures and processes. At the same time, war economies are managed by elites that, in general, have a clear grasp of the situation. Though it is often devastating for subordinate groups, internal conflict is hardly irrational from the perspective of these actors. Transborder trade is capable of netting them considerable amounts of money. Between 1992 and 1996, for example, Charles Taylor is estimated to have made between U.S.$400 million and $450 million per year from the conflict in Liberia.[37] Since 1992, UNITA has consistently controlled around 60–70 percent of Angola's diamond production. To date, this is estimated to have generated U.S.$3.7 billion in revenue.[38]

Post–nation-state conflict has important implications concerning the organizational characteristics of violence. In this respect, the qualification of nation-state competence through the emergence of new international and local actors is instructive. Transborder trade has been a useful vehicle in both building up and projecting the influence of nonstate and qualified-state actors, such as warlord or mafia entities, together with the elites of so-called weak, ethnocentric, or fundamentalist states.

These new entities and structures add another dimension to the privatization of security. At the same time that international security is being privatized and a new security community is emerging, extralegal transborder trade and criminalized economic activity can be seen as effecting a corresponding and associated privatization of violence.[39] In this respect, Federico Varese has provided a useful analysis of the rise of the Russian mafia.[40] Though economic reform in the mid-1980s created many new owners of private property, a corresponding reform of the legal apparatus did not take place. The resulting vacuum within the legal system, especially the inability of the central authorities to provide recourse, encouraged Russia's emerging business elite to seek alternatives. This pressure coincided with the post–Cold War downsizing of the security establishment and the increasing availability of men trained in the use of arms. Demand met supply, and mafia groups providing private protection consequently expanded. At the same time, these same networks have become the means through which many of the regulatory and enforcement aspects of Russian business life are now conducted.

Although the example is specific to Russia, this model of the decentralization and reworking of power has a far wider significance. Not only does it find echoes in other parts of the European East, it also has parallels with the effects of globalization on the status of legal authority more widely. The rule of law and protection of customary rights have been an important casualty of the qualification of nation-state competence.[41] In general terms, market deregulation has meant that many Southern rulers now have an enhanced ability to realize local assets on global markets. The growing tension around the land issue and the exploitation of its associated resources in many parts of the South are symptomatic of the new opportunities created by globalization. While the North is downsizing its various security establishments (but not necessarily their capability), subordinate groups in many parts of the South are rearming themselves with automatic weapons. Ambiguity over law and customary rights, exacerbated by market liberalization, has led many to take the protection of their assets and livelihoods into their own hands. Though this is frequently interpreted as a growth in acts of banditry or lawlessness, one should not overlook its global implications. It is also the case that social exclusion as represented, for example, in ethnic cleansing also implies new forms of social *inclusion*. Some of the client regimes associated with emerging nonstate and qualified state entities have been forged from the anxieties of subordinate groups and their readiness at arms.[42] The distribution of actual rewards within some of these entities may be narrow, but they nevertheless have to operate a system of patronage. It should not be forgotten that for many people, even sectarian or ethnocentric regimes provide the only form of protection they have in an increasingly uncertain world.

War Economies and Commercial Complicity

War economies are highly criminalized. Asset realization usually involves activities that breach national legal codes. The resulting transborder trade is also of a type that contravenes international proscriptions. Unlike parallel trade in legal goods, war economies usually link into transcontinental smuggling and other gray commercial networks to satisfy their special requirements. Today's so-called warlords or failed states may act locally, but to survive they have to think globally. In this respect, a high level of complicity among international companies, offshore banking facilities, and Northern governments has assisted the development of war economies. There is a growing symbiotic relationship between zones of stability and instability within the global political economy. In the early 1990s, for example, the Liberian warlord Charles Taylor (now head of state) was supplying, among other things, a third of France's tropical hardwood requirements through French companies.[43] During the latter part of the 1990s, UNITA's contribution to the ferocious war in Angola has largely been underwritten by De Beers' no-questions diamond-buying policy and an unwillingness of many Northern governments to uphold UN trade sanctions.[44] Despite sanctions, since 1993 it is estimated that UNITA has made some U.S.$4 billion from illegal diamond sales and investments.[45] Regarding Iran, though not a war economy in the sense of the above examples, it is instructive that the 1996 U.S.-Iran-Libya Sanctions Act was being undermined by European and Asian oil companies anxious to secure lucrative contracts to pump Turkmenistan oil and gas across Iran.[46] Unable to effect an embargo, the United States has recently relaxed sanctions against Iran, Libya, and, for similar reasons, Sudan. The only losers in this situation have been law-abiding American companies. As in the environmental field, securing effective commercial and governmental compliance with UN and donor sanctions requirements has proved difficult. Most conflicts or areas of protracted instability, however, are not covered by formal sanctions regimes. In such areas, international means of regulation and forms of asset seizure remain underdeveloped. The actions by Northern companies in the supply of arms and munitions to the South are perhaps better understood as an extreme example of the commercial complicity that characterizes many parts of international business culture. Without this help, war economies would find it difficult to survive.

Given the dependence of war economies on international trade networks, they are vulnerable to a concerted application of appropriate compliance and regulatory measures. Reducing the profitability and effectiveness of conflict-related transborder trade networks should be seen as complementing more conventional confidence-building and political reform measures to establish peaceful relations within countries. One can only surmise that the lack of attention accorded the transborder nature of war economies and their dependence on Northern commercial complicity reflect the predominant free trade ethos. One reflection of this concerns current attempts to better enforce UN sanctions against UNITA. At the time of this writing, the UN sanctions committee for Angola had been given funds to investigate how UNITA funds its war aims and procures armaments. Depending on results, the UN is now said to be ready to name and shame the countries and companies involved.[47] Although this is a welcome move, rather than treating it as a general problem of parallel and transborder trade under conditions of globalization, the UN is approaching the matter as a specific policing problem. Current plans, for example, include the tracking and interdiction of illegal flights and the installation of customs monitors in surrounding and implicated African countries. In other words, it is an approach that resembles the so-far-unsuccessful attempts to limit the drugs trade.

Conflict Resolution and Market Regulation

Conflict-related nonstate and qualified state entities supported by extralegal transborder trade networks constitute the violent analogue to the aid community.[48] Whereas many actors within this governance network usually perceive their existence in terms of being a response to instability, both the emerging political complexes and the aid community have grown in parallel under the influence of globalization. Although globalization has allowed violent nonstate actors to gain in influence, effective forms of international regulation and accountability have yet to catch up. To state this another way, the increasing de facto involvement of the aid community with nonstate actors has yet to be examined in terms of its profound implications for existing state-based charters, conventions, and modes of regulation. The linkages, networks, and competing agendas of the aid community and the emerging political complexes have combined to produce what can be called a new development-security complex. Within this complex the organizational structures of privatized development and security are increasingly confronting and conjoining the actors of privatized violence. This new terrain poses novel uncertainties, threats, and problems of analysis. Commercial complicity and lack of compliance with existing forms of regulation are only a part of a complex structure of reinforcement, accommodation, and confrontation.

With the exception of the lone U.S. superpower, the new development-security complex is characterized by the declining significance of major states. At the least, through the expansion of governance networks, states have to increasingly rely on a combination of multilateral and privatized solutions. This leaching of state authority to increasingly privatized and marketized aid and security communities is a measure of the growing ineffectiveness of traditional forms of analysis and response. With the loss of the political certainty of the Cold War, military deterrence and use of superior force appear increasingly problematic given the globalized and networked character of current patterns of instability. Rather than ending wars, problems mutate and assume a protracted nature. Such developments, together with the challenges of the new development-security terrain, are shifting research on conflict and aid policy in a new direction. In relation to war economies, for example, there remains a dearth of ethnographic accounts of their political functioning and methods of economic resourcing. In terms of applied research, a better understanding of the globalized nature of war economies and their reliance on commercial complicity would encourage more discussion on new forms of market regulation, trade policy, forensic accounting, international mechanisms of asset seizure, and so on. Many of the chapters in this book represent an important contribution to this work. Such measures can be seen as contributing to the development of structural methods of conflict limitation and the design of more targeted and effective sanction regimes.

Notes

1. World Bank, *The State in a Changing World: The World Development Report* (Washington, D.C.: World Bank, 1997).

2. David Held, David Goldblatt, Anthony McGrew, and Jonathan Perraton, "The Globalization of Economic Activity," *New Political Economy* 2, no. 2 (1997): 257–277.

3. Philip G. Cerny, "Globalization, Fragmentation, and the Governance Gap: Towards a New Medievalism in World Politics?" Paper presented at Workshop on Globalisation: Critical Perspectives, University of Birmingham, March 14–16, 1997.

4. John Gray, *False Dawn: The Delusions of Global Capitalism* (London: Granta, 1998).

5. The terms *North* and *South* are used here to loosely distinguish those countries that are part of the regional economic alliances centering on North America, Western Europe, and East Asia (the North) from those that are either outside these regional systems or only partially integrated within them (the South).

6. Georgi M. Derlugian, "The Social Cohesion of the States," in Terence K. Hopkins and Immanuel Wallerstein (eds.), *The Age of Transition: Trajectory of the World-System, 1945–2025* (London: Zed, 1996), 148–177.

7. Bob Deacon, Michelle Hulse, and Paul Stubbs, *Global Social Policy: International Organisations and the Future of Welfare* (London: Sage, 1997).

8. Vesna Bojicic, Mary Kaldor, and Ivan Vejvoda, "Post-War Reconstruction in the Balkans: A Background Report Prepared for the European Commission," *Sussex European Institute Working Paper no. 14* (Sussex University: European Institute, 1995).

9. Katherine Verdery, *What Was Socialism, and What Comes Next?* (Princeton: Princeton University Press, 1996).

10. Manuel Castells, *End of Millennium* [Vol. III of *The Information Age: Economy, Society and Culture*] (Oxford: Blackwell, 1998), 166–205.

11. K. J. Gantzel, "War in the Post-World-War-II-World: Empirical Trends, Theoretical Approaches and Problems on the Concept of 'Ethnic War,'" in David Turton (ed.), *War and Ethnicity: Global Connections and Local Violence* (Rochester, N.Y.: University of Rochester Press, 1997), 115–130.

12. Francois Jean (ed.), *Life, Death and Aid: The Médecins Sans Frontières Report on World Crisis Interventions* (London: Routledge, 1993).

13. Global Witness, *A Rough Trade: The Role of Companies and Governments in the Angolan Conflict* (London: Global Witness Ltd, 1998).

14. Mark Duffield, "Post-Modern Conflict: Warlords, Post-Adjustment States and Private Protection," *Civil Wars* 1, no. 1 (1998): 65–102.

15. Gray, *False Dawn.*

16. Kate Meagher, "A Back Door to Globalisation?: Structural Adjustment, Globalisation and Transborder Trade in West Africa," unpublished manuscript, Nuffield College, University of Oxford, 1998.

17. Ibid.

18. World Bank, *World Development Report* (Washington, D.C.: World Bank, 1981).

19. World Bank, *World Development Report* (Washington, D.C.: World Bank, 1989).

20. Carl-Ulrik Schierup, "Quasi-Proletarians and a Patriarchal Bureaucracy: Aspects of Yugoslavia's Re-Peripheralisation," *Soviet Studies* 44, no. 1 (1992): 79–99.

21. Verdery, *What Was Socialism.*

22. World Bank, *The State in a Changing World.*

23. Meagher, "A Back Door to Globalisation?"

24. James H. Mittelman, "Rethinking the 'New Regionalism' in the Context of Globalization," *Global Governance* 2, no. 2 (1996): 189–213.

25. Kate Meagher, "Informal Integration or Economic Subversion? Parallel Trade in West Africa," in Real Lavergne (ed.), *Regional Integration and Cooperation in West Africa* (Trenton, N.J.: Africa World Press with International Development Research Centre, Ottowa, 1997), 165–187.

26. Ibid., 182.

27. Ibid.

28. Schierup, "Quasi-Proletarians and a Patriarchal Bureaucracy."

29. Verdery, *What Was Socialism.*

30. Meagher, "A Back Door to Globalisation?"

31. A. Jamal, "Funding Fundamentalism: The Political Economy of an Islamist State," *Middle East Report* 21, no. 172 (1991): 14–17, 38.

32. Schierup, "Quasi-Proletarians and a Patriarchal Bureaucracy."

33. Paul Richards, *Fighting for the Rain Forest: Youth, Insurgency and Environment in Sierra Leone* (London: University College, 1995).

34. David Keen, *The Benefits of Famine: A Political Economy of Famine and Relief in Southwestern Sudan, 1983–1989* (Princeton: Princeton University Press, 1994).

35. Hugh Griffiths, "The Political Economy of Ethnic Conflict: Ethno-Nationalism and Organised Crime," unpublished manuscript.

36. David Keen, "The Economic Functions of Violence in Civil Wars," *Adelphi Paper* 320 (Oxford: Oxford University Press for the International Institute for Strategic Studies, 1998), 1–88.

37. William Reno, Paper presented at UNU/WIDER–Queen Elizabeth House, Oxford, meeting on "The Political Economy of Humanitarian Emergencies," October 1996 (Helsinki, Finland: The United Nations University, World Institute for Development Economics Research), 10.

38. Global Witness, *A Rough Trade.*

39. Keen, "The Economic Functions of Violence in Civil Wars."

40. Federico Varese, "Is Sicily the Future of Russia? Private Protection and the Rise of the Russian Mafia," *Archives Européennes de Sociologie* 35, no. 2 (1994): 224–258.

41. Verdery, *What Was Socialism.*

42. Mark Duffield, "The Political Economy of Internal War," in Joanna Macrae and Anthony Zwi (eds.), *War and Hunger: Rethinking International Responses to Complex Emergencies* (London: Zed, 1994), 50–69.

43. Reno, paper presented at UNU/WIDER.

44. Global Witness, *A Rough Trade.*

45. Victoria Brittain, "The UN Gets Tough with UNITA," *The Guardian* [London], July 9, 1999, p. 14.

46. James Meek, "Iranian Pipelines Mock Blockade," *The Guardian* [London], February 3, 1998, p. 14.

47. Brittain, "The UN Gets Tough with UNITA."

48. Duffield, "Post-Modern Conflict: Warlords, Post-Adjustment States and Private Protection."

5

Doing Well out of War: An Economic Perspective

Paul Collier

The discourse on conflict tends to be dominated by group grievances beneath which intergroup hatreds lurk, often traced back through history. I have investigated statistically the global pattern of large-scale civil conflict since 1965, expecting to find a close relationship between measures of these hatreds and grievances and the incidence of conflict. Instead, I found that economic agendas appear to be central to understanding why civil wars start. Conflicts are far more likely to be caused by economic opportunities than by grievance. If economic agendas are driving conflict, then it is likely that some groups are benefiting from conflict and that these groups therefore have some interest in initiating and sustaining it. Civil wars create economic opportunities for a minority of actors even as they destroy them for the majority. I consider which groups benefit, and what the international community can do to reduce their power.

Economic Agendas as Causes of Conflict

A useful conceptual distinction in understanding the motivation for civil war is that between greed and grievance. At one extreme rebellions might arise because the rebels aspire to wealth by capturing resources extralegally. At the other extreme they might arise because rebels aspire to rid the nation, or the group of people with which they identify, of an unjust

regime. These two motivations obviously imply radically different types of policy intervention if the international community
wishes to promote the prospects of peace. The most obvious
way of discovering what motivates people is to ask them. However, here we immediately encounter a problem. Those rebel
organizations that are sufficiently successful to get noticed are
unlikely to be so naïve as to admit to greed as a motive. Successful rebel organizations place considerable emphasis on
good public relations with the international community. Narratives of grievance play much better with this community than
narratives of greed. A narrative of grievance is not only much
more functional externally, it is also more satisfying personally:
Rebel leaders may readily be persuaded by their own propaganda. Further, an accentuated sense of grievance may be functional internally for the rebel organization. The organization
has to recruit—indeed, its success depends upon it. As the organization gets larger, the material benefits that it can offer its
additional members are likely to diminish. By playing upon a
sense of grievance, the organization may therefore be able to
get additional recruits more cheaply. Hence, even where the rationale at the top of the organization is essentially greed, the
actual discourse may be entirely dominated by grievance. I
should emphasize that I do not mean to be cynical. I am not arguing that rebels necessarily deceive others or themselves in explaining their motivation in terms of grievance. Rather, I am
simply arguing that since both greed-motivated and grievance-
motivated rebel organizations will embed their behavior in a
narrative of grievance, the observation of that narrative provides no informational content to the researcher as to the true
motivation for rebellion. To discover the truth we need a different research approach.

The approach I take, which is the conventional one in social science, is to infer motivation from patterns of observed
behavior. If someone says "I don't like chocolates" but keeps on
eating them, we infer that she really likes them, and the question of why she says the opposite is then usually relegated to
being of secondary importance.

I try to determine patterns in the origins of civil war, dis-
tinguishing between those causal factors that are broadly consistent with an economic motivation and those that are more
consistent with grievance. I then try to predict whether each

country has a civil war during each five-year period from 1960 to 1995 in terms of the values of the causal factors at the beginning of each period. For example, I try to predict whether Kenya had a civil war during the period 1970–1974 in terms of its characteristics as of 1970. This approach only becomes reasonably robust if the coverage is large and comprehensive. I therefore follow current research practice in opting for global coverage, only dropping countries where there are too little data.

I first describe the proxies I use to capture the notion of an economic agenda. The most important one is the importance of exports of primary commodities. I measure this as the share of *primary commodity exports* in gross domestic product (GDP). Primary commodity exports are likely to be a good proxy for the availability of "lootable" resources. We know that they are by far the most heavily taxed component of the GDP in developing countries, and the reason for this is that they are the most easily taxed component. Primary commodity production does not depend upon complex and delicate networks of information and transactions, as with manufacturing. It can also be highly profitable because it is based on the exploitation of idiosyncratic natural endowments rather than the more competitive level playing fields of manufacturing. Thus, production can survive predatory taxation. Yet for export it is dependent upon long trade routes, usually originating from rural locations. This makes it easy for an organized military force to impose predatory taxation by targeting these trade routes. These factors apply equally to rebel organizations as to governments. Rebels, too, can impose predatory taxation on primary commodities as long as they can either interrupt some point in the trade route or menace an isolated, and difficult to protect, point of production.

For rebels, primary commodities have one further advantage over other sources of taxation that does not apply to governments. Sometimes, taxation can be much higher if it is levied in kind: The rebels directly extract a proportion of the production, rather than cash. This is particularly likely to apply where production is conducted by poor households rather than by large firms, and the households are themselves cash-scarce because they can only command a small fraction of the international value of their production. If rebels receive taxes in kind, they will need to be able to dispose of the output. Because rebel organizations are extralegal, the disposal of output on international markets potentially poses problems. The more identifiable is the original source of the output, the deeper will be the discount below the international price. Primary commodities have the considerable advantage to rebel organizations that they are generic rather than branded products, and so their origin is much more difficult to determine. The discount from reliance upon extralegal marketing channels can therefore be much smaller.

Although primary commodities are thus a good proxy for the lootable resources that greed-motivated rebels would seek to capture, there are other factors likely to matter for an economic agenda. The most important other factor is likely to be the cost of attracting recruits to the rebellion. Overwhelmingly, the people who join rebellions are young men. Hence, other things equal, we might expect that the *proportion of young men* in a society, say those between the ages of 15 and 24, would be a factor influencing the feasibility of rebellion: The greater the proportion of young men, the easier it would be to recruit rebels. Relatedly, the willingness of young men to join a rebellion might be influenced by their other income-earning opportunities. If young men face only the option of poverty, they might be more inclined to join a rebellion than if they have better opportunities. I proxy these income-earning opportunities by the amount of *education* in the society—the average number of years of education the population has received. In developing countries this education will have been disproportionately supplied to young men, so that differences in the average educational endowment between societies will reflect much larger differences in the educational endowments of young males. It might seem to some noneconomists that considerations of alternative income-earning opportunities do not enter into the decision process of potential recruits to rebellions. I will therefore give an example of where such considerations were hugely important. The largest civil war of the twentieth century was the Russian civil war of 1919–1920. Both the Red and the White armies were essentially scratch, rebel armies, since the Czarist army had collapsed. For both these rebel armies recruitment and desertion were huge problems. Between them they lost four million men to desertion. Thus, the desertion rate is large enough to be a social rather than just an idiosyncratic phenomenon. The desertion rate was ten times higher in summer than in winter.[1] The reason for this was obviously that both armies were composed of peasants, and during the summer peasants had much higher income-earning opportunities, notably the harvest, than in the winter.

To summarize, my measures of economic agendas will be primary commodities, the proportion of young men in the society, and the endowment of education. There are of course many other potential economic agendas in conflict, such as suppliers of armaments and opportunities for bureaucratic corruption. However, most of these are difficult to measure in a comparative way and so preclude the sort of analysis I undertake here. I now contrast these economic factors with those that proxy grievance.

Rebel narratives of grievance are focused on one or more of four factors. Probably attracting the most horrified fascination from Western media is the expression of raw *ethnic or religious hatred*. Though such narratives may contain a subtext of specific economic or social grievances, sometimes these refer to very remote time periods, or may appear to be merely illustrations or even pretexts for a deeper hatred. For example, this might seem to be the most obvious interpretation of the Serb attack on the population of Kosovo. I measure the tendency to such raw grievances by the extent to which the society is fractionalized by ethnicity and by religion. Specifically, I use indices constructed from historical work by anthropologists that show the probability that any two randomly drawn people from the society are from different ethnic and religious groups. I also multiply the two indices, which gives a measure of potential cross-cutting cleavages: Societies that are highly fractionalized by both ethnicity and religion will thus get the highest scores on this combined index. Of course, ethnic and religious identities are not given, fixed phenomena, but social constructions. However, they are rather slow to change. I measure them as of 1965 and attempt to explain conflict over the ensuing thirty years; over such a period they have probably changed little.

A second important narrative of grievance is focused on *economic inequality*. The grievance might refer either to unequal incomes or to unequal ownership of assets. For example, some of the conflicts in Central America are commonly attributed to one or other of these types of inequality. Both of these are now objectively measurable for most societies, although my measure of asset inequality is confined to the ownership of land. However, in low-income countries, land is the major single asset, and so inequalities in its ownership should be a good proxy for overall asset inequality.

A third narrative of grievance is focused on a *lack of political rights*. If the government is autocratic and repressive, people will have a natural and justifiable desire to overthrow it in the pursuit of democracy. For example, the 1989 uprising in Romania is usually seen as a demand for democracy. Political scientists have now carefully classified political regimes according to the degree of political rights, and I use the one on which most political scientists now base their analyses (the "Polity III" data set).

A final narrative of grievance focuses on *government economic incompetence*. If a government is seen to inflict sufficient economic misery on its population, it may face an uprising. The successful National Resistance Movement rebellion in Uganda in the early 1980s is often seen as being motivated by despair at gross economic mismanagement by successive regimes. I proxy such economic performance by the rate of growth of per capita income in the preceding five years. Other things equal, an economy that had experienced rapid decline might be more prone to rebellion than one that had experienced rapid growth and so offered hope.

I will now describe the results. The purpose of this chapter is to present results to people who are not necessarily familiar with (or interested in) modern social science research methods. I will simply note that the method used is a "probit" model, which predicts the occurrence of civil war in terms of these underlying factors. The results from this analysis tell the researcher both how important each factor appears to be and how much confidence we can place in that appearance. The results are reported formally in Collier and Hoeffler.[2]

The results overwhelmingly point to the importance of economic agendas as opposed to grievance. Indeed, the grievance factors are so unimportant or perverse that there must be a reason for it, and I go on to explain why, I think, grievance-based explanations of civil war are so seriously wrong. First, however, I describe the evidence on the importance of economic agendas.

The presence of primary commodity exports massively increases the risks of civil conflict. Specifically, other things
equal, a country that is heavily dependent upon primary commodity exports, with a quarter of its national income coming
from them, has a risk of conflict four times greater than one
without primary commodity exports. The result is also highly
significant statistically, meaning that there is only a very small
chance that it is a statistical fluke. The presence of a high proportion of young men in a society also increases the risk of conflict, whereas the greater the educational endowment, the lower
the risk. Education is relatively more important than the proportion of young men. For example, if we double the proportion of young men, its effect can be offset by increasing the average educational endowment by around two months. Each year
of education reduces the risk of conflict by around 20 percent.

Thus, some societies are much more prone to conflict than
others simply because they offer more inviting economic
prospects for rebellion. The risk factors multiply up. A country
with large natural resources, many young men, and little education is very much more at risk of conflict than one with opposite characteristics. Before drawing out the policy implications, I will turn to the results on grievance.

The only result that supports the grievance approach to conflict is that a prior period of rapid economic decline increases
the risk of conflict. Each 5 percent of annual growth rate has
about the same effect as a year of education for the population
in reducing the risk of conflict. Thus, a society in which the
economy is growing by 5 percent is around 40 percent safer than
one that is declining by 5 percent, other things equal. Presumably, growth gives hope, whereas rapid decline may galvanize
people into action. Inequality, whether measured in terms of income or landownership, has no effect on the risk of conflict according to the data. This is, of course, surprising given the attention inequality has received as an explanation of conflict. The
results cannot, however, be lightly dismissed. For example, the
measures of inequality have proved to be significant in explaining economic growth and so are evidently not so noisy as to lack
explanatory power. Nor is our result dependent upon a particular specification. Anke Hoeffler and I have experimented with
well over a hundred variants of our core specification, and in

none of these is inequality a significant cause of conflict. (By contrast, primary commodity exports are always significant.)

Political repression has ambiguous effects on the risk of conflict. A society that is fully democratic is safer than one that is only partially democratic. However, severe political repression yields a lower risk of conflict than partial democracy. These effects are of moderate size and only weakly significant: A fully democratic country has a risk of conflict about 60 percent lower than the most dangerously partially democratic societies. In related work, Hegre et al.[3] investigate the effects of political transition. They find that the transition from one type of political regime, such as repression, to another, such as partial democracy, itself temporarily increases the risk of conflict. However, they find that the increased risk fades quite rapidly. One year after the change, three quarters of the risks generated by political transition have evaporated.

The most surprising result for those who emphasize grievance as the cause of conflict concerns ethnic and religious fractionalization. We find that such fractionalization is significant in changing the risk of conflict. The effect is most pronounced and significant when we measure social fractionalization as the combination of ethnic and religious divisions—that is, the potential cross-cutting fractionalization created by multiplying the two underlying indices. Thus measured, ethnic and religious fractionalization significantly *reduces* the risk of conflict. Fractionalized societies are safer than homogenous societies. For example, a highly fractionalized society such as Uganda would be about 40 percent safer than a homogenous society, controlling for other characteristics.

The grievance theory of conflict thus finds surprisingly little empirical support. Inequality does not seem to matter, whereas political repression and ethnic and religious divisions have precisely the opposite of their predicted effects. Why might this be the case?

I think that the reason that the grievance theory is so at variance with the actual pattern of conflict is that it misses the importance of what social scientists call the "collective action problem." Justice, revenge, and relief from grievance are "public goods" and so are subject to the problem of free-riding. If I am consumed with grievance against the government, I may well prefer to rebel than to continue to suffer its continuation.

However, whether the government gets overthrown does not depend upon whether I personally join the rebellion. Individually, my preferred choice might be that others fight the rebellion, while I benefit from the justice that their rebellion achieves. This standard free-rider problem will often be enough to prevent the possibility of grievance-motivated rebellions. However, it is compounded by two other problems. In order for a rebellion to achieve justice it probably needs to achieve military victory. For this it needs to be large. Small rebellions face all the costs and risks of punishment without much prospect of achieving justice. Hence, grievance-motivated potential rebels will be much more willing to join large rebellions than small ones. Obviously, however, rebellions have to start small before they can become large. It is quite possible that many people would be willing to join a large rebellion but that nevertheless it does not occur, because only few people are willing to join a small rebellion and so it does not scale up. Social scientists think of this as a coordination problem. The final problem is that rebels have to fight *before* they achieve justice. The rebel leader may promise to assuage grievances, but once he has won he may have an incentive to behave much like the current government. More generally, the rebel leader has a much stronger incentive to promise things than he has subsequently to deliver them. Because potential recruits can recognize this problem, they may not be able to trust the rebel leader and so may decide not to join the rebellion even though it promises relief from grievances. Social scientists term such a phenomenon a "time-consistency problem."

The free-rider, coordination, and time-consistency problems together pose formidable obstacles to rebellions motivated purely by grievance. How might a rebel leader overcome them? All societies face collective action problems of a great many varieties. Many are not overcome, and others are overcome by the function being taken over by government, supported by taxation and enforcement powers. However, where they are overcome less formally, in a way that could be pertinent for a rebellion, the usual way is through what we now term "social capital"; that is, the trust generated by participation in informal or formal groupings of people into networks, clubs, and societies. Through such interactions people learn to set each decision in the context of past and future decisions about other matters: I'd better not free-ride now because other people didn't free-ride last time, and if I do, they might free-ride next time. Thus, a rebel leader might seek to overcome the collective action problem by drawing upon existing social capital. This, I think, is why ethnic and religious fractionalization reduces rather than increases the risk of rebellion. Social capital usually does not span ethnic and religious divides. Thus, in highly fractionalized societies it is much harder to mobilize large numbers of people than in homogenous societies. It may only be possible to mobilize the people within a particular ethnic-cum-religious group, but if this is only a small part of the national population, the prospects of victory are poor and so the prospect of assuaging grievance is poor. Grievance-motivated rebellions by small minorities are liable to be quixotic. The pattern of rebellion is sufficiently strongly related to the proxies for greed, and sufficiently negatively related to ethnic and religious fractionalization, to suggest that most rebellion is not quixotic.

The remaining strategy for a rebel leader is to rely upon greed. Greed-motivated rebellion does not face any of the collective action problems of grievance-motivated rebellion. There is no free-rider problem because the benefits of the rebellion can be confined to those who participate in it. There is no co-ordination problem because the rebellion does not need to be so large as to be victorious nationally in order to gain spasmodic control of some territory and so be predatory on the export trade in primary commodities. There is no time-consistency problem because if rebellions are able to cream off some of the rent from primary commodity exports during the rebellion, then rebel recruits can be paid during the conflict rather than be dependent upon promises. Hence, we might expect that those grievance-motivated rebellions that actually take hold do so by combining some material payoff with the grievance. We see this in many rebellions. For example, in Colombia, groups that began as grievance-based organizations (of the political extreme left and extreme right) have evolved into drug baronies.

To conclude this section, rebellions based purely on grievance face such severe collective action problems that the basic theories of social science would predict that they are unlikely to occur, and the empirical evidence supports this prediction. Societies indeed differ markedly in the underlying objective causes of grievance. We can reasonably expect that a society that is fractionalized into many ethnic and religious groups, with high income and asset inequality, and which has a government that represses political rights will have many more grievances than a homogenous, equal democracy. Yet this does not translate into a higher risk of conflict. I suggest that what it does produce is a high-pitched discourse or narrative of grievance. There is a disconnect between these narratives and action. Even in apparently highly charged ethnoreligious conflicts such as the former Yugoslavia, there were apparently cases of one side renting tanks from the other side! Such behavior could not occur if the objective of conflict was simply to harm the opposing ethnic or religious group, but it can be explicable if there are economic advantages to the control of territory. To understand action we have to shift our focus from the discourse to the *economic agenda*. For the reasons I discussed above, this economic agenda will be concealed. The true cause of much civil war is not the loud discourse of grievance but the silent force of greed.

Who Gains During Conflict?

Civil wars inflict very high costs on an economy. I estimate that on average during civil wars the economy as a whole declines by around 2.2 percent per annum relative to its underlying growth path.[4] This may seem a small number, but it implies that after a decade of war a society will have an income 20 percent lower than it would otherwise have been.

Despite these overall losses, civil wars create some opportunities for profit that are not available during peace. These fall into four groups.

First, life during civil war tends to become less predictable. As a result, people shorten their time horizons, or equivalently, discount the future more heavily. This changes the calculus of opportunistic behavior. In normal circumstances people tend not to be opportunistic in business relationships because such behavior damages their reputations and so makes it more difficult for them to reach agreement on deals in the future. The less predictable is the future, or the more peculiar are current circumstances, the less worthwhile it is to sacrifice current opportunities for profit in order to maintain reputation. Hence, civil war societies tend to become opportunistic. This will affect business practices, so that some firms will thrive through sharp practices while others become their victims. Profit rates will therefore become more dispersed and increase for the opportunistic.

Second, there is likely to be an increase in criminality. Governments reduce expenditure on the police during conflict as they increase spending on the military. As a result, the risks of punishment for criminal behavior decline. The main economic activity of criminals is theft, and this reduces asset-holding through two routes. An increase in theft makes assets less attractive. Hence, households will tend to run their assets down or shift them out of the country. For example, a common phenomenon during civil wars is for the livestock herd to decline quite drastically. Further, the criminals themselves face an even more acute asset-holding problem than their potential victims. If a criminal accumulates assets through theft, he lacks good title, and so his possession is insecure. A likely response is to shift the assets out of the country, either directly, as when stolen cattle are moved over the border, or indirectly, as when their value is first converted into some other asset.[5]

Third, markets during civil war become disrupted. In normal circumstances the main force keeping marketing margins down, and indeed profits more generally, is competition. If there is good information and easy entry into trading, marketing margins will be driven down to the point at which traders earn no higher incomes than they would in any other activity. Civil wars make information much more costly and particular. Further, they make entry into the activity much more difficult. Existing traders may be able to resort to illegal means to discourage entry, and as opportunism becomes more rife, viable trading will contract to those relationships that can still be trusted. Thus, competition during civil war tends to break down. Trade becomes increasingly monopolistic, and so marketing margins increase. Of course, during conflict the actual volume of transactions will decrease, but if margins are initially narrow and widen sufficiently, then the profits from trade can actually increase.

Fourth, the scope for rent-seeking predation on trade increases for rebels and may even increase for government officials, as their actions become less open to scrutiny. Indeed, in some instances the very distinction between rebels and government can become blurred: Government soldiers by day become rebels by night. The rebels are not rebelling against the government at all; they are simply taking off their uniforms in order to reduce detection and thereby increase the opportunities their official weapons provide for predation. In the limit, if such rent-seeking becomes too competitive, it can kill trade off. Imagine that primary commodities must be transported from their point of production to the coast. If at many points along the road each locally powerful rebel, off-duty army officer, or official exacts a charge in an uncoordinated way, then the combined extractions can be so high that they make exporting unprofitable: The competitive predation simply kills the activity. Thus, sufficiently decentralized greed-motivated rebellions tend to kill off the economic goose and so die out. If there is no trade, there is no loot. To prevent this, a rebel movement will try to create a monopoly of predation, and for this it must generate a monopoly of rebel violence. This may be why a very common characteristic of rebel movements is that they go through a phase in which considerable military effort is expended on fighting other rebel groups. To be economically successful, a rebel group does not need to defeat the government, but it does need to replace the government monopoly of violence with a rebel-government duopoly of violence. Fully competitive rebellions will not normally be profitable except in the short run. This suggests that even when a country collapses into anarchy, such a state of affairs will seldom persist. There will be strong economic forces creating sufficiently large units of power that the primary commodity export trade will not be killed off.

Rebellions in which no group can impose its authority may thus fade out. Evidence for this is that the duration of rebellion, as opposed to the risk of its occurrence, is prolonged if the society consists of two ethnic groups.[6] Both ethnically homogenous and ethnically highly fractionalized societies have shorter conflicts. When there are two ethnic groups, probably one being the government and the other the rebels, the rebel organization has the best chance of imposing a cohesive monopoly on rebellion.

The implications of the above are that various identifiable groups will "do well out of the war." They are opportunistic businessmen, criminals, traders, and the rebel organizations themselves. The rebels will do well through predation on primary commodity exports, traders will do well through widened margins on the goods they sell to consumers, criminals will do well through theft, and opportunistic businessmen will do well at the expense of those businesses that are constrained to honest conduct.

If some people do well out of civil war they may not be particularly concerned to restore peace. Whereas they have increased incomes, all other groups will suffer sharply declining incomes and so have a strong interest in peace. Overall, the losers lose more than the winners gain, so that potentially there is scope for a mutually beneficial peace settlement. However, there are reasons to expect that it will be very difficult to achieve peace through a settlement in which all these groups are confident of being better off. There are two major problems. The first is that even if a settlement can be found in which all groups are better off, it is unlikely that the settlement can be trusted. Settlements face the "time-consistency" problem discussed above in the different context of whether potential rebels can trust their leader. The application to a peace settlement is as follows. Usually, a settlement will involve some military disbandment of rebel forces. As a result, the balance of military advantage is likely to shift to the government. As a result, the government will have an incentive to promise, ex ante, things it will not have an incentive to adhere to ex post. Because shrewd rebels can see this problem, they may rationally decide to decline a peace settlement that would ostensibly benefit them. The second major problem is that it is not realistically possible to construct a settlement in which all of the four groups who benefit from civil war are bought off. For example, although the offer of modest financial incentives to the leadership of RENAMO proved feasible, and may have been critical in ending the conflict in Mozambique, it is morally and politically much harder to offer drug barons the large financial incentives that would be needed to switch their interest from the perpetuation of conflict to the conclusion of a peace settlement.

Hence, although the costs of war appear to offer the potential for mutually beneficial peace settlements, in practice peace will depend upon those groups that gain from peace being more influential than those that gain from continued war. The relative power of economic interest groups is the classic question posed by modern political economy. The literature tells us that small, cohesive groups will be disproportionately influential. Unfortunately, because most people lose from war, the pro-peace group faces a massive free-rider problem in lobbying for peace. By contrast, because the beneficiaries of war are a much smaller group, some of whom gain very large amounts, the free-rider problem of the pro-war lobby is very much less severe.

An implication is that peace may sometimes prove illusive because the small groups that have an economic interest in sustaining or reviving conflict are disproportionately influential. Because the private interests of these groups are very much against the public interest, their true agendas will be actively concealed. Thus, the true motivations for the perpetuation of conflict are normally unobserved, not simply because they get crowded out by the discourse of grievance but because they will be kept secret. If such interest groups cannot be bought off, then they have to be overcome. Interventions that reduce their profits from conflict can work both to reduce their incentives for conflict and, perhaps more important, to reduce their capacity to influence decisions.

One test of these ideas is whether conflict becomes more likely as a result of previous conflict. If grievance is the main driver of conflict, then for sure a powerful impetus to grievance will be previous conflict. Conflicts leave a legacy of atrocities crying out for revenge. By contrast, the greed-based approach to conflict would argue that it is the underlying economic conditions that create the risk of conflict. Some societies will have repeated conflicts, not because of the cumulative legacy of the desire for vengeance but because war is profitable for some groups. Although the evidence is only preliminary, at present it supports the latter interpretation. Once we allow for the risk factors described above, countries that have had a conflict are not more likely to have a further conflict than countries that have been conflict-free. To the extent that this is correct, it is good news for the international community. It implies that conflicts are not deeply intractable in the sense that they are driven by historical loyalties. The loyalties of local communities may indeed be so determined, and the observed discourse may reflect these loyalties, but there is a wide gulf between this and actual large-scale conflict. If only the international community can change the economic incentives for conflict, it can substantially reduce their incidence, even in societies riven by long-standing hatreds.

Reducing the Incentives for Conflict

How can international policy reduce the economic incentives for conflict? For this we must work through the list of causes of conflict and determine where there is scope for intervention.

Recall that the most powerful single driver of the risk of conflict is for an economy to have a high proportion of primary commodity exports. This gives the international community some opportunity for risk reduction. Most of the international markets for primary commodities are highly centralized, with a small number of key intermediaries. The most extreme case of this is probably the diamonds trade. One reason for centralization is that there are almost always questions of product quality: Primary commodities are not completely standardized. To the extent that it is possible to curtail the sales of primary commodities that are financing conflict, the prospects for peace are increased. For example, diamond exports from Sierra Leone probably account for the high incidence of conflict in that country. Many of these exports originate in highly informal marketing channels but find their way onto world markets. Of course, some markets, notably those for narcotics, are illegal throughout their entire chain, making them uncompetitive and thus providing very high profits to traders. In most markets, however, the task may be to prevent illegitimate supplies from gaining access to legitimate channels. This will drive down the incomes of the illegitimate acquisition of the commodities and thereby reduce the incentive to contest the control of primary exports.

A further way in which the international community can reduce the risks generated by primary commodity exports is to assist in the diversification of the economies of those societies that are most at risk. The instrument for this is development assistance. Obviously, substantial development assistance is usually only feasible during peacetime conditions, so that its role is preventative, whereas the control of marketing channels may also be able to influence the incentives for settling current conflicts. Whether aid programs can succeed in diversifying an economy depends both on the underlying comparative advantage of the country and on its absorptive capacity for aid. A well-located country without major natural resources, such as Mozambique, has a better chance of export diversification than a landlocked country with large natural resources.

If an economy has a high absorptive capacity for aid, development assistance can reduce the risk of conflict not just through increasing diversification but through reducing poverty and increasing the growth rate. Recall that both poverty and economic decline increases risks. The absorptive capacity of an economy for aid depends primarily upon the economic policies governments adopt. Recent work using the World Bank's scoring system for twenty different aspects of policy finds that those developing countries with average policy scores have an absorptive capacity for aid about double that of countries with fairly poor scores.[7] Hence, if governments adopt policy environments that are highly discouraging for economic activity, there is rather little that donors can do to offset these effects through large aid flows. However, where governments adopt policies that are more conducive to growth, donors can do a great deal to accelerate the process of development and thereby reduce the risks of conflict. The limitations of aid, in that it cannot offset the effects of highly damaging policies, should not blind us to the considerable contribution that aid can make to enhancing peace in most environments.

I have suggested that marketing margins tend to widen during conflict, creating some lucrative monopolistic trading opportunities and giving these traders an incentive for conflict continuation. To the extent possible, policy should therefore be focused on making markets as competitive as possible. Competition will reduce profits to normal levels and reduce the attraction of conflict for wartime traders. Agencies of the international community, broadly defined, are themselves often major purchasers during conflicts. If their own purchasing practices are insufficiently cost-conscious, they will become a source for supernormal profits.

The international community (though obviously not the World Bank) may also increase the incentives for peace through political actions. First, the time-consistency problem surrounding peace settlements implies that there is a role for external guarantors of the settlement terms. The incentives for settlement maintenance may range from the military, through the diplomatic, to the financial. Second, the above analysis implies that full democratic rights are an effective means of reducing the risk of conflict, and that, although political transition temporarily increases risks, these risks do not persist for long. Indeed, a slow transition from repression may be dangerous because it implies a long period of partial democracy, during which the risks are at their peak. There may therefore be a role for assisting countries during a brief phase of rapid transition to democracy.

Finally, were the world to be composed of small, ethnically and religiously homogenous states, the statistical evidence suggests that it would have a much higher incidence of civil war. I have already discussed the result that ethnic and religious fractionalization actually make states safer rather than more dangerous, so that ethnic cleansing is not only repellent in itself but would result in more dangerous political entities. A result I have not yet described is that large states are proportionately much safer than small states. The risk of civil conflict occurring somewhere on the territory of one large state is approximately one third lower than if the same territory is divided into two identical states. Thus, the political forces for self-determination of small, ethnically or religiously homogenous groups may not be benign.

Economic Policies in Postconflict Conditions

Finally, I briefly consider economic policy priorities in postconflict societies. Such societies need to reduce the underlying risks of conflict. This will involve the same policies that are appropriate in conflict prevention, such as diversification and poverty reduction. However, there are also some economic legacies from conflict: particular interest groups that develop during the conflict and that have little interest in peace. These interests need to be weakened as rapidly as possible.

A civil war society tends to favor the opportunistic and the criminal, and to permit the encroachment of monopoly. These characteristics persist after the conflict has ended. Yet the groups who benefit from these characteristics have an interest in perpetuating wartime conditions. One approach is therefore to weaken these groups as rapidly as possible by reducing their profits.

Market integration can be promoted by deregulation, improved transport, and improved market information, for example, by means of better communications. In postconflict Uganda, when the government deregulated the transport of coffee, the road haulage industry expanded; this new entry into the sector broke the road haulage cartel that had informally operated during the conflict. As a result, road haulage rates approximately halved, and so rural produce markets in turn became more competitive. In the process, the politics of conflict probably changed. A larger, more competitive transport and trading sector that has made investments that depend upon the continuation of peace is a strongly pro-peace lobby. The former interest of a small cartel enjoying monopoly profits has disappeared.

Opportunism thrives on conflict. For example, in Uganda a trader who purchased mattresses on credit from the local manufacturer to sell in the North claimed that his purchases had been stolen by rebels. The manufacturer suspected that this claim was false but could not prove the contrary and so had to accept the default of the trader. The opportunistic trader thus has an interest in unrest. A firm can guard against such opportunism by improving its information. If the manufacturer had a better network of contacts in the North or a better network of information from other suppliers to the trader, it would be more difficult for the trader to be opportunistic. But information networks are costly. Particularly where the telephone system is poor and where newspaper circulation is low, information is expensive and so limited. The Ugandan government has indirectly reduced postconflict opportunism by encouraging cell phones, radio, and a free press.

Crime thrives on low detection and poor justice systems. The rehabilitation of the police and the courts is thus a postconflict priority, partly to ease problems of contract enforcement. There is also a need to professionalize the army. As discussed, sometimes during conflict the government army will itself be an important source of crime and predation, so that it will have little interest in peace. For this reason, demobilization may not be as problematic as is commonly feared. Ill-paid government soldiers may be less of a threat once disarmed, disbanded, and dispersed to their farms than when they are together in barracks. The Ugandan demobilization actually reduced crime rates despite the widespread fear that it would do the opposite.[8]

Conclusion

Discussion of civil conflict is dominated by the narrative of grievance. Hence, policy toward conflict tends to be focused upon on the one hand assuaging perceived grievances, and on the other, attempting to reconcile populations that have deep-rooted hatreds. The evidence on the causes of conflict does not really support this interpretation. The objective factors that might contribute to grievance, such as income and asset inequality, ethnic and religious divisions, and political repression, do not seem to increase the risks of conflict. Indeed, to the extent that they have any effect, it is to make societies safer. I do not wish to imply that the parties to a conflict do not hold grievances and historical hatreds, and it is indeed sensible to attempt to reduce them. However, the evidence on the causes of conflict points to economic factors as the main drivers of conflict. The combination of large exports of primary commodities, low education, a high proportion of young men, and economic decline drastically increases risks. Greed seems more important than grievance.

Although societies as a whole suffer economically from civil war, some small identifiable groups do well out of it. They thus have an interest in the initiation, perpetuation, and renewal of conflict. Naturally, these interests tend to remain low-profile. Hence, the discourse of grievance is much louder than that of greed, even if it is less significant. Policy intervention should, however, focus rather more than in the past on these economic agendas. Effective policy should reduce both the economic incentives for rebellion and the economic power of the groups that tend to gain from the continuation of social disorder. The restriction of access to international commodity markets for illegitimate exports from countries in conflict, and the targeting of development assistance to high-risk countries not currently in conflict, are both feasible strategies for the international community.

Notes

1. Orlando Figes, *A People's Tragedy* (London: Pimlico, 1996).

2. Paul Collier and Anke Hoeffler, "Justice-Seeking and Loot-Seeking in Civil War," mimeo (Washington, D.C.: DECRG, World Bank, 1999).

3. Havard Hegre, Tanja Ellingson, Nils Petter Gleditsch, and Scott Gates, "Towards a Democratic Civil Peace?" mimeo (Oslo: International Peace Research Institute, 1999).

4. Paul Collier, "On the Economic Consequences of Civil War," *Oxford Economic Papers* 51: 168–183.

5. Paul Collier and J. W. Gunning, "War, Peace and Private Portfolios," *World Development* 23 (1995): 233–241.

6. Paul Collier, Anke Hoeffler, and M. Sodersbom, "On the Duration of Civil War," mimeo (Washington, D.C.: DECRG, World Bank, 1999).

7. Paul Collier and David Dollar, "Aid Allocation and Poverty Reduction," mimeo (Washington, D.C.: DECRG, World Bank, 1999).

8. Paul Collier, "Demobilization and Insecurity," *Journal of International Development* 3 (1994): 343–351.

6

The Resource Curse:
Are Civil Wars Driven by
Rapacity or Paucity?

Indra de Soysa

Men of a fat and fertile soil are most commonly effeminate and cowards;
whereas contrariwise a barren country makes men temperate by necessity,
and by consequence careful, vigilant, and industrious.
> —Jean Bodin (1576)

Whatever the soil, climate, or extent of territory of any particular nation,
the abundance or scantiness of its annual supply [output] . . . [funda-
mentally depends on] the skills, dexterity, and judgement of its labor.
> —Adam Smith (1776)

Whereas recent systematic analyses of civil conflict find that an
abundance of natural resources leads to greed-motivated rebellion, others have argued forcefully that it is the scarcity of natural resources that sparks civil war. Arguments favoring the
abundance perspective have relied on a measure of primary
commodity exports as a proxy for greed-motivated violence,
and abundance is assumed. This study tests the competing hypotheses with a more precise measure of scarcity and abundance, the per capita stock of natural capital, both renewable
and nonrenewable, and finds that an abundance of mineral
wealth is positively and significantly related to armed conflict.
The results favor the proposition that countries with an abundance of mineral wealth are likely to suffer greed-motivated
rebellion. Contrarily, there is little evidence to suggest that
scarcity of renewable resources is a significant predictor of

armed conflict. This study concludes that mineral wealth may also be associated with conflict through deleterious economic and political effects of "Dutch Disease."

* * *

For centuries, it has been argued—and disputed—that an abundance of natural resources may be either a boon or a curse for the possessor.[1] Recently, the resource endowment of a state has also been linked directly to its propensity for causing armed conflict. Indeed, the search for environmental factors behind state collapse and civil conflicts has received the highest priority in U.S. foreign policy, in no small measure due to Vice President Al Gore's personal interest in the subject.[2] However, at least two distinct schools of thought are emerging on the issue of natural resources and armed conflict. The first sees criminal agendas as a primary driving force of civil conflict, where the availability of natural resources acts as a catalyst for violence. These analysts suggest that rebellion is driven by the desire for loot—thus violence is motivated by rapacity. The other, more celebrated, argument suggests that it is the scarcity of natural resources that causes conflict. Thus, violence results from paucity and want.[3]

It is abundantly clear today that the collapse of ideology with the end of superpower rivalry has not served to dampen Third World conflicts. It is also apparent that the nature of internal war looks very different from that witnessed during the Cold War. This has led some to speculate that the fundamental change in the nature of warfare is a result of changed agendas—war itself seems to have become privatized.[4] "State failure," "complex emergencies," and "ethnic cleansing" have now become *the* buzzwords in security studies. International agencies and governmental actors are increasingly called upon to supply relief during warfare, to act as peacemakers and intermediaries, and to bear the costs of postconflict reconstruction. A proper understanding of the role of "the resource curse" on states and societies is crucial if appropriate policies are to be formulated to deal with these crises. Examining questions about resources and conflict is not a purely academic exercise: Wide-ranging policy implications stem from the answers to such questions as whether criminal motivations drive civil wars or whether want and attendant grievance generate violence. Clearly, international responses to greed-motivated, criminal violence will have to be drastically different in approach and content than to paucity-motivated violence. In the following, I delineate the contending arguments on the role of natural resources as a cause of civil conflict and utilize standard social science methodology to test empirically whether civil conflict is driven primarily by rapacity, or by paucity of natural resources.

Paul Collier's work represents some of the first systematic analysis of conflict from a microeconomics perspective.[5] He finds strong empirical support for the proposition that natural resources motivate rapacious behavior, thereby causing civil wars. This research shows that a high dependence on primary goods exports is significantly and robustly related to the incidence of civil war.[6] In essence, this position is based on the premise that the availability of natural resources (exported as primary commodities) spawns violent conflict because it provides incentives for rebel groups to form on the basis of capturing loot, which also sustains the activities of these groups. Moreover, mineral resources are also easily captured. It is commonly propounded that the wars in Angola, Liberia, the Democratic Republic of Congo, and Sierra Leone arise from the struggle for control of oil, diamond mines, timber, and other resources.[7] Likewise, various conflicts in Asia and Latin America are fueled by the profits from trade in illegal commodities such as weapons and drugs, or hardwood timber and other renewable resources such as rubber.[8] In short, resources are seen to act as a "honey pot" that provides incentives for profit-seeking groups to engage in violent actions. As Collier notes, war is detrimental to society at large, but small, organized groups stand to "do well out of war."[9] This logic explains why conflict appears and reappears frequently despite the deleterious effects of wanton destruction in civil war situations.

Collier systematically challenges well-established theories that see civil war as a manifestation of grievance by gauging the relative significance of variables that proxy grievance and greed. According to Collier, the discourse of conflict itself is dominated by stories of grievance. For example, two drunks may come to fisticuffs with each other because they were drunk, but if asked why they fought they are liable to justify their drunken behavior with explanations of grievance about why each of them fought, such as "he struck me first." The true cause of conflict, drunkenness, is therefore masked by the discourse of grievance. In real-world conflicts, this discourse of grievance, whether along ethnic, political, or economic lines, also masks underlying realities about where the origins of conflict lie. In order to get beyond the discourse of conflict, Collier gauges which of the proxies of greed and grievance predict conflict best. He finds that the economic variables that proxy greed-motivated rebellion outperform the proxies for grievance-motivated rebellion (see Chapter 5).

Collier finds that ethnic heterogeneity and income inequality are mostly unrelated to conflict. Primary goods exports and average years of schooling in the male population, however, are strongly related to conflict. A large share of primary goods in exports provides a revenue stream easy to capture, offering the motivation for rebels to coalesce in seeking loot. The average years of schooling in the male population measures the opportunity costs for young men to join greed-motivated rebellion. This variable is significantly negatively related to conflict: The higher the level of education among males, the less likely they are to engage in risky endeavors such as armed conflict. A country more than one-fourth dependent on primary commodity exports emerges as four times more likely to be engaged in a conflict than one that is not. Similarly, even a slight increase in the level of education can decrease the risk of conflict. As Collier puts it, "A country with *large natural resources,* many young men, and little education is very much more at risk of conflict than one with opposite characteristics" (italics added).[10] He concludes that the "true cause of much civil war is not the loud discourse of grievance, but the silent force of greed."[11]

This proposition—that the "honey pot" effect of natural resource abundance causes civil wars by providing incentives for greed-motivated rebellion—clashes with the neo-Malthusian view that has gained much credence in the field of conflict studies recently. Thomas Homer-Dixon, the lead researcher of the Environmental Change and Acute Conflicts Project (ECACP), has argued forcefully that environmental degradation, which has led to scarcities in natural resources, is fueling civil conflicts within the poorest states in the international system.[12] The "Toronto Group" and the Swiss Peace Foundation's program on environmental conflicts (ENCOP) represented by the work of Günther Baechler have spearheaded a vast research program on "ecoviolence."[13]

From the environmental security perspective, ecological transformation alters the sociopolitical fabric of society, disrupting productive relationships and ultimately adversely affecting established constraints on and mechanisms of social peace. The clearest articulation of how environmental factors affect conflict is found in the connection between the incapacitating effect of resource scarcity on the adaptability of poor societies to socioeconomic pressures. This position is espoused most ardently by Homer-Dixon and associates. According to the scarcity and conflict perspective, conflict is generated by the scarcity of natural resources in two primary ways. The first mechanism is that resource scarcity drives elites to "capture" resources, marginalizing powerless groups in the process. According to Homer-Dixon, "Resource capture occurs when the degradation and depletion of renewable resources interact with population growth to encourage powerful groups within a society to shift resource distribution in their favor."[14] Such a process is often cited in connection with the recent violence in Chiapas, the conflict in Rwanda, and the peasant uprisings in the Philippines.

The second way in which scarcity is seen to cause conflict is through its debilitating effect on economic and social innovation—what Homer-Dixon terms the "ingenuity gap." According to Homer-Dixon,

> many developing countries face increasingly complex, fast-moving, and interacting environmental scarcities. These scarcities can overwhelm efforts to produce constructive change and can actually reduce a country's ability to deliver reform. Consequently, environmental scarcity sometimes helps to drive society into a self-reinforcing spiral of violence, institutional dysfunction, and social fragmentation. . . .[15]
>
> A persistent and serious ingenuity gap raises grievances and erodes the moral and coercive authority of government, which boosts the probability of serious turmoil and violence. . . . If these processes continue unchecked, countries with a critical ingenuity gap therefore risk becoming trapped in a vicious cycle.[16]

The argument is that poor countries stay poor and suffer armed conflict because resource scarcity acts to prevent socioeconomic innovation. The link between environmental pressure and conflict then is mediated in part by the ability of societies to achieve such collective goods as economic growth and innovation, thereby adapting to changing economic conditions and societal pressures generated by resource scarcity. To deal with scarcity, a society needs ingenuity—but the very scarcities demanding social ingenuity act as constraints on innovation. According to Edward Barbier and Homer-Dixon, endogenous growth theory, which stresses the importance of endogenous technical change for sustained economic growth (a proxy for economic capability and innovation), fails to take into account resource scarcity as a restraint on a society's ability to innovate.[17]

The idea that scarcity affects conflict by perpetuating underdevelopment is a novel one. It offers a more clearly testable model than most other analyses of environmental conflict, which tend to be explained through rather complex causal mechanisms. Indeed, some critics of the environmental security approach have pointed out biases resulting from the selection of cases and unsound reasoning, and they have even questioned the motives behind this line of research.[18] As Nils Gleditsch has suggested, more limited modules explaining environmental factors behind conflict with clearer specifications should be put to the test first before a causal connection between the environment and conflict can be made.[19] The scarcity/innovation/growth connection offered by Homer-Dixon and associates makes such a test possible within the realm of standard social science methodology. The connection between scarcity and growth as elucidated in the literature is discussed below.

Endogenous growth theory (or new growth theory) arose in response to neoclassical growth theory, which held that capital-poor developing countries would catch up with the rich ones because of diminishing returns to capital. These models predicted that capital would flow from rich to poor countries and create a higher rate of growth in the backward economy, and that growth in capital-rich states would then slow down.[20] However, there was very little evidence to suggest that this was happening. New growth theory tries to explain why convergence failed to take place as expected. New growth theorists saw the main problem as lying in the assumption that rich states experience diminishing returns to capital. According to these theorists, convergence did not take place given increasing returns to capital because of new ideas and technical innovations that keep capital at home and sustain growth within the richer states.[21] There is in fact a large body of empirical evidence indicating that economic convergence between rich and poor states is conditional on a given level of human capital, based on ingenuity and the stock of knowledge available to a society. In other words, poor countries would grow faster than richer countries *if* they had sufficient human capital.[22]

Homer-Dixon and Barbier do not take a position on human capital but suggest that resource scarcity prevents endogenous technical change by perpetuating the ingenuity gap in the following ways. I summarize some important points made by Homer-Dixon:

- Scarcity of resources leads to collective action problems and rent-seeking behavior, resulting in distorted markets and "social friction."
- Social friction prevents the proper functioning of institutions essential for maintaining conditions that foster innovation.
- Scarcity of resources affects poorer states because resource scarcity prevents the generation of new capital that is essential for generating knowledge; the elite within these states will monopolize the available capital.
- All of these factors will act as "constraints on science" by weakening institutions and creating social instability.[23]

The argument is that whatever the level of human capital, resource scarcity can prevent poor countries from achieving endogenous technical change, perpetuating poverty and generating violence. Barbier and Homer-Dixon cite the high dependence of poor countries (presumably the slow growers) on primary exports as support for their thesis. They do not test their thesis empirically against growth but merely supply a table showing that poor countries are highly dependent on the export of primary goods. Export dependence on primary goods, however, is not an indicator of scarcity. They make the assumption that countries that are dependent on primary goods exports are facing scarcities, but they provide no evidence to support this rather crucial assumption.

A country could, however, possess significant quantities of a given resource, which would also happen naturally to make up the largest share of its exports. This is precisely Collier's assertion, which suggests that resource-rich countries have a higher probability of conflict than resource-poor ones. Again, however, abundance is only asserted, since a measure of trade composition cannot show whether the exporting states are facing scarcities of the commodities that they are dependent on.[24] In a similar vein, Jeffrey Sachs and Andrew Warner have presented strong evidence supporting exactly the opposite of the Homer-Dixon thesis, which is that resource abundance leads to lower economic growth through Dutch Disease.[25] *Ceteris paribus*, countries with an abundance of natural resources are likelier to innovate at a slower pace than resource-poor states. Sachs and Warner also employ a measure of trade composition and make the assumption that a higher share of primary goods in exports signifies abundance of natural resources.

According to the Dutch Disease perspective, endogenous technical change does not occur in resource-rich countries because these societies become dependent on natural resources and fail to innovate. However, this happens not because of scarcity, as Barbier and Homer-Dixon would have it, but because the availability of a resource affects the incentives for allocating capital, labor, and innovative energies to other sectors, especially to manufacturing. This perspective relies on arguments that base economic development and innovation on "linkages" between and within sectors. The greater the linkages, the more robust an economy will be. Innovation progresses more rapidly within the manufacturing sector, as opposed to agriculture, because this sector is linkage-strong and offers greater opportunity for "learning by doing."[26]

These arguments are also salient to the issue of land scarcity, which has been touted as one of the root causes of the genocidal violence in Rwanda, the rebellion in Chiapas, and many violent conflicts in South America and South Asia.[27] Closely linked are arguments about population density in general. However, formal models of innovation offer counterperspectives that suggest agricultural growth occurs when population density and land scarcity lead to the intensification of agricultural practices, and thereby to innovation. Excess labor is then freed for other economic activities that support intensive farming.[28] A similar argument is offered by Kiminori Matsumaya, who has demonstrated that the abundance of arable land leads labor and capital away from manufacturing, thereby stemming the progress of invention that follows the logic of "learning by doing" from industrial activity.[29]

Although Sachs and Warner find robust evidence suggesting that a larger share of primary exports in total trade leads to slower growth—support for the Dutch Disease hypothesis—this does not account for scarcity per se. The content of exports says little about whether or not *scarcity* was present to lower or boost growth. When Sachs and Warner find that a higher share of primary goods exports leads to lower growth, growth performance may indeed be affected by the inability of these resource-vulnerable states to innovate their way out of dependence because of the scarcity-induced problems pointed out by Homer-Dixon and other neo-Malthusians. Thus, the Dutch Disease may come about not from a failure to innovate as such but from the inability to command enough resources to aid the processes behind innovation.

In any case, the Dutch Disease perspective also bears heavily on the issue of resources and conflict beyond merely the effects of natural resource abundance on economic performance. For example, theories of the "rentier state" are based on arguments that suggest that resource abundance, and the revenue streams that it generates, affects the proper development and functioning of state institutions, fueling corruption and leading to perverse subsidization policies and budgetary mismanagement. In such situations, the rentier nature of economic activity creates cultures of dependence, clientelism, and patrimonialism.[30] Such revenue streams act crucially to prevent long-term, cooperative state-society arrangements that derive from bargained outcomes that ensure the provision of public goods, good economic and social policies, higher economic performance, and perhaps equity and peace.[31]

In other words, the results of empirical analyses that find a strong positive connection between natural resource abundance and conflict may in fact be capturing the grievance effects generated by the perverse sociopolitical conditions associated with the distorting effects of reliance on convenient resource streams. Moreover, violence may also be generated by the weakening institutional structures that usually safeguard property rights, collect taxes, provide other public goods, and ensure growth in sectors other than the extractive (leading) sector, all thought to be symptoms of countries suffering from

Dutch Disease. Even though Collier finds strong effects of primary-export dependence on conflict, net of such factors as democracy and economic growth, it is still not clear as to how and to what extent "state failure" factors emanating from Dutch Disease are behind armed violence. William Reno has offered insight into how state institutions are circumscribed by elites to create what he terms "shadow states" in resource-rich African countries and how indeed such processes lead to conflict (see Chapter 3).[32]

Abundance and Scarcity, Greed or Grievance

The task of this chapter is to address abundance and scarcity as factors directly affecting the incidence of civil conflict, whether we choose to view such violence as being motivated by greed or by grievance.

In the following, I test whether the abundance of natural resources leads to conflict, holding constant several relevant factors thought to influence its occurrence. As argued above, export composition measures say little about the availability of resources. Thus, I use a measure of natural resource stock per capita. This measure is composed of the absolute value of the stock of cropland (agricultural resources), timber resources, other forest resources, pasture, and subsoil assets in per capita terms. The World Bank defines the stock of natural capital as the "entire environmental patrimony of a country."[33] These values represent the inherent surplus value in the extraction and harvest of a resource because they take into account the difference in the market price and the cost of extracting, processing, and marketing (the Ricardian rent). The rent represents the surplus value of a given resource relative to another. Therefore, if there is overexploitation of a resource, the market value will fall relative to the price of extraction (as capital and labor costs will eat into the surplus), which then acts to reduce the *natural* profit of this resource.[34]

A highly pertinent question relating to scarcity concerns what *type* of natural resources matter for conflict. Much of the environment and conflict literature discusses renewable resources, but many times all resources are grouped together. Homer-Dixon mentions scarcity of "non-renewables like petroleum and ores, and renewables like cropland, forests, fresh water and fisheries."[35] Barbier and Homer-Dixon present a table in their appendix showing high export concentrations of nonrenewables and renewables among the poorest countries, suggesting the importance of scarcity of *all* export commodities upon which these states depended.[36] However, the export share of primary goods (used by Collier and by Sachs and Warner) covers both agricultural and mineral wealth. Primary goods are usually composed of agricultural and mineral commodities alike. Stories of Dutch Disease are based on the abundance of renewables and nonrenewables, the dependence on either of which affects the development of manufactures. This is particularly true of Matsumaya's model. Nevertheless, if elites engage in "resource capture," which can lead to violence, the type of resource is salient, because the revenue stream is likelier to be greater with mineral wealth than with cropland. For this reason, I draw a distinction between the availability of renewable and nonrenewable resources, and model their independent effects on conflict. The crucial question is: Are civil wars driven by rapacity, or by paucity?

Results

What we are concerned with here is simply natural resource scarcity as an explanation for civil war, gauging whether greed or grievance can explain the connection between natural resources and conflict.[37] Greed-motivated rebellion will be proxied by the lootable income inherent in natural resources, especially subsoil assets. Scarcity-motivated rebellion is proxied by the availability of renewable resources. Ethnicity and democracy proxy the social bases of potential grievance-motivated rebellion. Economic growth and the openness of the economy also proxy grievance-based explanations.

The statistical results of the direct test of resource scarcity on conflict are presented in the appendix. The results suggest that the incidence of civil war is completely unrelated to the per capita availability of natural resources, defined as the stocks of both renewable resources—such as cropland, pasture, and forests—and nonrenewables (all known mineral deposits). However, the higher the per capita availability of subsoil assets (or mineral wealth), the greater the incidence of conflict. This result is highly significant ($p < .01$). All of the other variables perform as expected. In my model, population size does not impact on conflict if openness is included in the model, suggesting that larger populations are more conflict-prone as a result of closed economies.[38] Population density, on the other hand, is significantly and positively related to conflict, but only when growth is accounted for. This suggests interestingly that densely populated countries, which are also stagnant, are likelier to experience conflict.[39] Like Collier and others, I find a curvilinear relationship between democracy and civil conflict. There is little evidence to suggest that ethnicity drives conflict. The strong positive sign for mineral wealth suggests that there is a "honey pot" effect resulting from the abundance of this type of natural resource. My results thus support the findings of Collier, who uses a measure of trade composition. This result suggests that the abundance of renewable resources is not an important predictor of conflict, whereas mineral wealth is (*net* of income, strong democracy, and the innovation proxies of growth and openness). Although renewable resource abundance seems negatively related to conflict, this does not mean there is support for the scarcity and conflict position. Many countries with a high level of per capita renewable resource wealth (such as the rich countries that depend less on such resources) are also peaceful. Since Homer-Dixon's argument is that renewables matter for conflict only in the poorest societies, which happen to be the most dependent on primary commodities, I explicitly test whether countries that are poor (in per capita wealth) and resource-poor (natural capital per capita) are especially vulnerable to conflict. I find no evidence to support such a hypothesis.[40] I have also explored the issue of natural resources and growth elsewhere and do not find that an abundance of renewable resources contributes to the growth of per capita income. In fact, my results confirm the Dutch Disease position of Sachs and Warner, as I find that mineral wealth has a strong negative effect on growth.[41] These results together possibly explain the resource curse and conflict as being both greed-motivated at the micro-level and grievance-motivated through its effects on economic growth.

Policy Recommendations

The empirical findings of this study suggest that the abundance of mineral wealth is strongly related to the incidence of civil conflict. This result confirms the findings of others who have simply used measures of export composition rather than measures of availability. The studies that find a positive effect of a high share of primary exports merely assume abundance: It is not at all clear from those results whether it is the poverty associated with such states that motivates violence through grievance, or resources promote rebellion through greed. Moreover, the strong theoretical challenge from neo-Malthusians, who argue that poor countries are prone to violence because of resource dependence and scarcity, necessitated testing this issue by means of a direct measure of the availability of resources. This study has corrected the problem of the assumption of abundance by testing the competing propositions by utilizing a more precise measure of scarcity. Herewith, I summarize the major findings and offer policy recommendations.

First, an abundance of subsoil assets has a direct positive effect on intrastate armed conflict, net of variables controlling for economic, political, and social factors. An abundance of natural capital that is purely renewable, such as agricultural and timber assets, has a weak negative effect on conflict, net of variables proxying innovation. However, there is no evidence to suggest that poor countries with scant renewable resources per capita are likelier to be more conflict-prone than others. The strong association between mineral wealth and conflict suggests that the high stakes associated with controlling mineral wealth are likely to be a cause of conflict. This effect is also independent of growth, suggesting that the "honey pot" effect itself is influential in causing armed violence. In contrast, societal and political degradation may lead to conflict if the abundance of mineral wealth also leads to the Dutch Disease and perpetuates bad governance, capricious political processes, underdevelopment, and ultimately grievance. The evidence suggests strongly that resource scarcity as such may not generate armed violence, whereas failure to innovate economically and politically can hinder institutional development that prevents capricious behavior.

It might very well be that dependence on subsoil assets, which provide quick profit and largely require material resources rather than extensive human cooperation for their extraction, prevents the development of good governance and consensual political processes that result from bargained outcomes between state elites and the mass of society. In this way, Dutch Disease and political factors such as rent-seeking, corruption, and other dysfunctional political processes are likely to be locked in a vicious cycle of underdevelopment and armed conflict. Moreover, resource dependence also creates the politics of the rentier state, which in the long run leads to the decline of state capacity, the subversion of formal institutions, and the withholding of the public goods that can ensure economic development and social peace.

The question is, How can a country escape from resource dependence and manage to innovate? Economic growth is vital because the raising of per capita income proxies innovative capabilities. Bringing about economic growth through development assistance is one obvious answer. Countries with higher per capita wealth are far less likely to suffer internal conflict and are more likely to exhibit strong democracy—which is widely seen as promoting peace and conflict resolution. Thus, renewed efforts at promoting economic growth and democratic institutions seem to be the best long-term strategy for creating what UNESCO has termed "a culture of peace" in the developing world.

Much evidence suggests that countries have far brighter longer-term economic prospects if they are not dependent on resources, especially mineral wealth.[42] If export concentration and the abundance of mineral wealth prevent development and create conditions for conflict by providing the incentive for greed-motivated rebellion, then the international community will have to act in concert to prevent (and, in some cases, counteract) the criminalization of the primary commodity trade. As Collier has pointed out, this could be done by preventing illegitimate actors from gaining easy access to legitimate channels of international trade. This short-run strategy can be especially effective if development assistance and international pressure are used to promote democratic institutions and marginalize the criminal elements (state and nonstate) by blacklisting such actors both politically and from economic markets. Such actions send strong signals to civil society within these states, which may then seek to counter the activities of the incipient criminal elements more effectively.

Higher levels of development usually mean the growth of a stronger manufacturing base and the diversification of exports. Because exports of primary commodities are strongly related to conflict, such development will also help reduce the incentives for greed-motivated violence. Again, development assistance can be targeted toward this end. If resource abundance acts to distort the processes that lead to better policies, the donor agencies should seek to counteract trends toward Dutch Disease. To this end, donor agencies could insist on sounder fiscal policies, prevent the adoption of policies that promote rent-seeking, help identify and alter perverse subsidization that benefits merely the urban elite, and build institutions that protect property rights.[43] Moreover, the international community can help with transfer of technology to developing countries and support the processes of harnessing that technology by promoting investment in human capital. Providing assistance toward better educational systems will not only discourage recruitment of youths into rebellion but will also strengthen the longer-term prospects of economic growth and development. Investment in education will also encourage better government in the longer run that will result in informed participation in political and economic life. As recent studies of aid effectiveness find, aid can work wonders in the right policy setting, but it fails in bad ones.[44] The right policy conditions cannot simply be imposed but must be accepted by those who benefit from such policies. Acceptance of certain policies can be achieved only if people are able to understand them.

Conclusion

In conclusion, this study finds that rapacity encouraged by an abundance of natural resources tends to fuel civil conflict. Paucity of natural resources, on the other hand, does not seem to be such a strong factor in determining the likelihood of civil strife, despite the recent upsurge of interest in environmental degradation and scarcity as a source of conflict. It seems that the insights of Jean Bodin and Adam Smith are as valid today as when they observed, centuries ago, that economic progress has much to do with the incentives that motivate innovation. As they suggest, resource availability may have little to do with economic innovation, compared with other social and political factors. Environmental degradation, in contrast, is possibly part of a vicious cycle of poor governance, underdevelopment, and conflict. For example, farmers in a bad policy environment have little incentive to adopt environmentally friendly technologies; instead, they will practice subsistence farming, opening up new lands by deforesting, or simply abandon land.[45] Conflict also leads to environmental degradation when farmers abandon land in "search of cool ground" and become refugees somewhere else.[46] Disentangling the complex relationship between the "honey pot" effect, Dutch Disease, dysfunctional politics, and conflict may provide a promising agenda for future research on internal conflict. Judging by the other contributions to this volume, it seems that such a research effort is already beginning to yield substantial dividends.

Appendix

Table 6.1   Probit Estimates of the Relationship Between Scarcity of Natural Resources and Civil Conflict, 1989–1998

Variables	1	2	3	4
Income 1990 (log)	–.542[a]	–506[b]	–.458	–.681[c]
	(–3.1)	(–2.1)	(1.5)	(–1.7)
Population 1990 (log)	.194[b]	.125	.141	.252
	(2.0)	(0.7)	(0.8)	(1.1)
Population Density 1990	–.000434	.000749[c]	.00299	.00365
	(–0.2)	(1.8)	(1.4)	(1.3)
Democracy 1989	.0448[c]	.0768[b]	.0674[c]	.103[b]
	(1.8)	(2.2)	(1.7)	(2.3)
Democracy^2	—	–.0177[a]	–.0233[a]	–.023[a]
	–.0129[a]	(–3.2)	(–3.7)	(–2.9)
	(–2.6)			
Ethnic Pluralism 1990	.0178			
	(0.2)			
Trade/GDP 1990		–.0111[c]	–.00931	–.013
		(–1.8)	(–1.5)	(–1.2)
Economic Growth/pc 1985–1990		–.0954[c]	–.118[c]	–.155[c]
		(–1.8)	(–1.9)	(–1.8)
Total Natural Capital/pc 1990 (log)			.030	–.629
			(0.1)	(–1.5)
Subsoil Assets/pc 1990 (log)				.413[a]
				(2.5)
N	116	100	87	63

Note: Dependent variable = incidence of internal armed conflict (threshold of 25 battle deaths), 1989–1998. Significance: a = < .01; b = <. 05; c = < .10. T statistic shown in brackets. Huber-White corrected standard errors were computed in all tests (see *Stata Manual*, 1998). The N differs because of availability of data for some variables.

Like Collier, I use a standard social science technique to gauge the relative significance of the availability of natural resources (renewable and nonrenewable) in multivariate models that simultaneously account for important factors affecting conflict. I utilize probit analysis, which is a statistical technique for predicting a dependent variable with one or many independent variables. I follow Collier's models with some variation. Importantly, my dependent variable has a much lower threshold of violence for inclusion as civil conflict. Instead of the threshold of 1,000 battle-deaths used by the Correlates of War (COW) data, I employ data that use a lower threshold of

25 battle-deaths.[47] This lower threshold captures a level of conflict that may fit in with societal conflict that falls short of civil war and reflects the nature of "ecoviolence" and/or crime as discussed in the literature. Further, I test the post–Cold War era (1989–1998) because of the recent date of the natural-capital stock figures. Thus, I estimate the probability of conflict with 25 battle-deaths or more occurring between 1989 and 1998 with a set of independent variables, the key variables being the natural capital stock per capita in total terms and as subsoil assets measured at 1990.

My base model, like Collier's, accounts for the size of the population, since countries with larger populations are likelier also to suffer higher absolute numbers of casualties in conflict situations. Also, the larger the number of agents, the more likely it is that one or more groups will be dissatisfied with the policy preferences of the center.[48] Although these explanations may be correct, an alternative hypothesis is that the effects of population size on conflict are spurious, but that it captures instead the effects of trade openness on conflict. Because big markets are likely to be less open, perhaps large countries are susceptible to conflict because of capricious political processes and lower economic performance operating through a closed economic system. Using a dependent variable (civil war) with the lower threshold for battle-deaths is ideal for testing this proposition, as the threshold effect should not be present as much when using these data. Unlike Collier, however, I add population density in the model, as this is frequently cited as a source of conflict and should capture some of the curvilinear effects of population size.

I account for the level of institutionalized democracy, and model the "inverted-U hypothesis" of democracy and conflict, by adding a squared term of democracy.[49] The result that conflict is likelier at moderate levels of democracy is well established theoretically: Democratization in general generates a certain degree of instability. I use the Polity III data on democracy.[50] I control for the degree of ethnic fractionalization, which is derived as 100 minus the population share of the largest ethnic group $(100 - x)$. Thus, the smaller this number, the more limited is the dominance of the largest group, and the less ethnically homogenous is the society.

Collier proxies the opportunity cost of rebellion with a measure of the average years of schooling of the male population. Intuitively, it would seem that the greater the human capital the less likely it would be that greed-motivated rebellion substitutes for income-earning opportunities in the regular economy. Instead of schooling, I use per capita income, which is generally a significant predictor of peace.[51] Higher incomes give governments a larger tax base with which to pacify opposition—or crush it. Richer governments are also in a better position to provide public goods such as schooling, health care, and institutional capacity for policing and peace. The schooling variable used by Collier does not capture the likelihood of sanctions, although that is surely part of the calculus of all potential rebels and criminals. Nevertheless, education and income are generally very highly correlated (I computed a score of $r = .88$ for 1990).[52] Moreover, because schooling is also likely to reflect factors of good governance, it is unclear whether this factor really captures greed or grievance. Per capita income, in contrast, should proxy a host of political and social factors, such as the provision of health services, infrastructure, and other public goods.

I also add average economic growth during the period 1985–1995 to this model of conflict to test whether economic growth actually has a pacifying effect. Growth rates were obtained from the World Bank, *World Development Report* (1998). Growth is assumed, as in Barbier and Homer-Dixon, to signify the ability of states to adapt to changing economic conditions and as a measure of the innovative capability of a society. One other measure of the innovative capability of society is the total trade to GDP ratio, or openness. The level of trade is important because it has been found to have the most significant negative effect on the incidence of humanitarian crises from among a large set of variables.[53] The openness of the economy is measured as the average level of trade between 1985 and 1990; it consists of exports plus imports as a share of GDP (total trade 1985–1990/GDP1990). Finally, I add the crucial scarcity variable, which is the available stock of natural capital and subsoil assets per capita, as expressed in dollars. These tests allow us to judge simultaneously the relative importance of economic, social, and natural factors on conflict.

Notes

I am grateful to Nils Petter Gleditsch, Susan Høivik, and David Malone for helpful comments and suggestions. A grant from Future Harvest, an organization promoting international understanding on agricultural issues, and the Norwegian Foreign Ministry facilitated parts of this research. The author is solely responsible for the views expressed and for any errors.

1. For an excellent review of the recent literature, see Michael L. Ross, "The Political Economy of the Resource Curse," *World Politics* 51 (1999): 297–322.

2. The vice president's office initiated the "state failure project" to study the role of environmental factors (among others) behind state collapse and internal war; see Daniel Esty et al., *State Failure Task Force Report: Phase II* (Washington, D.C.: State Failure Task Force, 1998).

3. See Edward Barbier and Thomas Homer-Dixon, *Resource Scarcity, Institutional Adaptation, and Technical Innovation: Can Poor Countries Attain Endogenous Growth?* (Toronto: The Project on Environment, Population and Scarcity, 1996); Günther Baechler, "Environmental Degradation and Violent Conflict: Hypotheses, Research Agendas and Theory Building," in Mohamed Suliman (ed.), *Ecology, Politics and Violent Conflict* (New York: Zed, 1999); Thomas Homer-Dixon, "The Ingenuity Gap: Can Poor Countries Adapt to Resource Scarcity?" *Population and Development Review* 21, no. 3 (1995): 587–612; Thomas Homer-Dixon, *Environment, Scarcity and Violence* (Princeton: Princeton University Press, 1999); John Markakis, *Resource Conflict in the Horn of Africa* (London: Sage, 1998); and Mohamed Suliman, "The Rationality and Irrationality of Violence in Sub Saharan Africa," in Suliman, *Ecology, Politics and Violent Conflict.* For a collection of more skeptical views on environmental issues as security issues, see Nils Petter Gleditsch (ed.), *Conflict and the Environment* (Dordrecht: Kluwer Academic, 1997), and the special issue of *Journal of Peace Research* 35, no. 3 (1998).

4. Mark Duffield, "The Political Economy of Internal War: Asset Transfer, Complex Emergencies and International Aid," in Joanna McRae and Anthony Zwi (eds.), *War and Hunger: Rethinking International Responses* (London: Zed, 1994); Mary Kaldor, *New and Old Wars: Organized Violence in a Global Era* (Oxford: Polity Press, 1999); and Donald M. Snow, *Uncivil War* (Boulder, Colo.: Lynne Rienner, 1996).

5. Paul Collier, "Doing Well out of War," paper presented at the conference on Economic Agendas in Civil War, London, April 26–27, 1999.

6. For details of models, data, and variables, see Paul Collier and Anke Hoeffler, "Justice-Seeking and Loot-Seeking in Civil War," paper presented at the World Bank conference on Civil Conflicts, Crime and Violence, Washington D.C., February 22–23, 1999.

7. See William Reno, *Warlord Politics and African States* (Boulder, Colo.: Lynne Rienner, 1998).

8. Some groups even organize to benefit from relief operations during warfare by taxing relief agencies, stealing food and other aid for resale in the black market or neighboring countries, selling protection, and so on. See also Mats Berdal and David Keen, "Violence and Economic Agendas in Civil Wars: Some Policy Implications," *Millennium* 26, no. 3 (1997): 795–818; William Reno, "Commercial Agendas in Civil Wars," paper presented at the conference on Economic Agendas in Civil Wars, London, April 25–26, 1999.

9. Paul Collier, "Doing Well out of War," paper presented at the conference on Economic Agendas in Civil War, London, April 26–27, 1999.

10. Ibid., 5.

11. Ibid., 8. There also seems to be room for frankness. Consider the quote in Reno, *Warlord Politics,* 15, by an NPFL fighter in Liberia: "the Kalashnikov lifestyle is our business advantage."

12. See Thomas Homer-Dixon, "The Ingenuity Gap: Can Poor Countries Adapt to Resource Scarcity?" *Population and Development Review* 21, no. 3 (1995): 587–612; Thomas Homer-Dixon, *Environment, Scarcity and Violence* (Princeton: Princeton University Press, 1999); Thomas Homer-Dixon and Jessica Blitt, *Ecoviolence: Links Among Environment, Population and Security* (Oxford: Rowman and Littlefield, 1998).

13. See Baechler, "Environmental Degradation and Violent Conflict"; Günther Baechler, "Why Environmental Transformation Causes Violence: A Synthesis," *Environmental Change and Security Project Report* 4 (Spring 1998): 24–44.

14. Homer-Dixon, *Environment, Scarcity and Violence,* 177.

15. Ibid., 5.

16. Ibid., 7.

17. Barbier and Homer-Dixon, *Resource Scarcity, Institutional Adaptation, and Technical Innovation.* This view stands in opposition to induced innovation theories such as Esther Boserup's theory on population pressures and agricultural productivity; see Esther Boserup, *The Conditions of Agricultural Growth: The Economies of Agrarian Change Under Population Pressure* (New York: Aldine, 1965).

18. Marc A. Levy, "Is the Environment a National Security Issue?" *International Security* 20, no. 2 (1995): 35–62.

19. Nils Petter Gleditsch, "Armed Conflict and the Environment: A Critique of the Literature," *Journal of Peace Research* 35, no. 3 (1998): 381–400.

20. Robert M. Solow, "A Contribution to the Theory of Economic Growth," *Quarterly Journal of Economics* 70 (1956): 65–94.

21. Paul Romer, "Increasing Returns and Long-Run Growth," *Journal of Political Economy* 94 (1986): 1002–1037; Robert E. Lucas, "On the Mechanics of Economic Development," *Journal of Monetary Economics* 22 (1988): 3–42.

22. Robert J. Barro, *Determinants of Economic Growth: A Cross-Country Empirical Study* (Cambridge, Mass.: MIT Press, 1998).

23. Thomas Homer-Dixon, "Ingenuity Gaps: Can Poor Countries Adapt to Resource Scarcity?" *Population and Development Review* 21, no. 3 (1995): 587–612; Homer-Dixon, *Environment, Scarcity and Violence.*

24. Although Collier assumes abundance based on the trade composition measure, the link he makes between the motivation of greed and violence is that primary commodities are easily captured and resold. Whether these commodities are scarce or abundant is largely irrelevant to the issue of conflict. However, his findings are subject to criticism by neo-Malthusians, who would argue that the strong effects of resource dependence on conflict are in reality effects of scarcity.

25. Jeffrey Sachs and Andrew Warner, "Natural Resource Abundance and Economic Growth," *NBER Working Paper* 5398 (Boston: National Bureau of Economic Research, 19.

26. Arrow argued that trade (manufacture) promoted learning by doing; see Kenneth J. Arrow, "The Economic Implications of Learning by Doing," *Review of Economic Studies* 29 (1962): 155–173.

27. See Thomas Homer-Dixon and Jessica Blitt, *Ecoviolence: Links Among Environment, Population and Security* (Oxford: Rowman and Littlefield, 1998).

28. See Boserup, *The Conditions of Agricultural Growth.*

29. Kiminori Matsumaya, "Agricultural Productivity, Comparative Advantage, and Economic Growth," *Journal of Economic Theory* 58 (1992): 317–334.

30. Hussein Mahdavy, "The Pattern and Problems of Economic Development in Rentier States: The Case of Iran," in M. A. Cook (ed.), *Studies in Economic History of the Middle East* (London: Oxford University Press, 1970).

31. See Michael L. Ross, "The Political Economy of the Resource Curse," *World Politics* 51 (1999): 297–322; Mondonga Mokoli and Hans P. Binswanger, "Prerequisites for a Development Oriented State in the Republic of Congo," *Policy Research Working Paper* 2018, Rural Development and Environment Department, Africa Region (Washington, D.C.: World Bank, 1998); Terry Lynn Karl, *The Paradox of Plenty: Oil Booms and Petro States* (Berkeley: University of California Press, 1997); and Michael D. Shafer, *Winners and Losers: How Sectors Shape the Development Prospects of States* (Ithaca: Cornell University Press, 1994).

32. See also William Reno, *Warlord Politics and African States.*

33. World Bank, *Expanding the Measure of Wealth: Indicators of Environmentally Sustainable Development* (Washington, D.C.: World Bank, 1997), 30.

34. See ibid. for details on data and measurement.

35. Homer-Dixon, "Ingenuity Gaps," 1.

36. Homer-Dixon now stresses that it is with the scarcity of renewables that he is largely concerned (personal communication with author).

37. Methodology is included in the appendix to this chapter.

38. It seems that the threshold effect is also absent because of the smaller threshold for civil war used in the definition of my dependent variable. With the COW data, I too find a positive and significant effect.

39. I tested this variable against alternative models, but the effect was always statistically weak. A squared term did not yield promising results either. Testing linguistic heterogeneity and religious heterogeneity in this basic model revealed that the latter is significantly and negatively associated with conflict, net of the control variables.

40. Using a simple statistical tool, whereby I add an interactive term (the product of a dummy variable identifying the poorest countries and renewable resource stock per capita) to the model, enables me to see whether scarcity and poverty interact to cause conflict. I find no significant interactive effect.

41. The paper on resources, growth, and conflict was presented at a panel on environmental conflicts at the International Studies Association's annual meeting in Washington, D.C., February 16–21, 1999. The paper is available from the author upon request.

42. United Nations Development Program, *The Human Development Report* (New York: Oxford University Press, 1998), p. 93. The UNDP reports that in the 1990s, developing countries subsidized energy to the tune of $200 billion, twice the amount spent by the OECD countries. OECD countries, in contrast, heavily subsidize agriculture, which may also inhibit exports and promote mono-culture production rather than diversification in the developing countries.

43. R. M. Auty, *Resource-Based Industrialization: Sowing the Oil in Eight Developing Countries* (New York: Oxford University Press, 1990); Sachs and Warner, "Natural Resource Abundance and Economic Growth"; Karl, *The Paradox of Plenty.*

44. World Bank, *Assessing Aid: What Works, What Doesn't and Why* (Washington, D.C.: World Bank, 1999).

45. Luther Tweeten and Donald McClelland (eds.), *Promoting Third World Development and Food Security* (Westport, Conn.: Praeger, 1997).

46. Tim Allen, *In Search of Cool Ground: War, Flight, and Homecoming in Northeast Africa* (Geneva: UNRISD, with James Currey and Africa World Press, 1996).

47. Peter Wallensteen and Margareta Sollenberg, "Armed Conflict and Regional Conflict Complexes, 1989–1997," *Journal of Peace Research* 35, no. 5 (1998): 621–634.

48. In Collier's more recent work, he emphasizes a cuvilinear relationship between population size and conflict. In other words, large and small countries have more conflict whereas peace is strongest in midsized countries.

49. Håvard Hegre et al., "Towards a Democratic Civil Peace? Opportunity, Grievance, and Civil War, 1816–1992," paper presented at the World Bank conference on Civil Conflicts, Crime and Violence on February 22–23, 1999, Washington, D.C.

50. See Ted Robert Gurr, Keith Jaggers, and Will Moore, "The Transformation of the Western State: The Growth of Democracy, Autocracy, and State Power Since 1800," *Studies in Comparative International Development* 25 (1990): 73–106.

51. Wenche Hauge and Tanya Ellingsen, "Beyond Environmental Scarcity: Causal Pathways to Conflict," *Journal of Peace Research* 35, no. 3 (1998): 299–317.

52. Data on the years of schooling of the male population were obtained from the World Watch Institute's *World Resources Data,* and the income data are from the Penn World Tables, 5.6a.

53. See Esty et al., *State Failure Task Force Report.*

7

The View from Below

Musifiky Mwanasali

The tragedy that engulfed Rwanda in 1994, with the subsequent flight of refugees—hundreds of thousands of Rwandan civilians and armed elements—to eastern Zaire (now Congo) unleashed an economic as well as political shock wave that still affects the central African subregion. This change manifested itself in two ways: first, through the influx of U.S. dollars in local economies and the rise of the dollar as the preferential currency in local economic transactions; and, second, through the overall climate of economic uncertainty created concurrently by the use of the U.S. dollar and the presence of various armed elements and extremist groups on Congolese territory, which became the proximate cause of the two recent Congolese "wars of liberation" (1996–1997 and 1998).

The scope of this chapter is local and confined to the economic activities and trade networks that link the eastern provinces of Congo, more specifically the Oriental Province, to neighboring countries in the Great Lakes region.[1] This chapter has three purposes. First is to describe the economic transactions and trade networks that existed in the former Eastern Zaire prior to the two rebellions of 1996 and 1998. Next is to show how these rebellions have changed the local political and economic landscape in the Oriental Province. Here I will identify the linkages that the belligerents in the ongoing rebellion have established with local markets and the preexisting informal trade networks.[2] This section also shows how local productive systems and exchange networks have been affected by the

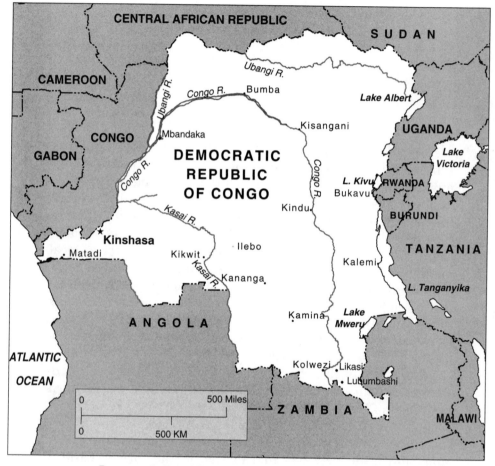

Democratic Republic of Congo and Adjacent Countries

new dynamics introduced by the civil war. Finally, I will emphasize the need for a field-based understanding of local survival
strategies and coping mechanisms as a prerequisite for lasting
peace, sustained economic growth, and effective governance in
the postconflict era.

Informal Trade Networks in Eastern Zaire

Civil wars cause major disruptions in the economic and political life of a country, parts thereof, or the entire surrounding region. At the same time, the parties to the conflict often graft
themselves onto surviving institutions, markets, and trade networks in the pursuit of their undertakings. The more informal
the nature of local political and economic transactions, the
greater the ease with which civil war factions can use them to
achieve their goals.[3] This is apparently so because informal
transactions and loose trade networks provide the kind of clandestine cover needed by the belligerents in the course of their
military-cum-commercial operations.

An investigation of the nature of the local economy (in this
case, the informal economy) is therefore paramount to any
meaningful grasp of the way local markets cope with the conditions brought about by the civil war, as well as how the latter
may be halted. Yet informal productive and exchange systems
that sustain the livelihood of entire communities in regions affected by civil wars seldom figure among popular scholarly topics and policy debates on peacemaking, peace building, or postconflict reconstruction.

The informal economy is central to this investigation of
local coping mechanisms in civil war contexts because it serves
as an important link between the actors involved in the economic activities that are usually called informal and civil war
protagonists. By linking local markets and transboundary networks of production and exchange, the informal economy
often provides needed outlets for the channeling of critical resources to (and for the benefit of) the warring factions.

Before the Rwandan massacres of 1994, trade networks extended throughout the Great Lakes region, which covers the
troubled quadrangle comprising Uganda, Rwanda, Burundi,
and Congo, and reached out across Kenya and Tanzania to the

Arabian emirates. Four major trading routes existed. The first route carried agricultural products and manufactured goods between Kampala in Uganda and Bukavu in the former Zaire via Goma, Rutshuru, and several villages along the way. The second axis was used primarily to transport goods and people between the port-city of Bujumbura in Burundi and the town (and port) of Uvira. Traders and shoppers routinely crossed the border daily in both directions—Burundian businessmen in search of foreign exchange in Uvira's unregulated currency exchange places, and Congolese traders flocking the open market in Bujumbura looking for manufactured goods.[4] The third axis linked the Oriental Province of Congo directly to Uganda and all points beyond (i.e., Nairobi and Dubai) through the well-known commercially active towns of Beni and Butembo in Congo. Along this route, traders of mainly Nande origin transacted in coffee, precious minerals, manufactured goods, and foreign currencies. The fourth major route had two branches. The first branch linked across Lake Tanganyika to the port-towns of Kalemie in Congo and Kigoma in Tanzania, whereas the second branch connected the city of Lubumbashi in Congo to the port-city of Dar-es-Salaam in Tanzania, via the town of Kapiri Mposhi in Zambia and the Tanzanian-Zambian railway network. Essentially, only manufactured goods were transacted along both routes, with some food traveling mainly between Zambia and Congo.

This vast network of informal trade linked the eastern part of Congo directly to the markets in eastern and southern Africa, and several others beyond. It was partly owing to the ingenuity of local entrepreneurs that the former Zaire was able to ward off the harsh blows of a decade-long flight of foreign capital and cuts in economic assistance. Private businesses, transportation companies, and tax-collecting bureaucracies throughout the region benefited significantly from the informal sector and the income opportunities it provided.

Occasionally, a neighboring country became the direct beneficiary. At the height of the political chaos in the former Zaire, some neighbors became exporters of raw materials such as gold or cobalt even though they did not naturally possess them. Looted from Zaire and exported "fraudulently" through the black market, timber, palm oil, coffee, elephant tusks, and precious minerals have now become a main source of foreign exchange for Congo's resource-deprived neighbors. Several years ago, a private bank was reportedly set up in Dar-es-Salaam, Tanzania, for the purpose of recycling earnings from smuggled precious minerals.

Coping with Civil Wars

As stated in the introduction, the Rwandan war had serious impacts for eastern Zaire, as manifested by the influx of U.S. dollars and the attendant economic uncertainty. Elsewhere in the former Zaire, the dollar had become the currency of choice in the early 1990s as a result of the currency speculation initiated by political incumbents who carelessly flooded informal foreign currency markets with hard currencies such as the U.S. dollar and the Belgian and French francs. In eastern Zaire, however, the rise of the dollar as the preferential currency was brought about by the influx and proliferation of international humanitarian agencies that rushed to the rescue of the Rwandan refugees.

The first "liberation war" of 1996 was so short that it did not seriously damage local economic activities. After initial hesitations (and even resentment) toward the essentially foreign nature of the war, a majority of the Congolese population rallied behind the rebellion in the hope that a victory against the corrupt regime of President Mobutu would usher in a new era of peace and prosperity for all. Local communities supported the war effort by sending their own children to defeat Mobutu's army. They also openly defied the authority of the embattled government by supplying the rebels with food and occasional information about the position of the Zairian army.[5]

This form of overt collaboration with the enemy has not occurred during the current rebellion. Set off in 1998 by a faction of the ruling Alliance of the Democratic Forces for the Liberation of Congo (AFDL) to combat "the dictatorial and genocidal impulses" of President Kabila, this second Congolese war seemed to lose its legitimacy right after its onset, as local communities overwhelmingly opposed the invasion of the country by foreign armies. Parents rejected the rebellion's call for more young recruits. Young children were kept home in some instances out of fear of their being drafted by rebel armies. Entire villages were burned because of the population's lack of enthusiasm for a rebellion whose political goals were not justified in their eyes.

The situation became even more ambiguous for local businessmen and traders. Recent reports issued by Congolese human rights organizations, such as the African Association for Human Rights (ASADHO), have denounced the harassment and arrest (on the grounds that they are conniving with the "enemy") of several prominent Nande traders by both the rebels and the embattled Congolese government. In other rebel-occupied zones, peasants have been forced to sell their produce only to specified rebel groups. In the Equator Province, coffee producers have been coerced to sell their coffee beans to the Mouvement de Libération du Congo (MLC) leadership and designated Ugandan buyers, generally at very depressed prices. Palm oil producers in Kisangani are compelled to sell their produce to Rwandan intermediaries below the market price.

The collection of taxes and customs duties constitutes another bone of contention among the three rebel factions and their respective backers. The Ugandan forces and their Rassemblement Congolais pour la Démocratie (RCD) allies have taken possession of the customs post of Kasindi in North Kivu, which produces a monthly revenue of approximately U.S.$24,000. They also control the newly created province of Kibali-Ituri in the Oriental Province, which includes the gold- and coffee-producing towns of Isiro, Bunia, and Butembo. The gold-producing towns of Bunia and Watsa (where the Kilo-Moto gold mines are located) are also under the exclusive control of Ugandan troops and their RCD allies. More coffee, timber, and, according to some sources, elephant tusks are regularly exported to Uganda by the MLC and its Ugandan partners.

Rwanda and its allies are not faring as well as Uganda as far as precious minerals and taxes are concerned. The Rwandan-backed RCD controls the Great Kivu area, which comprises the three provinces of Maniema, North Kivu, and South Kivu. Since the bankruptcy of the Société Minière du Kuvu (SOMINKI) gold mine in Kalima, the Kivu provinces are not very productive. Additionally, the alluvial diamond deposits in Banalia and Bengamisa in the Oriental Province cannot be exploited industrially, as some Rwandan businessmen have expected.

In the absence of important mineral reserves, the Rwandan-backed RCD has resorted to the collection of various types of fees from local producers and Lebanese intermediaries. In Bukavu, an entrepreneur wishing to operate as a "commission-naire" or intermediary between local (peasant or artisan) producers and the market is required to pay to the RCD a fee in the amount of U.S.$1,300 to be issued a license, and roughly U.S.$3,000 as a "deposit." Because local businesspeople generally cannot afford these exorbitant fees, this niche is dominated by foreigners mainly of Indian and Lebanese origins. Rwanda and its RCD partners are also involved in the palm oil business, the only commodity produced in Kisangani, which is regularly exported to Kigali via military planes. According to my informants in Kisangani, palm oil producers are paid normally, but at a very low price. In contrast, textile imports from Rwanda are competing with SOTEXKI products.[6]

The aftermath of the 1994 communal violence in Rwanda and the onset of the 1996 and 1998 rebellions in Congo have completely changed local productive and trade systems in the eastern provinces of the DRC. Previous trading routes in the Great Lakes region are currently beset with violence and littered with small weapons, armed rebels, and regular troops. Production has collapsed in Rwanda, Burundi, and the eastern part of Congo, whereas the movement of people and goods is seriously hampered by the general insecurity. The continuous influx of refugees from Congo has raised security concerns in neighboring Zambia, a situation that led the Zambian government to significantly curtail the movement of informal traders. As a result, economic activity along these routes has dropped to almost nothing.

Cut off by the violence from import and export channels, most traders have now abandoned their trading activity out of fear for their lives. Those who still operate along these perilous routes have been obliged to cooperate with the rebel armies and the troops of the countries that back the rebellion. In Kisangani, some traders supply the troops with cash payments, food, clothes, goods of basic necessity, and other wares in return for personal protection and safety along trading routes. A handful of the very few affluent businessmen sponsor the rebel movement financially. Although some in the music and sex industry continue to live their lives normally, the majority of the people have maintained a prudent and distant attitude toward the rebellion and its sponsors.

In Kisangani, the Rwanda-backed RCD has prohibited *taxi-vélos* on the ground that the operators are sympathetic to the Ugandan-backed RCD.[7] Local consumers, for the most part, are said to be resigned to these new circumstances and do business with their occupying forces and their traders. In Butembo, however, the Nande population appears determined not to do business, particularly with the Rwandan-backed RCD. Nande customers only buy from fellow Nande merchants who, in turn, rarely sell to non-Nande consumers. Several Nande traders in the Beni-Butembo area continue to transact with their counterpart in Uganda, ironically despite the fact that this country has sponsored two of the three rebel factions intent on overthrowing Kabila's government. In North and South Kivu, however, in order to minimize the hostilities of most Congolese merchants and allow economic and commercial transactions, the government of Rwanda and its RCD allies have resorted to a policy of twinning Congolese and Rwandan cities and towns.

Greed, Grievances, and the Rationality of Civil Wars

In a civil war context, warring factions and informal traders live off each other in a complex way. Examples abound concerning how small arms and ammunition find their way inside a country through loose trade networks. Disguising themselves as charcoal producers, Zairian rebels smuggled arms and ammunition in preparation for the 1977 Shaba war in southern Zaire. A significant portion of the agricultural and mineral products that are making the fortunes of some Ugandan, Rwandan, and foreign traders and politicomilitary elite is looted, confiscated from local producers, and exported fraudulently through Kampala and Kigali.

Paul Collier's distinction between greed and grievance offers a useful starting point for a discussion of economic or commercial motivations (and/or crimes) in a civil war context. In his chapter entitled "Doing Well out of War," Collier remarks, "At one extreme rebellions might arise because the rebels aspire to wealth through capturing resources extralegally. At the other extreme they might arise because rebels aspire to rid the nation, or the group of people with which they identify, of an unjust regime." Collier believes that in spite of rebels' own pronouncements, it is not easy to precisely determine whether greed or grievance is the rebellion's driving force. For him, "even where the rationale at the top of the [rebel] organization is essentially greed, the actual discourse may be entirely dominated by grievance." This is so because the rebels need effective propaganda to muster outside support and strengthen their movement internally. To this end, "[n]arratives of grievance play much better with [a] community than narratives of greed, [and] by playing upon a sense of grievance, the [rebel] organization may therefore be able to add more recruits cheaply."[8]

Collier then makes a distinction between the main factors that constitute purely economic causes of war (greed) and those factors that might broadly be ascribed to grievance. He uses three main "proxies," or conceptual devices, to describe and measure the "economic agendas" of rebellions. Among them is the availability of "lootable resources," that is, primary commodity exports. Primary commodity exports present several advantages to the belligerents. Because they are generic products, rather than brand names, their origin can easily be concealed. They are usually the most heavily taxable, especially in kind, and their production or marketing does not require complicated processes, as is the case of manufactured goods. Coffee, timber, gold, diamonds, and other agricultural products are the key primary commodities used by the belligerents involved in the personal enrichment scheme in Congo.

It is therefore appropriate to question, as do Mats Berdal and David Keen, the usefulness of theoretical propositions and policy prescriptions that argue about the "irrationality of war." Berdal and Keen rightly suggest that "the continuation of seemingly 'senseless' civil wars is sometimes linked to the 'rational' pursuit of economic goals" by the warring factions.[9] Presumably, as for Collier, the main task for them is that peacemakers identify the economic agendas as well as their beneficiaries, and raise the opportunity costs of pursuing them through warfare.

Unfortunately, it is not always easy to identify with certainty the multiple economic agendas and actors behind a civil war. According to the classical definition, civil war situations usually involve the use of force by one of several organized groups against the established government. From the perspective of the embattled government, civil wars are always illegal. They violate the political principles, ruling institutions, and law of the land, and are to be dealt with by force. Governments usually refer to internationally accepted principles and norms to support and legitimize their determination to restore law and order by force if necessary. For the most part, the international community endorses such claims and usually tends to uphold the rights of its members to maintain law and order within the internationally recognized borders of their territory.

Rebel forces have a different view of their campaign. They generally invoke the illegal character of the state and its lack of legitimacy as the determining factor in their decision to overthrow it by use of military might. From their perspective, war is the only effective means of toppling an unwanted political regime, ridding the country of corrupt leadership, and achieving radical transformation of the governing structure and institutions. When abducted Ugandan children wanted to know the reasons for their harrowing ordeal, they were told by the Lord's Resistance Army (LRA),

> The president of Uganda is biased and only developing the west and south, and is neglecting development in the North. . . . [The LRA rebels] capture people because they wanted to disappoint Museveni and to break the government. . . . [The rebels] don't want this man Museveni who is ruling Uganda because he has killed a lot of Acholi, he has killed a lot of their brothers, mothers, fathers, aunts and sisters.[10]

The LRA or RCD rebels may have in President Yoweri Museveni or Laurent-Désiré Kabila a clearly defined enemy and a "rational" justification, or grievance in Collier's terms, for their decision to take up arms in defense of their interests. In reality, however, civil wars tend to generate a multiplicity of autonomous power centers and agendas as well as a continuous shift in the identity of the key actors. When significant economic interests are involved, the decision to start, prolong, or end a civil war is also made possible by the nature of the economic system and the kind of economic gains and incentives it offers the belligerents in their pursuit of their political agenda.

Credible accounts, including from the Uganda-based RCD leaders, have denounced the looting, exports of precious minerals, and destruction of property by the rebel forces and their backers in the Kivu and Oriental Provinces. Recent hostilities and tensions between the armies of Uganda and the joint rebel-Rwandan troops in Kisangani have been attributed to quarrels over control of economic resources by Ugandan and Rwandan commanders. The Ugandan government has even suspended the license of a Ugandan private airline whose major business consisted of chartering looted products from the Congolese northeastern region to Ugandan and other external markets. Military aircrafts are regularly used for the transport of troops and merchandise between Rwanda, Uganda, and the rebel-occupied Congolese provinces. Unconfirmed reports indicate that Rwanda and Uganda have become major exporters of primary commodities they do not possess.

Angola is another example. More than a quarter of a century ago, the National Union for the Total Independence of Angola (UNITA) took up arms against the government led by the Popular Movement for the Liberation of Angola (MPLA). In theory, the war was the result of irreconcilable differences between two inflexible political parties supported by two equally resolute and well-equipped armies. Over the years, it became apparent that Angola's was not a civil war in the classic sense of the term.

First, despite regular references to both UNITA and the MPLA as homogenous groups, it is increasingly apparent that neither warring party is as popular or unified as it claims to be. Among the present UNITA leadership are several former MPLA caciques and defectors as well as lukewarm partisans of a ruthless movement whose raison d'être, according to some Angolan sources, seems psychological rather than political. Similarly, the MPLA fractiousness is as notorious as is the general dislike of its ruling establishment. Witness the regular criticism against the established authorities aired by private radio broadcast in the MPLA-controlled areas.

Second, UNITA appears to be a strong and well-equipped army, owing in large part to the ruthless treatment inflicted on undisciplined or deserting soldiers. But the MPLA does not fare better. It has chosen "bribery" in order to attract and keep young people in an army that they see no reason to die for. Well fed, well paid, and well dressed in comparison to the rest of the Angolan poor, MPLA soldiers now seem eager to enjoy the perks associated with their job, but they show little enthusiasm for fighting a civil war whose objectives are increasingly unclear to them.

Finally, while their respective armies are slugging it out in various battlefields, in the diamond-rich Lunda Province it seems that some kind of tacit alliance exists between UNITA and MPLA top commanders and administrators in the diamond business. Thus, while rebel and government authorities obtain personal enrichment through the diamond trade, all the rank and file can do is loot and ransack private homes.

There are even cases where international actors become involved in providing the protagonists with the requisite means to achieve their goals. Private businesses are a case in point. When they do not instigate rebellions, as they did during the 1960 Katangese secession in the newly independent Congo-Kinshasa, private individuals and companies may reap huge benefits from their collaboration with rebel forces and "legitimate" governments.

One of its major partners is the South African transnational corporate giant De Beers, which is notorious for its astute control of the global diamond market. This company is now involved in litigation with another smaller corporation over mineral contracts in the former Zaire. The plaintiff, American Mineral Fields (AMF), once rallied around the rebels seeking to overthrow the defunct regime of President Mobutu in the hope of securing lucrative contracts in Congo's geological scandal. To its great surprise, AMF was excluded from major deals, as President Mobutu's successors chose to sign mining contracts with "credible" companies, including that particular AMF rival. Though the trial is yet to take place, AMF is allegedly providing financial support to the RCD rebels who are now set on overthrowing the government.

Cases like these abound in countries torn by or emerging from civil wars. The Sudan, Cambodia, Yemen, Somalia, Liberia, Sierra Leone, and Lebanon are replete with stories of individuals, groups, private corporations, and governments that profit from domestic violence. Faced with such an intricate web of political and economic interests and agendas, at what point in this chain of transactions does the shift in the economic agenda occur? Moreover, can macroeconomic accounts fully reveal the economic agendas of external actors for fueling violence and perpetuating hostilities in neighboring countries?

Determining Economic Agendas

Even if it were possible to identify the primary motives for civil wars and to determine who sets the agenda for the pursuit of economic gains through warfare, there still remains the problem of how to capture the full volume of economic transactions carried out informally. One cannot rely solely on the statistics produced by leading international development agencies. Perhaps because of the difficulty of incorporating the informal sector within conventional economics, the key macroeconomic indicators used by leading international development agencies rarely include the economic transactions typical of local markets.

Collier's framework is useful in that it helps the international community focus on greed or economic gains as a primary motive for warfare. It thus provides a stepping-stone for a further exploration of effective economic incentives for promoting lasting peace at the local level. But this effort needs major improvements, especially when the economic agendas of the belligerents are hard to quantify and the volume of primary commodity exports does not show up in national accounts. In Uganda's national accounts, where does the "in-kind taxation" (to use Collier's terms) appear that is provided to the LRA by Ugandan-abducted girls? We know from their stories that these children were used as farmers, porters, and nurses. Fourteen-year-old Thomas described his duties as consisting mostly of farming. He says, "I would dig fields and plant maize beans. I spent most of my time digging." According to Sarah, aged sixteen, a top rebel commander by the name of Kony "wanted those [children] who had been in schools to be trained as nurses, to give first aid to the rebels." Much worse happened to children like sixteen-year-old Susan. By her own account, "one week after [she] was abducted, [she] was given to a [thirty-year-old] man called Abonga. Two girls were given to him. . . . [She] was taken away from him when [she] got to Sudan because [she] had syphilis."[11]

It is an arduous, if not impossible, task to identify with certainty the multiple economic agendas behind a civil war, even more so to determine who defines them and how they change as the war progresses. Civil wars create a dynamic situation with new stakeholders as well as a whole new set of winners and losers in the political, economic, and security arenas. They represent complex episodes in the political life of a country as one or several groups, alone or with external help, seek radically to transform the existing framework of social, political, economic, military-strategic, institutional, and sometimes territorial structures and dynamics in order to implement their own vision of society.

In such a highly volatile context, economic agendas shift in accordance with new constraints and opportunities, rewards and punishments, incentives and disincentives for various sets of belligerents. At the local level, where the effects of the war are the most drastic, civilians caught in the hostilities are concerned primarily with basic survival. Theirs is generally an opportunistic adaptation to the conditions that have been forced upon them. Their need for the normalcy of life (education, health care, social safety nets) further dictates the activities and networks that they engage in during and after a civil war.

It is equally tempting to regard these acts as criminal. However, one should bear in mind that the moral restraints that usually function in times of peace against "criminal" activities such as smuggling, looting, gun running, drug cultivation, or prostitution very often break down in do-or-die situations, particularly when the situation is a prolonged war. Additionally, one must realize that the mechanisms, networks, habits, and activities that develop during the conflict often survive long into the postconflict period. In many cases, they may become the seedbeds for further conflict. Civilians caught in hostilities may be offered rewards or subjected to punishments of different kinds by different belligerents if they accept or refuse to participate in these "criminal" activities. This has been the case with drug cultivation in the Bekah Valley in Lebanon, in Afghanistan, and in Colombia. War may represent a rational pursuit of economic interests for some, but it remains a senseless destruction of life and property for many others.

What Is to Be Done?

The world community appears unenthusiastic about an open scrutiny of the economic motives behind the official justifications of the relentless pursuit of war. Yet in countries and regions steeped in civil wars and rebellions—and amidst the ensuing lawlessness and political chaos—ransoms, clandestine arms trade, drugs trafficking, money laundering, looting, and smuggling continue unabated, making the resolution of violent conflicts even more problematic.

The international community has outlawed torture, abduction, unlawful detention of civilians, forced labor, rape, and sexual abuse. It has set up a sanctions regime and institutions to prosecute these crimes and punish the criminals. Civic groups and humanitarian agencies have used different creative methods to protect the civilians caught in civil wars. Ransoms have been paid to the rebels in Chechnya, for instance, to secure the freedom of abducted foreign businessmen, journalists, and famous and ordinary civilians. The Roman Catholic Church hierarchy in Colombia recently decreed the excommunication of the Colombian National Liberation Army (ELN) for the abduction of innocent civilians during Sunday mass.

Human rights groups and humanitarian organizations routinely call upon the combatants to respect the relevant international conventions regulating the conduct of war and the protection of civilian lives in wartime. The usual recourse is to refer to existing international conventions and ask the belligerents to eradicate the abhorrent practice. Occasionally, specific governments or rebel forces have been identified by name and compelled to stop the abuses.

Protests have been organized and restrictions imposed on the Sudan to exert pressure on "rogue states" to enforce international covenants outlawing practices like abduction, rape, or slavery. Recently, a group of American students went so far as to raise funds to free child slaves from the Bahr El Ghazal region in the Sudan. Human Rights Watch has asked that "the Lord's Resistance Army should comply with its obligations under international humanitarian law, and the Government of Uganda should take all possible steps to protect the rights of Ugandan children, as required by the Convention on the Rights of the Child."[12] UNICEF issued similar statements about Uganda and called on the Sudan to end the trade in children as slaves.

Statements like these are commendable. However, civil wars often result in a total or partial breakdown of law and order in large areas of embattled countries. They can hold an entire population hostage to the enrichment motives of the belligerents. Human rights pronouncements will have little effect in these circumstances, particularly on the rebel forces. And, how can an embattled government be expected to carry out its international legal obligations when it does not control vast portions of its own territory?

Reconstruction of the legitimacy of credible local authorities and the establishing of islands of peace in local communities may be a more imaginative way for the international community to create incentives for lasting peace at the local level. Care should be paid to promote and encourage local peace entrepreneurs at the same time that efforts are being deployed to reconcile feuding rivals. Frequently, the international community is too concerned with the latter, even though it is apparent that the belligerents have no reason or incentive to stop the war. In this sense, postconflict rehabilitation and reconstruction must be approached very carefully, so as to avoid the reproduction or perpetuation of the conditions that led to the conflict or that arose in the course of the civil war.

Finally, in tackling postconflict peace building, there is a clear need for a deep understanding of the political economy and the economic geography of the affected society prior to the onset of civil war, and how these have been altered. More context-specific, microlevel analyses are needed, particularly if they can help change the nearly exclusive emphasis on the economic agendas of the elite, warlords, governments, and donor communities. If we are to make a difference for the majority of the people who suffer the horrible effects of civil wars, we ought to also focus our research on how ordinary people adjust their lives to cope with the constraints and opportunities brought about by civil war. It is for this reason that I have deliberately shifted the focus away from macrolevel analysis and policy prescriptions that are generally based on a snapshot rather than a dynamic view of the changing situations on the ground.

Notes

This chapter presents preliminary findings from a study that is a collaborative project led by Arun Elhance, an economic geographer, and myself. Entitled "Surviving and Coping with Civil Wars: Perspectives from Below," it concerns four cases: the Democratic Republic of Congo (DRC), Cambodia, Colombia, and Lebanon. The first monograph on the DRC is due in October 2000. The objective of this study is to produce field-grounded knowledge that would help policymakers understand the changing political dynamics created by civil wars; the various adaptive responses by the affected communities; and the nature of economic activities, trade networks, and governance mechanisms and practices that persist after hostilities have ceased. Such an understanding is crucial to the success of all efforts for peace building, economic rehabilitation, and good governance. Several people have contributed data and editorial and substantive comments on various drafts. I thank Arun Elhance, Edith Oyulu, Gloria Ntegeye, and Ciara Knudsen for their perceptive comments. Special thanks are due to Kinyalolo Kasangati, Jean-Pierre Badidike (of the Kisangani-based NGO Justice et Liberation), and several friends and relatives in eastern DRC, who kindly provided the bulk of information presented here. Needless to say, I take responsibility for all errors contained herein.

1. The data presented here have been collected since 1992, mainly in the Maniema, the two Kivu, and the Oriental Provinces of the Democratic Republic of the Congo (DRC).

2. This rebellion started on August 2, 1990, when a faction of the ruling Alliance of the Democratic Forces for the Liberation of Congo (AFDL) broke away and, with the help of the armies of Uganda and Rwanda, took up arms to overthrow the government of President Kabila. Naming itself Rassemblement Congolais pour la Démocratie (RCD), the rebel movement eventually split into two opposing factions backed by Rwanda and Uganda respectively. There is a third rebel movement, the Mouvement de Libération du Congo (MLC), which is also backed by Uganda.

3. A voluminous literature has been produced on the "informal economy," notably by the International Labor Organization, which helped publicize it. Since Keith Hart's use of the term "informal income opportunities" in 1971, a plethora of new terms have been proposed to describe this phenomenon. I have reviewed this literature in my Ph.D. thesis, entitled "Accumulation, Regulation and Development: The Grass-roots Economy in the Upper Zaire Region (1970–1990)" (Evanston, Ill.: Northwestern University, 1994).

4. Trade with Rwanda has generally been negligible.

5. It was local fishermen who provided the AFDL troops with the military intelligence and logistical support that allowed the fall of the town of Kindu in the Maniema province in early 1997.

6. SOTEXKI is the French acronym for Société des Textiles de Kisangani, a major textile factory that was recently looted and destroyed by Rwandan and RCD troops after the battle in which they had fought Ugandan troops and their own RCD allies.

7. *Taxi-vélos* are a common mode of transportation used by informal traders to carry products from the countryside to the city of Kisangani. For a small fee, they can also be rented for transport within the city.

8. These passages are excerpted from the paper Collier presented at the conference on Economic Agendas in Civil Wars (London, April 26–27, 1999).

9. Mats Berdal and David Keen, "Violence and Economic Agendas in Civil Wars: Some Policy Implications," *Millennium* 3 (1997): 816.

10. Human Rights Watch, *The Scars of Death: Children Abducted by the Lord's Resistance Army in Uganda* (New York: Human Rights Watch Africa, 1997), 25.

11. Ibid., 26–29.

12. Ibid., 82.

PART TWO

Confronting Economic Agendas in Civil Wars

8

Arms, Elites, and Resources in the Angolan Civil War

Virginia Gamba and Richard Cornwell

This chapter examines the regulation and self-regulation of the private sector during civil wars, with a special focus on the issue of arms as a commodity of war, and through the lens of the current civil war in Angola. The first section of the chapter illustrates the ease of acquiring weapons in Angola, and the second section presents possible ways of addressing this situation. Any discussion of regulation and self-regulation of the private arms-producing sector is largely academic. The existing civil war in Angola and the levels of armaments available to both parties in this war are sufficient proof that neither regulations at national/regional level on arms industries nor self-regulation by the arms industry itself is working. If weapons will always find a way to reach a client who can pay, the focus on regulations must shift from the commodity itself to the elites who consume them and the financial resources used to pay for them. Finally, for a better understanding of the arms industry in Angola, this chapter looks at the dynamics of power in relation to the civil war and at the resources employed by the warring parties in acquiring and maintaining a military option.

The Arms Dimension

The weapons fueling armed conflict in Angola today have three sources: They are still part of the stocks freely dumped in the country by sympathetic governments to the different warring parties during the Cold War era, they are old stocks of small arms recirculating in the region of Southern Africa from conflict area to conflict area, and they are new supplies sold and transferred to Angola to serve the Angolan government or UNITA forces. The first two sources, which are a remnant of decades of warfare in Angola and elsewhere in Southern Africa, are very difficult to assess both in relation to original suppliers and to patterns of their present dissemination through illicit channels in the region. Over and above the interface between Angola and the ongoing armed conflict in the Democratic Republic of the Congo that is fueling its own "procurement" wars, the situation of circulating stocks in Southern Africa—although difficult to pinpoint with precision—can be commented upon.

In Mozambique alone, the estimates of weapons imported during the civil war range from 500,000 to 6 million. During the United Nations peacekeeping operation (ONUMOZ 1993–1995), nearly 190,000 weapons were collected. Most of these were not destroyed, however; they soon were again on the streets of Maputo or being moved into neighboring states. In four distinct recovery operations conducted between South Africa and Mozambique since 1995, a total of 11,891 firearms, 106 pistols, 6,351 antipersonnel mines, 88 land mines, 1,260 hand grenades, 424 hand grenade detonators, 7,015 mortar bombs, 263 launchers, 8,138 projectiles, 1,242 boosters, 33 cannons, 3,192,337 rounds of ammunition, and 5,912 magazines were seized and destroyed.[1] Given the differences between weapons accounted for and those not, it is not too much to assume that some of the weapons unaccounted for have made their way to the Angolan theater. A typical route for this to occur is either from South Africa via Namibia or from Mozambique via Zambia.

In Angola it is virtually impossible to estimate the number of weapons in circulation and use after two decades of war. Nevertheless there are some figures to go by; for example, it was reported that in 1992, 700,000 weapons were distributed to civilians by the government following the renewal of fierce fighting after the aborted elections. During the demobilization component of the most recent United Nations peacekeeping operation (UNAVEM III), however, only 34,425 weapons were collected, many of which were old and unserviceable.[2] This, combined with the small number of police and soldiers who were demobilized, suggests that most weapons and soldiers were kept out of the now broken peace process. Furthermore, besides the arms stockpiled during the 1970s and 1980s, Angola continued to receive weapons on a regular basis after 1992. Though UN sanctions to cut off UNITA's supplies were introduced in October 1997, Savimbi, the rebel group's leader, has been able to find alternative routes of supply.[3] Without doubt, the continued availability of small arms in the Angolan conflict has contributed significantly to a renewal of civil war in that country. The same is true of the resumption of war in 1992.

The phenomenon of a transitional process without accompanying disarmament operations in Southern Africa is also pertinent in the cases of Zimbabwe, Namibia, and South Africa, although the latter has now adopted a policy that encourages the destruction of surplus stocks of light weapons and small arms rather than their sale.[4] Thus, and despite some progress on control and reduction of existing stocks in Southern Africa, the situation is such that all countries in the region are threatened by the excessive accumulation of small arms and the increasing availability of illicit stocks circulating in the region.

The movement of small arms in the region can be viewed from two different perspectives: intrastate and interstate movements. The intrastate movement of small arms is characterized by the way weapons change hands both from legal to illegal possession and among illegal possessors. The interstate movement looks at cross-border movement of arms taking place legally and/or illegally.

Internally, the circulation of weapons is aggravated by increasing crime and the lack of effective policing, which in turn is partly caused by the transition processes; the increasing number of private security companies using weapons; and demobilization and disarmament in situations where mechanisms for the reintegration of demobilized soldiers and the control and regulation of arms and military skills are inadequate.

Externally, apart from exceptional cases such as Zimbabwe, Namibia, and Angola in their supply to the DRC government in response to the emerging requirements of the conflict there, there are no other major legal transfers of weapons between Southern African countries. The cross-border movement of illegal weapons, however, is quite commonplace. This cross-border arms trafficking is broadly facilitated by the existence of increasingly well-organized transnational criminal organizations, the existence of well-established covert arms supply networks across a region of extensive borders, and little potential for effective physical control (this being particularly true of air entry points).[5]

Aside from the problems associated with existing illicit stocks and their circulation to fuel conflict, new weaponry is also flowing into Southern Africa. In the case of the civil war in Angola, there are credible reports that UNITA's war-fighting capacity has been augmented by some high-tech acquisitions reportedly including North Korean versions of the Frog-7 ground-to-ground missile system, Mi-25 attack helicopters, and possibly fixed-wing ground attack aircraft from the Ukraine.[6] Not to be outdone, the Angolan Defence Forces have also been reequipping themselves in similar fashion.

The Potential for Control

Although the availability of weapons might not be the primary cause of conflict, it does exacerbate it, and it also bears much of the responsibility for the upsurge of criminal violence. These considerations in themselves should provide enough justification for a more coordinated and prioritized approach to the curbing of light weapons proliferation worldwide. As Lucy Mathiak explains, "light weapons play critical roles both as commodities and as instruments of the modes of violence that are central to the new era of insecurity in the transnational, global and local contexts. . . . At the same time, states have increasing incentives to resist efforts to bring light weapons under control at either the national or international levels. States that have turned to weapons production as a form of economic development are unlikely to accept restrictions that would harm their markets, for example."[7]

Despite the inherent difficulties of controlling both the supply of and demand for light weapons today, there are ways in which these ends might be made feasible. Robert Naylor, for example, suggests that "the curtailment of production and of dispersion of small arms is justified on the basis that there are three approaches that could be taken: combating the actual trafficking, challenging the supply side, or changing the demand side."[8] Naylor dismisses the first option, because for him traffickers need something to sell and someone to sell it to, implying that the problem is related to the supply and demand side. On the supply side, Naylor distinguishes between primary, secondary, and tertiary suppliers. These correspond to the categories of production of new weapons, distribution of old stocks, and dispersion of arms to the user population.[9]

The solutions, according to Naylor, have to be adapted to the level of supply. He suggests that encouraging conversion policies in primary suppliers, tightening regulations on the transfer of existing stocks, and the voluntary disarming of populations are the only possible ways to proceed on the supply side. It is on the demand side, however, that Naylor sees the greatest difficulties for action. According to him, the solution to demand lies "in the shifting of loyalties back away from the clan, sect and tribe in favour of rebuilding civil society *and* rectifying gross inequalities in the global and local distribution of income, wealth and ecological capital."[10] Although this formula should not be ignored, the obstacles for implementation are formidable.

Be that as it may, and as William Benson indicates, light weapons arrive in regions of conflict by a number of routes: through legitimate state-to-state sales prior to the outbreak of war; through illegal supply by states, often in contravention of an arms embargo; supplied illegally, directly, by individuals operating outside the conflict zone; and supplied indirectly (smuggled) via a complex series of transactions having been "diverted" from the possession of the original recipient. Approaches aimed at stemming the proliferation of light weapons have included strengthening and enforcement of existing national controls, increased coordination and cooperation within regional groupings (through the agreement and implementation of criteria governing arms transfers), and demand-side measures on the ground, such as microdisarmament initiatives.[11] Obviously—and taking into consideration the relative weakness of the industrial base in the South—it is more important to ponder regulations to be applied at national and regional levels from the supplier side in the North than it is to reduce the demand factors from the recipient's side.

From the supplier side, regulations can be put in place nationally through tighter licensing procedures in relationship to arms exports, through the integration of light weapons into national control systems, and by looking at the ultimate destination of weapons to be sold. The most promising regulating mechanisms are a mix of incorporating accepted principles of export controls (such as those of the Wassenaar arrangements) to cover light weapons and small arms exported from a weapons-producing region such as the European Union elsewhere. Other methods include end-user certification and monitoring, with verification of delivery and restrictions on reexport.

These measures coupled with the adoption of specific "Codes of Conduct" would allow for a minimum standard to be met by all member states without fear of undercutting each other's defense industries. In recent years, much work has been undertaken, particularly for the regulation of weapons exports produced by member states of the European Union. A compilation of best practices produced by the United Kingdom's Saferworld indicates that a number of policies could be undertaken, such as:

- Increased coordination between the ministries involved
- Categorizing weapons to be subject to more rigorous restrictions
- Agreement on the application of common criteria specifically aimed at controlling exports of light weapons
- A method whereby the licensed delivery of arms is verified as having taken place in accordance with the specifications on the end-use certificate, and a requirement that the recipient must consult with the authorities before reexporting the goods
- Legislation to be extended to cover the activities of nationals involved in brokering arms transfers between third parties
- An annual report to be presented to parliaments on arms exports entering the public domain, setting out details of exports by type, destination, quantities, and values.[12]

All these initiatives might be useful in improving accountability, transparency, and perhaps in reducing the flows of legal transfers, but they do little to stem the flow of illicit weapons. The latter are more commonly controlled through broad-ranging trade and/or customs agreements or through informal cooperation agreements between governments—the European Union's program for preventing and combating illicit trafficking in conventional arms (COARM) and its subsequent initiative to combat illicit small arms trafficking being a region-to-region attempt at assisting Southern African states to regulate and reduce their illicit arms trade. By the same token, the international effort at obtaining a United Nations convention to control and ultimately reduce the operations of transnational criminal organizations is also looking at a protocol to control illicit firearms flows.

The problem with regulations attempting to control and induce greater accountability and transparency with the legal arms trade is that these do not carry with them a certainty that the weapons—however legally sold and transferred—might end up ultimately in the hands of the recipients for which the deal was initially brokered or enter a region in the same conditions that existed at the time of the approval of the transfer. Moreover, and according to Naylor, it is not a question of reforming rules (gaps in legislation exist for a reason) but of generating the will in states to enforce existing regulations.[13] There seems to be no real volition in the international community to police effectively what legislative and administrative measures have already been adopted.

Nor is it yet clear that many manufacturers of weaponry in Europe or elsewhere are interested in sustaining a corporate code of conduct over and above the minimum requirements imposed upon them by national regulations. Unlike the nuclear technology debate with specific reference to the production and export of dual-use technologies, which generated a spate of corporate codes of conduct (particularly in Western Europe), the production of conventional and light weapons does not seem to attract the same type of restraint. One issue that might account for this is that at the end of the Cold War, the world was left with extensive stockpiles of unused weapons and financially strapped countries, such as those comprising the old Soviet sphere of influence, that no longer placed great emphasis on the conversion of their military industries. They were reluctant to hamper an industry that provided revenue and employment for many at a time when the recognizable enemy had quit the scene. If anything, there was now an incentive to export weapons more widely because they were available and because they were no longer needed in vast quantities for home defense. In this light, it is not surprising that even a European Union code of conduct on arms exports remains insufficient when placed against the balance of the unregulated exports of conventional material coming from elsewhere in Europe and Asia.

The Disintegration of the Postcolonial State: Angola as a "Shadow State"

Some experts argue that what we are seeing is the disintegration of the postcolonial state project in Africa. Obviously this phenomenon, if accurately identified, would have major implications for the relationship of international institutions such as the World Bank and even the United Nations, to the states of the continent. By the same token, it has introduced a different dimension to the dealings of the international business sector in Africa.[14] Peter Lock has suggested that rather than seeing the boundaries of postcolonial states as the framework of understanding the continent we should instead see how Africa is essentially divided in the considerations of external players into *Afrique utile*—usable or useful Africa, linked in various ways to the global economy, and *Afrique inutile*—useless, unprofitable, or disposable Africa. In this view, those parts of the continent that are regarded as useful or as containing exploitable resources are provided a modicum of protection and are linked to the global economy. Those that are devoid of such attractions are consigned to the margins and left to their own devices, so that, in effect, we have a new "apartheid" of administration and security.[15] In effect, Africa is again divided, between those that are under protection and those without. The implications for the political and economic future of Africa are profound. For most of Africa's peoples, the state has long since ceased to be the provider of security, physical or social.[16]

Other considerations about the nature of state security in Africa also have to be borne in mind. Christopher Clapham's work on the African state has identified the difficulties of applying Western assumptions about the nature of state security in much of Africa. He points out that in many cases concerns for state survival are subordinate to those connected with the personal security and well-being of the incumbent leadership. The apparatus of juridical statehood is then appropriated to serve the requirements of this fixation.[17] A method employed by rulers in circumstances in which little more remains of the state than the abstract and juridical is to create a parallel political authority, where personal ties and controls replace failing institutions.[18] William Reno has termed this "the shadow state" in his path-finding work on Sierra Leone, which examines the role of informal markets in the construction of alternative extrastate power networks, underpinning political and economic privilege.[19] So potent and pervasive are these networks that by manipulating the vestiges of state power, they are able to frustrate and bend to their own purposes interventions by the international financial and donor community designed to undermine the informal sector and strengthen the structures of the state.

Perhaps nowhere is the "shadow state" more obvious than in Angola. In the 1960s, this former Portuguese colony in Southern Africa became a major battleground between the superpowers that financed rival factions, each of which was seeking to oust their Portuguese masters. The war between the Cuban/Soviet-backed MPLA and the U.S./South Africa–backed UNITA and Front for the National Liberation of Angola (FNLA) was fueled by covert financial assistance and continued long after independence in 1975. The past twenty-five years have seen intermittent civil war, which has left over 100,000 people dead, and a legacy of economic and social ruin. And yet Angola is one of the major oil-producing countries of Africa and boasts vast diamond-mining areas. It also produces gold and—were it not for environmental degradation and a legacy of millions of land mines strewn in its land—has one of the best agricultural profiles in Africa. The revenues that the Angolan government enjoys from both the oil and diamond industries and the vast sums of money that UNITA commands in the trade of diamonds out of the areas under its control should have been enough to at least partially address the needs of the Angolan people; yet these revenues are consistently utilized in pursuit of two objectives: the personal well-being of a small elite of people belonging to both warring parties, and to continue to feed the arms race in the country.

It has been said of Angola that the discovery of diamonds should be seen as a benefit that will bring wealth and prestige.

However, in the case of Angola, diamonds are a curse that fuels greed and threatens the very existence of the country. Since 1992 UNITA has consistently controlled 70 percent of Angola's diamond production, generating U.S.$3.7 billion in revenue, enabling it to maintain its war effort. Its outputs have been channeled through various means, and more recently—as sanctions have been applied—to South Africa, Belgium, and Israel.[20] Because Angolan rough diamonds are easily recognized, and after the UN Security Council Embargo (Resolutions 1173 and 1176, which prohibit the direct or indirect export of unofficial Angolan diamonds) was passed in 1998, UNITA is not selling the diamonds in their natural state but ensuring a first polish probably undertaken in Israel and/or Ukraine. In any case, and aside from the diamond trade itself, UNITA has also built up substantial investment portfolios abroad to supplement these revenues. By the same token, the ongoing conflict has also benefited the pockets of a select military and political elite in the government. Although some of the MPLA's business elite wish to see an end to the war and economic turmoil, others have profited greatly from Luanda's war economy, especially in the allocation of scarce foreign exchange and import licenses. There have even been allegations that senior figures in the government's security forces and administration have been involved in selling war supplies to UNITA.

According to the nongovernmental organization Global Witness, the opaque three-way circuit followed by oil revenues and oil-backed loans from foreign banks between the oil company Sonangol, the presidential palace, and the central bank has been of even greater importance.[21] In times of major conflict with UNITA, this circuit has funded arms purchases of up to $1 billion per year, and it remains vital to the MPLA's war economy. It is also the main reason why formal arrangements with the IMF have not been established, despite the need for economic reconstruction and the rescheduling of Angola's U.S.$12 billion–plus external debt. Discussions with the IMF have resulted in agreement on an IMF staff-monitored program, with a view to agreeing upon a three-year Enhanced Structural Adjustment Facility in 1999. Although President dos Santos and other MPLA figureheads had accepted the need for such a relationship, renewed hostilities with UNITA—and the need to mobilize oil revenues for fresh weapons purchases—

have strengthened the hand of those in the leadership who oppose the radical overhaul of public finances and the unwelcome international scrutiny of the oil accounts this would entail.

The real problem behind the oil and diamonds resources in Angola at this time is the seemingly endless capacity both the government and UNITA have in extracting maximum personal bribes from the foreign investors and middlemen operating in this business while mortgaging many decades of Angola's future development. Surely this can only be explained if we come to the realization that Angola is in the hands of a group of people who care nothing about the country they control.

Today, a highly centralized government structure has been accentuated by the centralizing tendencies of the MPLA during its Marxist period. The president remains the most powerful figure in government, and it is he who generally chairs the council of state—not the prime minister, whom he may appoint or dismiss as he pleases. Provincial and local structures were embryonic even before independence and have been largely dislocated by decades of war. Large swaths of the country are under UNITA control or under no effective administration from the central government. The high-level, pervasive, and large-scale corruption surrounding those in power has not only alienated the government from popular support but has also engendered a different type of corruption among middle officials and skilled personnel. Most officials must indulge in "irregular" activities to augment salaries that no longer provide a living. Corruption is therefore pervasive in a bureaucratic system of almost Byzantine complexity that naturally lends itself to "rent-seeking" activities. Ironically, the replacement of an austere Marxism with aggressive free-marketeering in an economy of scarcity has probably contributed to a general acceptance of corruption and theft as normal practice.

In conclusion and as summarized by a recent U.S. State Department report discussing Angola, "the country's wealth continued to be concentrated in the hands of a small elite who used government positions for massive personal enrichment."[22] It is interesting to note that earlier in the same week that this report was issued, World Bank president James Wolfensohn spoke to a group of African cabinet ministers—no Angolan among them—who had come to Washington for Vice President Al Gore's Global Forum on Fighting Corruption. Wolfensohn said, "I do not start with finance. I do not start with water. I do not start with education. . . . If you cannot have in a country a sense of proper governance that is unambiguous in its opposition to corruption, then general statements or even specific statements that we make will fall to the ground."[23]

There is no point, in other words, in even talking about development strategies for countries whose governments are heavily involved in the theft of public monies. The collapse of the 1994 Lusaka Peace Accords and the return of the MPLA and UNITA to war are generally ascribed to UNITA's failure to comply with its treaty obligations to demobilize, surrender its weapons, and hand over areas under its control to state administration. That may well be the proximate cause. But what should be obvious by now is that neither side gives any consideration to the reconstruction of their country, or even to winning the affection or support of their countrymen. As UN Secretary General Kofi Annan observed, there has been no evidence of a genuine effort to build political support by improving the basic living conditions of the population.[24]

Despite all of this, foreign investors continue to flock to Angola in increasing numbers, particularly to the lucrative oil and diamond sectors. It can then be argued that it is this willingness to do business with specific groups in Angola that produces the resources that are ultimately used to keep the war going. It is here that the discussion of regulation and self-regulation of the private sector might in fact be a more interesting proposition than dealing directly with the arms industry that engages in the war in Angola. It is interesting to note that since an embargo was decreed on UNITA diamonds by the United Nations, much more debate on corporate practices in that sector is being conducted in a much more transparent manner than ever before. As Global Witness investigations into the trade in rough diamonds from Angola show, the lack of transparency and corporate responsibility in the diamond industry has been central to the continuing financing of UNITA and hence the fueling of civil war in Angola. If transparent and responsible business practices had been in place, as claimed in corporate statements, this situation would not have arisen. Bilateral and multilateral institutions such as the IMF, World Bank, the Organization for Economic Cooperation and Development (OECD), and the World

Trade Organization (WTO) now consider transparency and corporate responsibility to be essential to all areas of business.[25] However, the International Chamber of Commerce, WTO, and OECD all refuse to accept a need for legally binding codes of conduct for multinationals. This must change. The issue of natural resources and their use to fund conflicts is of major importance on the African continent, and its importance is set to grow. The process of pushing companies toward corporate accountability over their operations is already well developed in other extractive industries, for example Shell and RTZ. Diamond companies need to develop new ways of operating that will ensure that combatants in conflict zones such as Angola are not able to derive revenue from diamond sales.[26]

There are and should be vital changes in how corporations carry out their business. In the case of Angola this does not only apply to the UNITA diamond trade (i.e., the international trade, the operation of the market, and the middlemen in that process) but to the ethics of oil companies that consistently agree to pay signature bonus for the rights on oil exploration blocks (some amounting to $900 million), which effectively is nothing more than sophisticated "bribe" money to line the pockets of corrupt elites running a desperately poor country.

Conclusion

Africa has managed to resist conditionality, and democratization will not be the best lens through which to observe the continent as shadow networks of power emerge in reaction to the privatization of the state and the economy. Informal and illicit trade, financial fraud, systematic evasion of rules, and international agreements will be some of the means used by certain Africans to survive the tempest of globalization.[27]

What Patrick Chabal and Jean Pascal Daloz have called the political economy of disorder offers opportunities for those who know how to play the system.[28] *Informalization* affects politics as well as economics. In many respects what we are seeing in the conflict zones of Africa is the playing out of rivalries for the control of scarce resources and the manipulation of business links, licit and illicit, to the benefit of the entrepreneurs of violence. On the back of these resource wars vast profits are to be made on the transportation of other things, from guns to food. If this analysis of the African state is applied to the current wars raging in and around Central Africa, then we must adjust our thinking and assume that we are dealing with a set of pseudo-states in which the interest of the community and the rule of law count for nothing. The problem is that the current international diplomatic and security architecture is unable to cope with this type of crisis. It is partly a matter of scale, of course, the equivalent of a body being overwhelmed by massive infection. But it is also more than that. Current diplomatic and security arrangements are state-centered and predicated upon regarding states as the primary actors in international affairs. In Africa this is simply no longer so. Regional alliances are forming between private actors, and some leaders appropriate the framework of the state to their own ends and in their own private interest. In this environment the international community finds itself ill at ease, having to deal with individuals both as the source of power and wealth and as the origin of ambiguous signals in a rapidly changing environment. Hesitating between nonintervention and semi-intervention in the opaque world before them, institutionalized external actors find themselves uncertain of where to exert leverage and unwilling in any event to muster the political will to use force to back up their political pressure. It is in this environment that the issue of regulation and, above all, self-regulation of the private sector becomes key in determining the length, scope, and impact of conflict situations.

In this context the onus must again shift to self-regulation of the private sector. It may be very easy for companies to respond that it is not possible to alter the way in which they do business, but this response, especially when set against the scale of recurring tragedies across the African continent, is no longer acceptable. In the end any company should determine for itself if it can do business in Angola and remain in accordance with its own policies and ethical code of conduct. This is desperately needed.

Notes

1. Martinho Chachiua, "Operation Rachel: A Joint Effort to Retrieve Arms Surplus Between Mozambique and South Africa," Institute for Security Studies (ISS) Monograph, 38 (Halfway House: ISS, 1999).

2. See Jakkie Potgieter, "The Price of War and Peace: A Critical Assessment of the Disarmament Component of United Nations Operations in Southern Africa," in Virginia Gamba (ed.), *Society Under Siege: Crime, Violence and Illegal Weapons*, ISS book series (Halfway House: ISS, 1997).

3. Richard Cornwell and Jakkie Potgieter, "Private Militias and Arms Proliferation in Southern Africa," paper presented at International Conference on Southern African Security, Centro de Estudos Estrategicos e Internacionais (Maputo, November 19–20, 1998), 7.

4. As per the media statement by the chief of the defense corporate communication, Major General Chris Pepani, on destruction of small arms (Pretoria, February 26, 1999), the government has agreed to destroy 262,667 small-caliber weapons during 1999.

5. See Gamba, *Society Under Siege.*

6. As per indicators of the Early Warning Programme at ISS, March 1999.

7. Lucy Mathiak, "The Light Weapons Trade at the End of the Century," in Gamba, *Society Under Siege,* 95.

8. Robert Naylor, "The Rise of the Modern Arms Black Market and the Fall of Supply-Side Control," in Gamba, *Society Under Siege,* 67–69.

9. Ibid.

10. Ibid.

11. William Benson, "Regulatory Mechanisms Aimed at Stemming the Proliferation of Light Weapons," paper presented at a conference on light weapons in the Great Lakes region hosted by International Alert and CCR (Cape Town, July 21, 1997), 2.

12. Ibid., 16.

13. Ibid.

14. Richard Cornwell, "The End of the Post-Colonial State System in Africa?" *ISS Occasional Paper* (February 1999).

15. For a discussion of these developments see Peter Lock, "Africa, Military Downsizing and the Growth in the Private Security," in Jakkie Cilliers and Peggy Mason (eds.), *Peace, Profit or Plunder? The Privatization of Security in War-Torn African Societies* (Johannesburg: Institute for Security Studies, 1999), 29–31.

16. Ibid., 29–31.

17. Christopher Clapham, *Africa and the International System: The Politics of State Survival* (Cambridge: Cambridge University Press, 1996).

18. Cornwell, "The End of the Post-Colonial State System in Africa?"

19. William Reno, *Corruption and State Politics in Sierra Leone* (Cambridge: Cambridge University Press, 1995).

20. Global Witness, *A Rough Trade: The Role of Companies and Governments in the Angolan Conflict.* http://www.oneworld.org/globalwitness/reports/Angola/diy.html.

21. Ibid.

22. U.S. Department of State, *Angola Country Report on Human Rights Practices for 1998.* Released by the Bureau of Democracy, Human Rights and Labor on February 26, 1999. Available at http://www.state.gov./www/global/human-rights/1998-hrp-report/angola.html.

23. Simon Barber, "Leaders of Angola Are Not Interested in Peace, Only Profit," *Business Day,* March 3, 1999.

24. See UN Secretary General's report to the Security Council, January 17, 1999.

25. Global Witness, *A Rough Trade: The Role of Companies and Governments in the Angolan Conflict.* Available at http://www.oneworld.org/globalwitness/reports/Angola/diy.html.

26. Ibid.

27. Cornwell, "The End of the Post-Colonial State System in Africa?"

28. Patrick Chabal and Jean Pascal Daloz, *Africa Works: Disorder as Political Instrument* (Oxford: James Currey, 1999).

9

Targeted Financial Sanctions

Samuel D. Porteous

Over the past decade support for comprehensive economic sanctions has waned as the weaknesses of these systems, including their undesirable impact on civilian populations and their nonefficacious nature, became ever more evident. The failure of these comprehensive regimes has led to a fruitful rethinking of how best to use economic levers to alter the behavior of rogue regimes or leaderships engaged in unacceptable activity. Targeted financial sanctions that strike directly and decisively at the personal financial and commercial interests of the leadership responsible for the unacceptable behavior at issue are beginning to be recognized as the international community's last best alternative to costly and destructive military interventions.[1] This chapter will explore the goals of financial sanctions, how they might best be employed, the challenges and opportunities that could accompany their implementation, and the types of instruments and actors who could be involved in creating viable targeted financial sanctions policy, including a key role for the private sector.

Background

While the implementation of sanctions has multiplied during the 1990s, so have questions surrounding their efficacy and humanity.[2] Economic sanctions, such as trade embargoes or the withholding of development assistance, in particular have come under fire for the devastating impact they often produce on the general population of the target country.[3] This impact is regrettable since these populations, particularly in nondemocratic countries, often have little opportunity to influence the policy direction of their respective governments.[4] Acknowledging these failings, some supporters of sanctions, unwilling to forgo the use of what many consider both an alternative to indifference and, in some cases, the final option prior to military action, have suggested less blunt and more targeted forms of sanctions.[5] These "financial sanctions" would be directed at the offending country's leadership and its associates rather than the general population.

To date, most of the preparatory work in the field has been done at the Expert Seminars on Targeting UN Financial Sanctions in Interlaken in 1998 and 1999 (which has come to be called the "Interlaken Process"[6]), and the supplementary working seminars held in London in September 1998 and New York in December 1998. The Interlaken seminars were hosted by the Swiss government and brought together a variety of actors from different sectors to study the potential use of targeted sanctions. However, more work must be done to examine how these sanctions could be designed, implemented, and monitored.[7]

What Are Financial Sanctions?

The introductory paper for the Interlaken conference described targeted financial sanctions as "measures such as the freeze of foreign assets of specifically designated individuals, companies or governments that particularly contribute to the threat of peace and security."[8] It was intended that only an elite group determined by an official list would fall within the scope of this measure. The example provided at the conference was the 1994 edict issued by the UN Security Council to freeze funds and assets of Haitian elites.

Most financial sanctions pertain to asset freezing or asset blocking. The terms are interchangeable. If a property, be it a boat or a bank account, is blocked or frozen, title to this property remains with the designated country, individual, or entity. However, the exercise of powers and privileges normally associated with ownership is prohibited without authorization by the appropriate authority. "Refusal to deal" can be considered another form of financial sanctions and is a catchall phrase designed to prohibit any financial or commercial dealings of any kind with designated individuals or entities. What is important to consider with targeted sanctions of a refusal-to-deal nature is that they clearly broaden the impact of financial sanctions on individuals or entities from going after existing accumulated assets to disrupting the target's ongoing or future commercial and financial interests.

How Will the Leadership Group to Be Targeted Be Defined?

The targeting of individuals and companies or organizations is relatively rare, but it is not unknown.[9] The United States, not surprisingly, is the leader in imposing financial sanctions against individuals and organizations, with numerous executive orders freezing the assets and blocking financial dealings with a range of individuals and organizations. U.S. targets include "specially designated narcotics traffickers" (SDNTs). This list of affected individuals and organizations includes both "principals" in the drug trade and those who are determined to materially assist these individuals in some fashion. The list of designated SDNTs provided by the Office of Foreign Assets Control (OFAC) extends to fourteen pages in double columns of small type. Penalties for breaching the order range from ten years in prison to U.S.$500,000 in fines.[10] The United States has also set special provisions in place for targeting certain individuals and entities engaged in or supporting terrorism. As of OFAC's last count, its master list of "specially designated nationals and blocked persons" contained over 5,000 names of individuals, government entities, and companies located around the world.[11] If this sort of attention can be directed toward individual drug traffickers, terrorists, and their supporters, it seems appropriate that potentially more destructive and dangerous political leaders and those that materially assist their activities be treated in the same fashion.

It is important to ensure that the group targeted for financial sanctions is broad enough to encompass those who may not be directly part of the relevant leadership but whose support is essential to maintaining their hold on power. Therefore, both obvious decisionmakers and their sometimes less obvious enablers are targeted. Clearly, in some instances a comprehensive list of associates or enablers is not available. In these instances, efforts will be required to obtain the best intelligence available on these issues. Furthermore, a demonstrated ability to rapidly append to the target list individuals and entities determined to materially support the target group could dissuade those who have not yet been discovered to end their support and discourage any entity contemplating engaging in such support.

What Are the Goals of Financial Sanctions?

The primary goal of financial sanctions would be a change in the policy of the targeted leadership, be it ethnic cleansing or the prosecution of an aggressive war—civil or otherwise. This approach recognizes the importance of economic agendas in shaping the nature and direction of civil strife and assumes the targeted leadership will be influenced by financial pressure.[12] In some instances, with a true ideologue or ideologues, targeting the direct leadership will not be sufficient—their loyalty to the cause may override any concern with their financial interests. In these situations it becomes doubly important to ensure that the sanctions are broad enough to encompass those whose support is necessary to the leadership but who may not share its fervor for the cause. Once this group calculates the costs of supporting the regime to be greater than the benefits, support can begin to unravel quickly. For example, reports in May 1999 indicated that a member of Slobodan Milosevic's inner circle, Dragomir Karic, "a business tycoon, has been secretly negotiating with Russians and Americans in Vienna to allow foreign ground troops to enter Kosovo."[13] Karic, along with his brothers, runs the largest private-sector business empire in Yugoslavia.

Secondary goals would include penalizing the leadership and its associates for their behavior and revealing ill-gotten gains to the general population. This approach may undermine their support in a way that collective punishment for an entire population through trade sanctions never could.[14]

Finally, financial sanctions can be employed as a deterrent or warning to other leaders who may wish to contravene international norms of civil conduct.

How Can Financial Sanctions Be Enforced?

Financial sanctions are not easy to enforce. The international financial structure as it exists today is designed to operate outside state control, and it has to a certain extent achieved this "sublime" nature. It is a system designed to continually outrun state rules and norms. This otherworldly nature of the international financial structure is the reason why cash is targeted in most money laundering investigations. Once the electronic sphere is entered and physical assets are converted to numbers flashing across screens, the international financial structure typically ensures a safe haven from all but the most dogged pursuer.

There are, however, structures and systems that can be put in place to facilitate the implementation and enforcement of financial sanctions. The most sophisticated system administering financial sanctions is employed by OFAC. OFAC sets out a system of penalties for failure to abide by sanctions and allows responsible financial institutions and individuals to determine how best to comply. OFAC does little in terms of enforcement or compliance monitoring but attempts to ensure that all financial institutions and other groups affected by U.S. sanctions are aware of the individuals and companies on U.S. sanction lists. OFAC advocates that affected commercial entities employ what is known as *interdict software* to assist them in complying with U.S. law.

Interdict software, such as OFAC Tracker, acts as a filter through which all new financial transactions are screened. These systems are capable of checking over 4,100 names per second, or close to 15 million names an hour. Each match that is made results in an interruption of the transaction should a suspected individual or commercial entity be detected.

The Australian government had some success when it adapted a somewhat different computer program that had its origins in U.S. president Ronald Reagan's failed "Star Wars" defense initiative. The software had been designed to determine which of a thousand incoming missiles was the most dangerous. This software was adapted by the Australians to examine instead the thousands of international financial transactions occurring almost simultaneously to determine which were suspicious.[15] The system, known as ScreenIt, is now employed by AUSTRAC, Australia's money laundering authority.

These systems, as sophisticated as they may be, are only as good as the information that is fed into them. Although they can be refined to accommodate multiple spellings and minor spelling errors or changes in form, they become less useful when faced with common surnames such as Lee, Smith, or Abdhulla. They are also incapable of detecting deceit.

When target individuals and entities begin to use the same techniques employed by criminal money launderers and tax evaders, the financial sanctions challenge becomes even greater. Few targeted despots are likely to stumble late upon the fact the rest of the world disapproves of their acts and wishes them ill. Most would have started hiding their assets early in their careers. However, it would be incorrect to suggest that this challenge would be comparable to combating money laundering in general. The major hurdle facing those who combat money laundering is the staggering volume of potential offenders and the extraordinary resources required to deal effectively with the phenomenon in its entirety.

This is not true for the implementation of financial sanctions. Whereas there appears to be an unlimited supply of felons engaged in money laundering, only rarely will there be a multilateral condemnation of a country's leadership of a type that would lead to the implementation of financial sanctions. This would enable significant resources to be directed by the international community toward both the monitoring and the enforcement of these sanctions.

For analogies, one could look at the UN operation conducted against Iraq and UN Security Council Resolution 687 (1991) to ensure no weapons of mass destruction were developed. This was a massive effort that enjoyed support from intelligence services around the world. The information these services provided through signals, intelligence capacities, and other methods and sources provided useful and timely information to the relevant UN monitoring agency, UNSCOM. Such resources directed toward a different type of task—discovering hidden assets and financial covers—would be necessary to any new system set up to ensure that financial sanctions worked.

Drawing from the UNSCOM experience, both good and bad, a critical path and structure in enforcement and intelligence for financial sanctions could be developed in order to collect and analyze information provided by intelligence and enforcement sources around the world.[16] This would allow for a quick start to the work of establishing link charts and other necessary information when the mandate is set. This group could also act as a liaison with private-sector financial institutions and other commercial entities. In many ways, its work would be analogous to some done by the Financial Crimes Enforcement Network (FINCEN) of the United States. FINCEN provides analytical services to U.S. enforcement authorities by searching databases and other sources for evidence of relationships between targets and other persons or entities who may be involved in the money laundering process. In addition, they provide link analysis to identify relevant connections and interpret the results of their findings.

Monitoring and tracking financial transactions is not something that would be new to intelligence services brought in to support a financial sanctions regime.[17] The Promis software case allegedly portrayed a situation where "bugged" software was deliberately sold by Western intelligence services to international financial institutions and private banks in order to utilize a "trapdoor" secretly installed in the communication software. The door allegedly enabled intelligence agencies to surreptitiously monitor the communications between international financial institutions and potentially defaulting Mexican banks.[18] In a more recent incident, the British signals intelligence agency allegedly intercepted a 1997 wire transfer of U.S.$800,000 from Tariq Aziz, Iraq's deputy prime minister, to an account that was linked to Yevegny Primakov, the Russian prime minister.[19] As a *Pravda* correspondent in the Middle East, Primakov reportedly became friendly with Saddam Hussein and has since been suspected of working to assist Iraq's weapons program. The Russians have vehemently denied these accusations. Intelligence sources said they "vacuum" up information like this all the time. The implementation of targeted financial sanctions could certainly benefit from such activity.

Although signals intelligence would be important in these areas, old-fashioned human intelligence (or humint) often turns out to be the source of the information that ultimately leads to the assets or disguised financial flows. Most persons in positions of power involved in civil strife are justifiably somewhat wary about the people they have around them. Kroll Associates' experience in asset search indicates that leaders in these positions tend to feel the need to maintain some direct contact with their money and assets, no matter how desperately they wish to hide them. It is this need to maintain some control, often through a relative or close associate, that leads to the identification of the assets. In one Canadian example, assets of the leadership of an African country became revealed only after it was discovered through a source hostile to the regime that one of the wives of a member of the leadership group was in Canada engaging in financial transactions. Canadian financial authorities were informed of her identity and followed up on the disclosure.[20]

A Role for the Private Sector?

The creation of an elaborate government-run investigative and intelligence capacity to support targeted financial sanctions akin to FINCEN but on a global scale may, however, not be required for the successful administration of targeted financial sanctions. Private-sector forensic accounting companies and intelligence and investigative firms have already been employed in some instances by governments pursuing a leadership's hidden assets. After financial sanctions have been agreed upon, concerned countries could hire a private-sector group to locate the assets and then pass on the information to legal authorities, who would freeze or seize the assets. (See Appendix.)

Depending upon the scope of the investigation, the cost would be, at most, in the millions of dollars. The chances of success, defined as locating hidden assets or at minimum ensuring the leadership and its associates have little opportunity to enjoy them, would be rather good. Kroll Associates, which has been retained to search for the assets, inter alia, of Ferdinand Marcos, Baby Doc Duvalier, and Saddam Hussein, experienced considerable success in these cases. Working for the Kuwait Investment Office in London, Kroll located assets connected to Saddam Hussein worth tens of millions of dollars. They were found attached to a front corporation named Montana Investments, located in Switzerland. This discovery resulted from thorough investigation of public record materials and was assisted by the creation of large text databases capable of sorting names, bank accounts, and other data points according to exact instructions. One of the case-breaking clues was the discovery of a company with a director who was a known associate of Saddam Hussein. The goal of the Kuwaitis was twofold: first, to identify assets that could be seized for reparations; and second, to ensure Saddam Hussein had as few financial resources as possible to pursue his weapons program.

One of the drawbacks to private-sector involvement in searching out assets and links is the challenge of integrating valuable government intelligence resources, such as signals intelligence, into the process. This might best be resolved through a hybrid approach that allocates specific roles to public- and private-sector actors in the realm of financial sanctions.

At minimum, market mechanisms and the pursuit of personal gain that create many of the opportunities to evade these sanctions could also be harnessed to reinforce them through rewards for information and bounties. Offering bounties and rewards for information on front-company pseudonyms, numbered accounts, and hidden assets of the targeted leadership group could pay real dividends and create an atmosphere of suspicion that would bring added pressure to bear on that leadership.

Enforcement: The Need to Go Beyond Monitoring

Simple discovery of the assets or clandestine financial activity will not be enough. The UN, working with the European Union, the United States, and Canada, set up an elaborate monitoring system in the early 1990s to monitor the implementation of the increasingly severe economic sanctions imposed on the Federal Republic of Yugoslavia. Though the sanctions assistance missions (SAMs) were established at an unprecedented scale and coordinated through a communication center in Brussels, they lacked an enforcement capacity, and widespread sanctions-busting continued. This provided a steady stream of goods and supplies to the leadership in Serbia while the general population suffered considerably.[21]

If financial sanctions are mandated, they must be accompanied by the resolve necessary to ensure enforcement once clandestine financial activity or hidden assets are discovered. Clandestine financial activity must be disrupted and any hidden assets frozen. Absent a multilateral capacity and the political will to do this, the impact of financial sanctions will be greatly diminished. It is particularly important to ensure that there are no "haven" jurisdictions for those targeted by financial sanctions.

Countries otherwise uncooperative with anti–money laundering and clandestine finance programs could be convinced to
cooperate with an international effort on this level. Requests
for cooperation on targeted financial sanctions issues would be
relatively infrequent compared to what would likely accompany
any significant cooperation agreement on more general money
laundering issues. Thus, haven jurisdictions could slightly improve their tarnished international reputations without too
greatly disturbing their clientele.

Searching for Hidden Assets: The Challenges

Major Financial Institutions

After Bretton Woods, the world's major financial institutions
largely inherited the power from government to define what
money is and also took on partial responsibility of maintaining
the credibility of the international financial system. Fortu-
nately, this includes exercising a modicum of moral responsibility. Any cooperation to be expected by this group on targeted financial sanctions and the clandestine finance issues it
raises will stem from this responsibility. There is a limit, however, to the amount of cooperation on money laundering and
clandestine financial issues that can be expected from the
major financial institutions. Up to 95 percent of financial transactions are estimated to be clean. No matter how many billions
a few despots are able to stash away in the international financial system, even the largest of such fortunes will pale in significance when compared with total financial flows, which easily
account for more than $2 trillion a day. Although billions may
be hidden by targeted leaders, trillions are not, and the trillions will logically dictate what happens to the billions.

Major financial institutions may well adopt the Financial Action Task Force, or FATF's, forty recommendations, but this
says nothing about how hard they will work to truly "know their
customer" or question transactions arriving from countries or
institutions who have not adopted the forty recommendations.[22] The banks have been left to themselves to determine
what effort they put into pursuing money launderers or others
engaged in clandestine financial activity. Beyond the occasional

drug case they have, not surprisingly, shown little interest in driving away potential customers. But even the limited efforts put forth by the world's banks stand out compared to the lack of interest in the issue shown by other private financial actors.

This is significant since we are moving away from banks as a focus for money laundering or clandestine finance. With tightened regulations and increased international cooperation, major Western banks have become part of the problem facing those engaged in clandestine finance. Brokerage houses, insurance companies, and other nonbanking financial institutions are among their new targets. Some of these institutions, notably brokerage houses, have high-risk cultures more akin to those of the criminal milieu than those of staid banking circles. For example, stock brokerages now move as much money as banks, and brokers eager for commissions are being used by individuals wanting to hide their assets.

Non-Western Banking Systems

These are just some of the problems facing investigators fortunate enough to be dealing with Western financial institutions. Once beyond the confines of Western finance structures, significant concern for clandestine financing or money laundering is more difficult to identify. Asian countries are just beginning to address the challenges presented by clandestine finance. At a meeting of twenty-six Asian nations held in 1997, only eight countries had enacted anti–money laundering legislation.[23] As other regions enact tougher measures, an Asian region that does not will become relatively more attractive to those engaged in clandestine finance.

Whereas many non-Western formal finance structures may appear at best indifferent to clandestine finance, the underground banking systems found in many of these societies are actually designed to facilitate it. Well-established underground banking systems, such as the Hundi system in India or the Fei Chen or "flying money" system used in some Chinese circles, have existed for hundreds of years and evolved specifically to evade government control. There is little doubt that some of these ethnic underground banking systems are ideally suited to funneling financial resources to and from countries involved in conflict.

Cyber Banking

Not all the systems facilitating clandestine finance are centuries old. The creation of "cyber banks" that deal primarily in "digital credits" used in "debt" or "smart" cards presents money launderers and those engaged in clandestine finance with a new and attractive technique. Unlimited sums can be placed in digital credits and easily smuggled into any jurisdiction. Once a digital credit is created, it can be used for any transaction. Other than the user's telephone bill, there will be no record of these transactions, which will typically be protected from detection by a key encryption system (e.g., PGP, which is freely available on the Internet). Even the telephone record may not be available if certain "1–900" masking systems are used. Where cyber cash systems operate in conjunction with offshore banks, large sums of money can be transacted without any record and without the participation of major financial institutions that are more susceptible to pressure than their small, narrowly focused offshore counterparts. In this way the entire money laundering tax evasion control/deterrence structure envisaged by the FATF membership is evaded. These concerns have been confirmed by the FATF. According to the Paris-based organization, cyber payment developers are currently experimenting with fewer restrictions; these products have higher or no value limits and "most disturbingly, some will allow value to be accessed and transferred without the need for financial institution intervention."[24]

Conclusion

All these problems may support academic Michael Levi's contention that most money laundering legislation is ultimately best understood in symbolic rather than instrumental terms. However, in the case of the enforcement of financial sanctions, even the problems listed above may not pose too great a challenge. The enforcement of financial sanctions, though paralleling the battle against money laundering, in many ways is best thought of as a unique subset of that challenge, featuring resources and attention far beyond anything that could be imagined for ordinary money laundering cases. With financial sanctions, we can assume some sort of multilateral agreement and cooperation, including shared intelligence and intelligence efforts. These efforts could bring pressure to bear on even the most labyrinthine clandestine financial activities or asset hiding schemes.

Beyond the likely success in locating some assets, the relatively high cost of financial sanctions, in comparison to its alternative, must once again be emphasized. A thorough financial sanctions program requires only a tiny fraction of the financial resources a military deployment would. In sum, financial sanctions can serve a valuable role in punishing or seeking to change the behavior of offending authoritarian leaders. More work, however, needs to be done to establish the appropriate structures and systems necessary to establish an efficient financial sanctions enforcement mechanism acceptable to the international community. In light of this, the absence of evident political will to aggressively pursue this policy is difficult to fathom.

Appendix Timeline: Investigation and Analytical Approaches to Financial Sanctions

1. Receive the initial information indicating that a certain political leadership and associates may be targeted by financial sanctions. Develop a flow chart of all possible relationships including biological and business associates. Look for weaknesses in the interrelationships.

2. Develop informants and witnesses who have details on the leadership's financial operations. Deal with a lower member of the leadership and associates who may decide to assist the investigation. Also contact rivals of the leadership and associates or former spouses, if available, within and outside the country. They may be cooperative and have valuable information. Determine individuals or related entities, which may be holding assets for the leadership or their associates in their names.

3. Compile information on indications of wealth exhibited by the leadership and suspected assets. Perform a "net worth" calculation on significant leadership members and associates.

4. Consider an undercover operation to gather more information. Sometimes it may be useful to disrupt the activities of the leadership and its associates in order to make them more susceptible to an undercover operation.

5. Use signals interception technology ("sigint") to monitor communications of leadership and associates. Engage in traffic

analysis and examine frequently called numbers or foreign numbers.

6. As intelligence and investigation develops, further avenues of investigation may arise. Telephone or communication records may reflect contact with banks or other financial services. Checks on records of real estate transactions or other major purchases associated with the target group may reveal method of payment and source. Keep records of all assets suspected to be controlled ultimately by individuals associated with the leadership. (Bank records are one of the most important sources of leads to assets that can be seized.) Almost all financial transactions leave a record. The key is to be able to trace funds going into a financial institution and their destination when they leave the financial institution. FATF recommendations seek to ensure an environment where anonymous accounts or those obviously opened in fictitious names are not available. But they are, and few banks in "haven" countries make a serious attempt to establish the true identity of account holders and transactors.

7. Determine financial havens where a target may be hiding assets.

8. After the decision is made to apply financial sanctions, known assets of leadership and associates are seized. Names of leaders and associates are entered into interdict database, effectively cutting them off from legitimate commerce and finance.

9. Continued surveillance of leaders and associates may lead to additional banks or financial institutions associated with the leadership. As some financial resources are squeezed, others that have heretofore been dormant may be accessed, presenting opportunities for disclosure.

10. Hidden or nonhidden assets are seized as discovered. Appropriate action is taken.

Notes

1. Targeted financial sanctions are defined here as measures directed against specifically designated individuals, private legal entities, governments, or other organizations that have been deemed to particularly contribute to the threat of peace and security. These measures include edicts forbidding commercial or financial transactions with said individuals or entities and the freezing and seizing of said individuals or entities assets.

2. Former UN Secretary General Boutros Boutros-Ghali questioned "whether suffering inflicted in vulnerable groups in a target country is a

legitimate means of exerting pressure on political leaders." As cited in "Humanitarian Sanctions? The Moral and Political Issues," David Cortright, human rights brief, Center for Human Rights and Humanitarian Law at Washington College of Law, American University, 1.

3. In fact political masters within target countries often are able to profit from the sanctions placed on their countries. See Gary Clyde Hufbauer, Jeffrey Schott, and Kimberly Ann Elliott, "Economic Sanctions Revisited," Washington, D.C. Institute for International Economics, 1990; and Robert Stranks, "Economic Sanctions: Foreign Policy or Folly?" Canadian Department of Foreign Affairs, *Policy Staff Commentary*, no. 4 (May 1994).

4. Gary Clyde Hufbauer argues: "When dealing with authoritarian regimes, the president should direct sanctions at rulers, not the populace at large. Iraqis are not our enemies. Nor are the Cubans. We can single out individuals and agencies that give offense or outrage. We can devise civil and criminal penalties, buttressed by bounties, so that their persons and property are at risk whenever they venture outside their own territory." See Hufbauer, "The Snake Oil of Diplomacy: When Tensions Rise, the U.S. Peddles Sanctions," *Washington Post,* July 12, 1998, p. C01. John Stremlau notes, "There appears to be a growing consensus within the UN that sanctions should be more narrowly focused on specific leaders responsible for the situation that has caused the Security Council to take action. The freezing of assets and other financial sanctions fit this category"; quoted in John Stremlau, *Sharpening International Sanctions: Towards a Stronger Role for the United Nations* (Washington, D.C.: Carnegie Commission on Preventing Deadly Conflict, 1996), 5.

5. Hufbauer, Schott, and Elliott, "Economic Sanctions Revisited," 2.

6. Rolf Jeker, *Chairman's Report,* available Internet, http://www.smartsanctions. ch/int2_papers.htm.

7. See Swiss Federal Office for Economic Affairs, Department of Economy, "Expert Seminar on Targeting UN Financial Sanctions," March 17–19, Interlaken, Switzerland (available Internet, www.smartsanctions.ch/interlaken1.htm). The basic conclusions of the conference were that making financial sanctions effective would require clearer identification of the targets and enhanced ability to identify and control financial flows. Particular concern was expressed over the need to assist member states to improve legally and administratively the domestic implementation of any financial sanctions the UN may choose to mandate.

8. Ibid.

9. The UN has only twice targeted sanctions at an internal faction within a country. Once was in 1993 against the National Union for the Total Independence of Angola (UNITA). The Khmer Rouge in Cambodia was the other target. In March 1996 the United States called on other industrialized countries to join in freezing assets belonging to Nigeria's leaders. See John Stremlau, "Sharpening International Sanctions—Sanctions Innovations of the 1990s," Carnegie Commission on Preventing Deadly Conflict, Carnegie Corporation of New York; available Internet, www.carnegie.org/deadly/ su96–03.html at p. 10/14. In 1997 the United States imposed trade sanctions on five Chinese individuals, two Chinese companies, and one Hong Kong company out of concern for their activities related to arms proliferation in the chemical and biological weapons area. See the press statement by Nicholas Burns, U.S. Department of State Office of the Spokesman, May 22, 1997.

10. OFAC has imposed millions of dollars in fines on financial institutions that failed to block illicit transfers where one party or more was a target country or specially designated individual or entity. See *Foreign Assets Control Regulations for the Financial Community,* U.S. Department of the Treasury, February 23, 1999.

11. Ibid.

12. For more on this perspective, see Mats Berdal and David Keen, "Violence and Economic Agendas in Civil Wars: Some Policy Implications," *Millennium* 26, no. 3 (1997).

13. "Tycoon Brothers Join Cast in Diplomatic Effort," *National Post* (Toronto), May 6, 1999, p. A12. Apart from being a key adviser, Karic also represents a Yugoslav business community that clearly wants an end to the conflict. It is also interesting to note in this context that it was recently reported that "Swiss authorities said this week that they will freeze the assets of 300 people close to Slobodan Milosevic as part of the most intensive effort yet by Western countries to squeeze the Yugoslav leader." This tactic was turned to after Switzerland failed to locate assets that could be connected to Milosevic or four high-ranking allies. See "Swiss Freeze Assets of 300 Milosevic Associates," *New York Times,* July 18, 1999, p. 6.

14. According to some studies financial sanctions are the least costly and have been used alone more often and more effectively than trade sanctions alone. See Hufbauer, Schott, and Elliott, "Economic Sanctions Revisited," 8.

15. See John J. Fialka, "Computers Keep Tabs on Dirty Money," *Asian Wall Street Journal,* May 8, 1995.

16. See appendix for sample approach.

17. Intelligence agencies usually pursue the agendas of their own government, but in most of these cases they would be coincident with the multilateral group enforcing the sanctions.

18. Samuel D. Porteous, "Economic/Commercial Interests and the World's Intelligence Services: A Canadian Perspective," *International Journal of Intelligence and Counter-Intelligence* 8, no. 3 (Fall 1995): 291.

19. Seymour M. Hersh, "Saddam's Best Friend: How the CIA Made It a Lot Easier for the CIA to Rearm." *New Yorker,* April 5, 1999, p. 41.

20. Discussions with Canadian banking officials. Control over the banking system can be quite an asset to those engaging in clandestine finance. In one case, the former vice president of a middle European quasi-central bank, an Ivy league educated economist, ended up in Cyprus ably quarterbacking her country's sanction-busting efforts. There are, however, limits. A leadership's control over its internal banking system merits strict controls on dealings with banks from those countries. Despite control over its country's internal financial structure, it likely recognizes its own potentially transitory nature and will not feel secure leaving assets at home. Usurpation of leadership and ultimate loss of assets are always around the corner.

21. "International Sanctions Innovations of the 1990s": According to the U.S. Department of State, in 1995 there were approximately 240 customs monitors employed in this effort, sixty of which were contributed by the United States.

22. The Financial Action Task Force was established by the G-7 Summit in Paris in 1989 to examine measures to combat money laundering. In 1990 it issued forty recommendations of action against this phenomenon. These were revised in 1996 to take account of new techniques and trends. The FATF membership is comprised of twenty-six governments and two regional organizations.

23. Thailand is a particularly poignant example of a country negatively affected by money laundering. As much as U.S.$30.8 billion, 17 percent of that country's GDP, is attracted annually in illegal money from narcotics, prostitution, gambling, and smuggling. See Ted Bardacke, "Asia Warned of Money Laundering Dangers," *Financial Post,* February 28, 1997.

24. *FATF Annual Report 1995–1996,* Appendix 3, p. 6.

10

Aiding or Abetting?
Humanitarian Aid and
Its Economic Role in Civil War

David Shearer

The image of aid agencies as protectors of the weak and victims of violence has been tarnished by those who accuse them of helping warring parties, feeding fighters rather than beneficiaries—or, more seriously, fueling war economies and prolonging conflict. This chapter will survey these charges against the backdrop of the changing nature of war, the explosive growth in the humanitarian aid industry, and the diminishing political will on the part of states to intervene in domestic conflicts. First, it will outline the ways in which humanitarian aid has been implicated for exacerbating conflict, namely by causing the manipulation of populations and allowing the acquisition of resources by warring sides. Next, and despite these charges, it will document the fact that relief aid appears to have had little impact on the course of civil wars. Finally, it will discuss the changing role of humanitarian agencies in the face of declining political will to intervene and the fact that humanitarian aid has become a favored Western response to conflict or state failure. Unfortunately, aid agencies are only equipped to address the symptoms, and not the causes, of conflict.

* * *

Rakiya Omaar, referring to the emergency in Sudan in 1998, claimed that nongovernmental organizations need famine to "raise money and justify their existence," adding that "they will not ask themselves: are we prolonging the war?"[1] Edward Luttwak in a similar vein blames NGOs in Somalia for fueling the warfare "whose consequences they ostensibly seek to mitigate."[2]

From one point of view, the critics are right. Relief aid cannot be isolated from its environment. But is their mantra just as simplistic as the image that aid agencies have put forward? There is little doubt that aid can contribute to a war economy. But its significance is generally overstated. Much of the evidence that aid has distorted or prolonged wars has tended to rely on anecdotes from specific situations that are "universalized" more widely to other conflicts. The intensity of aid efforts has waxed and waned without any discernible change in levels of violence. And, the economic value from revenues derived from minerals, hardwoods, and drugs dwarf the impact aid can play on a war economy.

Relief aid is a Western response to conflict. Its importance has been cultivated by a coalition of interests within the humanitarian community. Donors have latched on to it as a substitute to political action in the strategic vacuum of the post–Cold War environment. Aid agencies thrust into the limelight have enjoyed the attention and insinuated importance far beyond their ability to really influence. It has also funded the expansion of aid agencies. The critics of aid, rather than analyzing its real impact, have taken this same inflated starting point to launch their attacks on the humanitarian effort. It is important to appreciate the negative effects that aid might have, as is outlined in the first part of this discussion. But it is equally essential to analyze their real significance to a conflict.

Aid's Downside

The intense violence of civil wars has placed civilians at the core of the conflict. At best, the distinction between civilians and combatants is blurred: Fighters mix freely with civilians, confusing the innocent and the military target. At worst, civilians are no longer merely collateral damage but tools to be manipulated for strategic purposes. If civilians are seen as strategic assets by warring factions, then humanitarian assistance that targets these same victims will inevitably be perceived as a political intrusion—not merely as an incidental fallout of violence. Alternatively it can be an economic resource to be tapped to aid a war effort, or a device to further one party's war aims. When this happens, humanitarian aid becomes inseparable from the conflict.

The negative impact of assistance has been described in a number of different ways. Mary Anderson notes that these side effects comprise two basic types: The first results from the transfer of resources, and the second involves "the ethical message conveyed by the provision of assistance."[3] Hugo Slim more broadly claims that relief can facilitate the isolation or displacement of particular populations, fuel the war effort by directly contributing or freeing up local relief resources for the war effort, escalate violence by attracting raiding, undermine coping strategies, and bestow unrepresentative legitimacy on warlords and the like.[4] The discussion below briefly examines two of the more directly observable and commonly cited effects—the manipulation of populations and acquisition of resources by warring sides.

Moving Populations

The movement of populations to suit warring sides has always been a key tactic of warfare. Naturally enough where aid is a feature of the conflict, it is manipulated to assist this process. In Sudan in the late 1980s, David Keen notes, famine relief was concentrated on refugee camps in neighboring Ethiopia and on government garrison towns in the south. This helped Khartoum to depopulate parts of the south, notably the areas where oil reserves were known to be concentrated.[5] In a similar way, international relief in Mozambique contributed to the government's ability to concentrate power. Before 1986–1987, large-scale international assistance was largely absent in both government and RENAMO rebel areas. But after 1987, and particularly after 1990, international aid expanded significantly.[6] Channeled through government outlets, it played a key role in expanding government military control in northern Mozambique by enabling large populations to live in government-held zones, thereby depopulating rebel-held zones. It also helped the government's legitimacy by facilitating its provision of services and helped the failing economy in the region. In short, it allowed an extension of state power at a local level.

Concentrating people into more controllable areas is a classic counterinsurgency technique that has been repeated most recently in Burundi and in the northwest provinces of Rwanda. Aid agencies in these places have supported, though often under protest, these new security structures by providing assistance to the new "villages." Conversely, in other violent situations, relief agencies have contributed to depopulating areas. During the Bosnian conflict, when aid convoys finally broke through to the isolated 9,000-strong enclave of Srebenica in March 1993 and unloaded, they were swamped by people desperate to flee. The aid agency Médecins Sans Frontières commented that by helping to evacuate civilians, aid organizations were confronted with the moral predicament that they could contribute to "ethnic cleansing." Faced with the distress of the population, the United Nations High Commissioner for Refugees (UNHCR) decided to evacuate people and did so under the gaze of the Serbs, "who could not have hoped for more."[7]

Theft and Extortion

Relief aid can be stolen or taxed, thereby contributing to the war effort of the controlling faction. The lure of relief goods can also encourage violence and open possibilities for extortion. During the height of the famine in Somalia in 1992, over 50 percent of all food brought into Mogadishu port was estimated to have been looted, either directly from the port or through the hijacking of aid convoys.

Gaining access to the seaport depended on the agreement of at least four clans whose disputes centered on their share of the economic benefits derived from taxes and fees. A similar standoff between the Hawadle and Habre Gedir clans over control of Mogadishu airport meant that aid agencies were forced to pay high fees for aircraft that landed. In the same way, the Liberian faction leader Charles Taylor frequently charged—or attempted to charge—an aid tax for relief brought into the area under his control. He clearly perceived aid as an additional source of funds for his war effort.

Factions also profited through extortion or the need to rent out security. In Somalia, to prevent the theft of vehicles, aid agencies hired Somali vehicles equipped with their own drivers and security. Employment by an aid agency became extremely lucrative. This only partially solved the problem of security, as frequently the drivers and guards were implicated in theft. For many agencies the resort to armed security clashed with their mandate. The International Committee of the Red Cross (ICRC) was criticized in the British press in January 1992 for its decision to carry weapons in its hired cars. Its response was to move in convoys of two vehicles, one directly attending to relief needs or transporting Red Cross personnel, followed by an unmarked heavily armed security car. The action merely doubled the amount the ICRC paid its Somali security.

Perhaps the most disquieting example of where aid has distorted a war economy in recent years was the relief assistance given to the refugee camps established in Eastern Zaire. Included with the refugees were the former soldiers and *interahamwe* who had been involved in the 1994 Rwandan genocide. Internally, the camps were organized by the same Rwandan administrators who had organized the genocide. These leaders saw the camps as a means to maintain control over the population and prepare for a future invasion of Rwanda. Documents found when the camps were overrun by soldiers from the nascent Alliance of the Democratic Forces for the Liberation of Congo (AFDL) and the Rwandan army confirmed that the camps had also received international shipments of weapons. As a result, the camps created an enormous potential as a source of future conflict.

Humanitarian assistance not only ensured the existence of the Hutu refugee camps in Eastern Zaire but also indirectly assisted the rearming of the former Rwandan army. In the Goma camps, for example, former military commanders of the Rwandese Armed Forces expropriated an estimated food tax of 15 percent from refugees that went to feed the ex-soldiers in the military-run Mugunga camp.[8] Hutu camp officials persistently thwarted any aid agency attempts to conduct a census of the camp populations that might expose what was widely suspected to be an exaggerated number of refugees and lead to reduced rations. The threat of riots stymied a UN-NGO census in September 1996. Any humanitarian imperative, therefore, was manipulated by the genocidal elements that controlled the camps.

An Exaggerated Tale

These examples seem to support the notion that aid has considerably distorted wars. Yet most analysis relies heavily on anecdotal evidence. Mostly it tends to be universalized from specific examples that have been applied more generally. Much of the field research—and evidence—for example, has focused on the Horn of Africa, notably Sudan and Somalia.[9] Yet these instances have tended to be shielded from international markets and places where mineral wealth or other major international inputs have played a smaller role in comparison with other conflicts. In the absence of other economic factors, aid plays a relatively much bigger role.

Rather, as Mark Duffield notes, the weight of experience suggests a different picture: that humanitarian assistance is only one part of a much wider framework of relations and actors. Rather than entrenching conflict, he notes, "it is usually better summed up as too little too late."[10] Moreover, on the other side, there is very little effort made to determine whether the political and military situation would have been significantly different had humanitarian assistance not been provided.

Wars Have Continued With or Without Aid

From a more macro perspective, relief aid appears to have had little impact on the course of civil wars. Most have proved extraordinarily resilient to peace. Sudan's war began in 1956 and with the exception of an eleven-year hiatus from 1972 to 1983 has continued unrelentingly. Prospects for a settlement look no rosier today than a decade ago. Given this wider picture, the assertion that aid is fueling war in Sudan ignores the historical realities.

Likewise, the course of Somalia's war has continued unchanged despite extreme vacillations in the amounts of aid given. There is little observable correlation between amounts of aid and levels of violence. In 1991 a combined force of Hawiye clans toppled Somali president Siad Barre. However, immediately after, intense fighting erupted between Mohammed Farrah Aideed from the Habre Gedir clan and the Abgaal leader, Mahdi Mohammed, over the future rule of Somalia. The fighting claimed the lives of an estimated 15,000 people. International relief during this time was negligible but rose substantially during 1992, when the conflict savaged the food-growing areas of the central Shabelle area and caused widespread famine. The armed intervention of UN Operation in Somalia (UNOSOM) from late 1992 until 1994 accompanied an almost unprecedented relief effort to meet Somalia's humanitarian needs. Violence continued—much of it aimed at international relief efforts—but at a lower intensity than in 1991–1992. In 1999, long after these international efforts had been branded a failure, the conflict has continued unresolved, its underlying causes unsolved. Relief aid at best provided a brief windfall to those with the power to exploit it.

Causal Mechanisms May Not Be as They Seem

On a micro level, quantifying the economic and organizational benefits brought to Somali faction leaders by relief programs is "impossible," Alex De Waal notes.[11] What appeared to be a process by which the powerful enriched their ability to wage war is not quite as it seemed. Individuals profited, but exactly how much of it ended up in the pockets of those political leaders who were directly prosecuting the war is unclear. Most payments to drivers and guards, in the experience of the author, stayed at the level of the direct family. Most weaponry, in contrast, came from either captured stockpiles of weapons and ammunition from Barre's armories or from Ethiopia after the fall of the Menghistu. The Somali diaspora outside the country also contributed to various factions. Humanitarian agencies certainly provided an economic bonus. For a period between 1992 and 1994, aid and the UNOSOM peacekeeping mission were easily the biggest economic forces in Somalia. The economic spoils provided by aid agencies in a devastated country that held few other economic prospects were a huge attraction for the undisciplined troops from all sides and the large number of armed bandits or *mooriyan*. But any economic gain that benefited these fighters was ultimately a distraction in a war that was fueled by more intractable impediments.

Aid as the Junior Partner

It is easy to overplay the magnitude of aid and downplay the importance of other economic incentives. Yet these dwarf the size of the aid basket. The UNITA faction in Angola, for example, is commonly believed to earn around U.S.$500 million from diamonds a year. These resources have directly financed its war effort against the Angolan government. In Colombia, the Revolutionary Armed Forces of Colombia (FARC) that is battling the government monopolizes the drug trade in the areas under its control, earning an estimated annual revenue of around U.S.$450 million. Of this, 65 percent comes from drugs, and the remainder from robbery, kidnapping, and extortion.[12] In Liberia, Charles Taylor's National Patriotic Front of Liberia (NPFL) faction was financed from its ability to export hardwoods outside the region he controlled.

Nicholas Stockton compares the annual value of $120 million in international aid to Afghanistan with the U.K. street value of Afghanistan's annual production of narcotics, estimated to be $15 billion, to contrast this difference.[13] Aid played virtually no part in Sierra Leone's brutal and ugly war. The Revolutionary United Front that has battled the government since the early 1990s has sought to control alluvial diamonds, which is the source of funds to arm and equip its fighters. The amount of food aid delivered to the interior of Sierra Leone has been minimal.

Food aid, in almost all cases, dominates the cost and volume of humanitarian assistance. Unlike diamonds, drugs, or even hardwoods, it is a bulky, low-cost item, difficult to steal and resell. That is not to say that stealing and rerouting food aid do not happen. Aid workers in Sudan are likely to admit that a proportion of the relief food flown or trucked into southern Sudan finds its way to the fighters in the Sudan Peoples Liberation Army. But even where relief food is in short supply, few wars have stopped for lack of food. Soldiers seldom go hungry. And there are few places where the truism "the army eats first" does not hold. The absence of aid, therefore, is not a limiting factor in violence. Its value compared to other "fuels" that propel war economies should not be overestimated.

Aid's Undeserved Position?

If the impact of aid and the attention it has attracted are exaggerated, why has this occurred? The debate on aid has very often been between those who denigrate the effects of aid and those who praise them. However, it is suggested here that both sides have tended to exaggerate the effects of aid—and have an interest in so exaggerating. Aid agencies have, for a number of reasons, overstated their ability to assist in conflict situations, and Western governments have colluded with them. Meanwhile,

the critics of aid have inflated the importance of their own critique by overstating the harm done by aid policies. There are
two key reasons why aid has gained such prominence in the
past decade.

Humanitarian Expansion

The first is a simple numbers game. Humanitarian agencies
have expanded geometrically in both size and number since
the end of the Cold War. In large part the expansion is because
of changes in approaches to sovereignty. In less than a decade,
gaining access to populations affected by war has been articulated as a humanitarian "right" radically transforming the nature of humanitarian assistance. This was not traditionally the
case. With the exception of the International Committee of the
Red Cross, humanitarian agencies during the Cold War worked
almost exclusively through governments, whose ability to refuse
humanitarian access was supported by their right of sovereignty. Interference by outside parties in the affairs of a state
was frowned upon. There were a few notable exceptions. Many
NGOs, for example, backed the Emergency Relief Desk for the
Eritrean Relief Association and the Relief Society of Tigray—
the "humanitarian" wings of the Eritrean and Tigrayan military
factions during the civil war against the Mengistu Haile Mariam
regime in Ethiopia.

Aid agencies today negotiate freely with warring parties. In
part, this change has also occurred because of the collapse of
some states and their government's inability to protect or meet
the needs of its own citizens. Nongovernmental organizations
in Liberia during the early 1990s negotiated directly with
Charles Taylor because his National Patriotic Front of Liberia
faction controlled 90 percent of the country. In Somalia after
1991 following Siad Barre's overthrow, agencies made their
own agreements with warlords and factions in the absence of a
central authority.

The Demise of Western Interests

Second, the growth of humanitarian agencies has also coincided with the decline in political interest by major international players to engage or prop up weak or collapsing states.
Humanitarian action has stepped in as an alternative—partly

replacing weak state activities as an alternative to Western power intervention or traditional societal support. It has been used as a tool or panacea for just about all aspects of political action. As Andrew Natsios, the former director of the U.S. Office of Foreign Disaster Assistance, notes:

> Diplomats now use disaster response as a preventative measure to stave off chaos in an unravelling society, as a confidence-building measure during political negotiations, to protect democratic and economic reforms, to implement peace accords which the U.S. has mediated, to mitigate the effects of economic sanctions on the poor, where sanctions serve geopolitical ends, and to encourage a political settlement as a carrot to contending factions.[14]

In the profusion of civil wars, Western powers have little strategic incentive to intervene and run the risk of casualties. Yet for their own domestic audiences presented with another African famine, for example, they cannot also be seen to be doing nothing. Humanitarian assistance, therefore, has filled a convenient gap. As most media focuses almost exclusively on the plight of victims of war, major donors have substituted humanitarian aid for political action. This has meant that civil wars are managed by dealing with their symptoms, not their causes. Donor funding to the refugee camps in eastern Zaire, for example, put on ice a highly volatile situation destined inevitably for a violent conclusion. Hutu militias, indiscernible from civilians, were fed and housed by donor largesse via humanitarian agencies while they prepared for war. With the problem redefined as humanitarian, the underlying political dilemmas remained untouched. While in Bosnia, Western powers frequently used humanitarian aid as an argument—or an excuse—against the use of air attacks on Serb forces.

Humanitarian aid, therefore, has become a favored Western response to conflict or state failure. Its intrinsic attributes make it highly suitable for the job. The aid message is simple: "give to alleviate the suffering of these people"—an appeal invariably linked to powerful visible images of suffering and dying. Aid agencies appeal for donor funds and to the compassion of domestic television audiences. Journalists seek out Western aid workers to describe the plight of the victims. Given this airtime, the Western public has been persuaded that aid is a significant intervention.

Donor agendas are clearly served by magnifying the importance of humanitarian aid. The more significant humanitarian assistance is portrayed, the more governments can use it as a substitute for more difficult political action. Western aid agencies have been content to accept their newfound importance. It has both increased their visibility—and power to lobby—and maintained their expanding institutions. In this way, the different agendas of the donors and the aid agencies coincide, elevating the influence that aid might have on a conflict beyond its real significance. But overplaying this hand has its downside for the victims of violence. Aid still connects the conflict to the West, possibly representing an international commitment or a link that hints at the promise of a more substantial intervention. Raised expectations may modify the behavior of belligerents. The less tangible effects of aid, therefore, may be more significant than what emerges from the back of the truck.

A Critical Cul-de-Sac

The problem is that the critics of aid—and those who have suggested that aid prolongs wars—have taken this exaggerated view as their point of departure. Few have questioned the analysis; instead, they have merely inverted the conclusions. Rather than aid being an important intervention to assist those in need, it is perceived as a significant intervention that can prolong wars.

Many critics have also taken their attack a further step and lashed out at the weakness of assistance for not doing more to resolve conflict.[15] On this point their thinking is muddled. Its effects might be overstated, but aid can only address the symptoms of a more fundamental problem. Yet they can be excused for misreading the messages arising from the aid industry. There is a trend by agencies to move closer to conflict resolution and social reconstruction as part of a belief that they can exercise greater influence over patterns of violence. The "do no harm" approach, for example, that outlines strategies to minimize the harmful effects of aid hints at the possibility of manipulating aid to produce desirable outcomes.[16] There are three problems with the politicization of aid in this way. First, aid agencies are notoriously clumsy at merely reaching their intended victims. Suggesting that they can in some way influence behavior or reward policies of warring parties implies a level of sophistication they simply lack. Second, this approach fails to appreciate the wider framework of other actors and economic influence in which aid plays a small part. And third, the approach intimates that aid can somehow "solve" a situation. It further absolves from action those most suited to engage politically or militarily with a conflict. The success or failure of an aid intervention, therefore, should be measured not by its ability to shift the policies of warring parties but by its ability to reach those victims.

The additional problem of aid's critics is that they suggest an end point where no aid is preferable to one that might cause some harm. As Mary Anderson notes, this position entails a logical and moral fallacy: "Demonstrating that aid does harm is not the same as demonstrating that no aid would do no harm."[17] Likewise, the conclusion that aid does harm does not justify the additional conclusion that providing no aid would result in good—in other words, that the removal of aid might improve the chances of resolution. The cost of not intervening is rarely calculated. Critics of humanitarian assistance—most commonly academics or journalists on fleeting visits—ignore the obvious: how many lives were saved by relief interventions. This side of the balance sheet is rarely addressed.

Finally, the critics have also attacked the motivations of aid agencies, as if in some way this has some bearing on the harmful effect that aid might have. "Their first priority," Luttwak notes, "is to attract charitable contributions by being seen to be active in high-visibility situations."[18] This echoes Alex De Waal's comments that aid agencies have two motivations: a "soft" one centered on helping the victim, and a "hard" interest to meet the demands of an organization's institutional needs. This, however, is a side issue to whether agencies contribute to prolonging or worsening a conflict. The accusations are undoubtedly true. Indeed, it would be surprising if agencies were not concerned about their survival, expansion, and meeting the needs of employees. In this respect, aid agencies are not dissimilar to other businesses that operate in a competitive environment. But this does not necessarily lead to a conclusion that aid prolongs or fuels conflict. It is merely a recognition of the true rather than romantic image held of aid agencies.

Conclusion

Nevertheless, in the past five years, in response to criticism that their activities promote war, humanitarian organizations have reexamined their operations. Numerous sets of guidelines and protocols have resulted—not unlike a form of industry standards—to which agencies have agreed to adhere. Previously, NGOs had drawn heavily on the principles from the Red Cross movement and the Geneva Conventions. To these are added a number of other initiatives, most notable being the Red Cross/NGO Code of Conduct. Recently there have been more explicit attempts to use these principles to determine humanitarian action among a group of agencies, notably the efforts made with Operation Lifeline Sudan, the humanitarian operation into the south of Sudan, and Joint Policy of Operation in Liberia.[19]

These protocols have undoubtedly contributed to more measured thinking about the implications of engaging in violent situations. The problem, and where the critics have some grounds to criticize agencies, is that when instances emerge where an agency would best serve a situation by keeping out, market forces push them to engage, regardless of these rules. Following the military overthrow of Sierra Leone president Tejan Kabbah in May 1997, for example, British aid agencies protested against the United Kingdom's Department for International Development decision not to fund their relief efforts. A rush of NGOs, the department rightly decided, would represent de facto recognition of the military junta and undermine the passive protest of Sierra Leonean citizens who were boycotting government ministries and departments on the grounds that the regime was illegitimate. As Rony Brauman notes, "deciding when to act means knowing, at least approximately, why action is preferable to abstention." Any plan of action, he goes on to say, "must incorporate the idea that abstention is not necessarily an abdication but may, on the contrary, be a decision."[20]

Humanitarian assistance will continue to function as a significant nonstate intervention into crises that Western governments increasingly choose to ignore. But its importance is more in the eyes of those implicated with giving aid than as an ingredient that fuels and prolongs conflict. In the end, the actions of aid agencies address only the symptoms, not the causes of conflict. Food and medical aid can never solve the factors that start wars. They may at times get in the way of a belligerent's aims, but solutions are ultimately political, a fact frequently forgotten in the fog and frustration of a brutal conflict. By criticizing aid agencies, the critics are elevating the effect of relief aid beyond its real impact. More important, they also distract attention from the more critical forces that sustain conflict.

Notes

The author would like to thank David Keen and Alice Jay for their useful comments on an earlier draft of this chapter.

1. Kevin Toolis, "The Famine Business," *Guardian Weekend*, August 22, 1998, p. 11.

2. Edward N. Luttwak, "Give War a Chance," *Foreign Affairs*, July/August 1999: 44.

3. Mary Anderson, "Doing the Right Thing," *New Routes*, no. 3 (1998): 9.

4. Hugo Slim, "International Humanitarianism's Engagement with Civil War, I, the 1990s: A Glance at Evolving Practice and Theory," a briefing paper for ActionAid UK, December 1997, 12.

5. David Keen, "The Economic Functions of Violence in Civil Wars," *Adelphi Paper* 320 (Oxford: Oxford University Press for the International Institute for Strategic Studies, 1998), 58.

6. David Keen and Ken Wilson, "Engaging with Violence: a Reassessment of Relief in Wartime," in Joanna MacCrae and Anthony Zwi (eds.), *War and Hunger: Rethinking International Responses to Complex Emergencies* (London: Zed, 1994), 213.

7. Francois Jean (ed.), *Life, Death and Aid: The Médecins sans Frontières Report on World Crisis Intervention* (London: Routledge, 1993), 93.

8. Unpublished UN report, September 1996, quoted in Alex De Waal, *Famine Crimes: Politics and the Disaster Relief Industry in Africa* (Oxford: James Currey, 1997), 205.

9. See De Waal, *Famine Crimes;* David Keen, *The Benefits of Famine: A Political Economy of Famine and Relief in Southwestern Sudan 1983–1989* (Princeton: Princeton University Press, 1994).

10. Mark Duffield, *New Routes* (March 1998): 14.

11. Alex De Waal, "Dangerous Precedents? Famine Relief in Somalia 1991–1993," in Joanna McRae and Anthony Zwi (eds.), *War and Hunger: Rethinking International Responses to Complex Emergencies* (London: Zed, 1994), 147.

12. International Institute for Strategic Studies, "Growing Conflict in Colombia," *Strategic Comments* 4 (June 5, 1998): 1.

13. Nicholas Stockton, "In Defence of Humanitarianism," *Disasters* 22, no. 4 (1998): 355.

14. Quoted in Refugee Policy Group, *Hope Restored? Humanitarian Aid in Somalia 1990–1994* (Washington, D.C.: Refugee Policy Group, 1994), 94–95.

15. Toolis, "The Famine Business," 11.

16. Mary Anderson, *Do No Harm: How Aid Can Support Peace—or War* (Boulder: Lynne Rienner, 1999).

17. Mary Anderson, "Some Moral Dilemmas of Humanitarian Aid," in Jonathan Moore (ed.), *Hard Choices: Moral Dilemmas in Humanitarian Intervention* (Rowman and Littlefield, 1998), 138.

18. Luttwak, "Give War a Chance."

19. See Nicholas Leader, "Proliferating Principles," *Disasters* 22, no. 4 (1998): 288–308.

20. Rony Brauman, "Refugee Camps, Population Transfers, and NGOs," in Moore, *Hard Choices*, 192.

11

Shaping Agendas in Civil Wars: Can International Criminal Law Help?

Tom Farer

Civil armed conflicts are nasty, brutish, peculiarly intractable and, these days, often long, even where one side is vastly stronger than the other. In earlier times, power asymmetries translated more readily into slavish submission, expulsion, or extermination of the weaker party. Today, the universalization of human rights as a kind of secular faith and a spreading (albeit by no means universal) conviction that gross violence within a country threatens the interests of other countries combine to inhibit that translation. But it may nevertheless occur. Ask the Tutsis of Rwanda—that is to say, ask the remnant who survived.

Normative restraints on the exterminating use of force rise amidst a necropolis of losers. The dead are thereby honored, but just as dead. If they are susceptible to comfort, then comfort they may have in the thought that their unintended sacrifice inspired the struggle to limit the play of ruthless power.

Today the structure of constraining rules and principles is largely complete. It bans, admittedly with somewhat varying degrees of clarity, brute repression as a means for resolving group conflict. The great remaining task, far more arduous than norm building, is enforcement. Over the decade, regional organizations and the United Nations, as well as ad hoc coalitions and individual states, have episodically tried to narrow the gap between norms and behavior by threatening or employing military and economic sanctions against pitiless governments and factions.

During the past decade, champions of a normative order informed by commitment to protect the weak and foment peaceful settlement have begun to invest hope in another enforcement vehicle, namely criminal punishment of those who lead or serve delinquent forces. Its threat, were it to appear real, could affect the behavior of the agents of civil conflict regardless of whether greed or grievance drives them. The extradition battle over Augusto Pinochet, the longtime Chilean dictator, and the treaty establishing a permanent International Criminal Court are milestones in the accelerating effort to add penal sanctions to the humanitarians' armory. My task, I take it, is to describe, analyze, identify the obstacles to, and anticipate the consequences of this admirable yet problematical initiative.

Why Penal Sanctions?

The purposes of penal sanctions in international law are largely coextensive with those in national legal orders. In both, sanctions are presumed generally to deter criminal acts, to protect society against confirmed delinquents by isolating them, to reinforce the authority of violated norms and of the rule of law generally, to comfort victims and their kin, and, by doing public justice, to reduce recourse to the private variety. "[It has become] an article of faith in the human rights community," Jonathan Bush wrote in 1993, "that judicial processes are a critical tool in ending and preventing violations of international law . . . [and as providing] catharsis, honoring victims, stigmatizing tyranny, restoring legality, 'bearing witness,' or otherwise having dignitary functions."[1] Exemplifying Bush's observation, the human rights scholar/activist Jelena Pejic wrote five years later, on the eve of the diplomatic conference establishing the International Criminal Court: "It is recognized that human rights and the protections guaranteed under international humanitarian law will not be translated into practice unless potential offenders realize that a price for violations must be paid."[2] But that is not all, she adds, for in addition to its deterrent and protective value, the criminal process plays a key role in facilitating national reconciliation following civil armed conflicts: for if there is no individual accountability for crimes, she asserts, victims will tend to impute criminality to the entire group from whose ranks the criminals sprang.[3]

The virtuous effects identified with criminal law are more easily assumed than proven, and at the margins, at least, they remain controversial. Scholars and practitioners of law debate the incidence and intensity of deterrence, the relationship in terms of crime reduction between deterrence and harsher sentences, the possibility and conditions of rehabilitation, and punishment's allegedly cathartic effect on victims and their kin. Less controversial are the claims that it inhibits recourse to private justice. These are old and complicated disputes. To join them would carry me too far from the main focus of my inquiry and would offer dubious advantage. For if, as appears to be the case, governments and humanitarians have rooted convictions about the efficacy of penal measures, convictions that scholarly debate has not altered, it would be pretentious to imagine that agnostic conclusion on my part would change anything. Moreover, these convictions spring from powerful intuitions or, one might say, from a collective projection by generally law-abiding people of what they take to be their own or at least their neighbor's reaction to the threat of criminal sanctions. In other words, on the basis of a subconscious canvass of their own hearts, people assume that in the absence of credible criminal sanctions, they and therefore others would far more frequently violate the law.

The Problem of Extrapolation

Belief about the potential efficacy of penal sanctions as vehicles for enforcing international law is a fairly straightforward extrapolation from the collective appreciation of law enforcement at the national level. Confidence in this extrapolation is not universally shared. Do contextual differences between national and international enforcement make behavior in the former a doubtful basis for anticipating responses to a criminal justice system in the latter?

One widely accepted dictum of domestic law enforcement is that a high probability of punishment generally deters more effectively than a very severe sanction rarely applied or, more simply, "relative certainty trumps relative severity" as a rule of thumb for the allocation of enforcement resources. The question, then, is whether the present and foreseeable nature of the international system reduces the risk of punishment to the point where on that ground alone it is unlikely to deter, even if on occasion persons are severely punished. By their very crimes, thugs may consolidate or seize control of sovereign states and thereby establish for themselves a comfortable refuge often with little fear of foreign intervention, particularly if they have succeeded in decimating opponents who might otherwise be transformed by external aid into a law enforcement vehicle for the global community.

A second question an agnostic might pose is whether a system shaped by the human rights sensibility in its most distilled form will tolerate effective procedures and intimidating punishments. Despite pleas from the post-holocaust government in Rwanda—in effect, therefore, from the survivors—the United Nations denied the ad hoc criminal tribunal for Rwanda the authority to impose capital punishment.[4] Even life terms, with or without the prospect of parole, are deemed "inhuman" by some European civil libertarians.[5] Moreover, those convicted by the tribunal will serve their sentence in a state designated by the international tribunal from a list of states that have expressed willingness to take the convicted, provided that the prisons meet internationally recognized prison conditions. At present, however, there is no prison in Rwanda that even approaches internationally recognized minimum prison conditions, raising the possibility that those convicted of masterminding the genocide will serve their sentences in country-club settings while those convicted by Rwandan courts will serve their time in appalling prison conditions.[6]

The same sensibility may also hamper effective prosecution in those exceptional cases where the criminals fail to control the state or are seized in their own territory by a decisive intervenor or unsuccessfully risk foreign travel. Notions of due process appropriate to well-developed democratic legal orders may place an insuperable burden on prosecutors when they are transferred wholesale to international criminal trials. Here too, the very extent of the crimes and brutality of their perpetrators may ironically facilitate the defense of the indefensible. For instance, if witnesses or their relations still live in territory controlled or threatened by the defendants' associates or principals, then unless the witnesses can testify anonymously, they may be reluctant and well advised not to testify at all. The ad hoc tribunal established by the Security Council in 1993 to prosecute "[p]ersons responsible for serious violations of international humanitarian law committed in the territory of the former Yugoslavia"[7] has in fact received anonymous testimony and promptly been criticized for doing so.[8]

Convicting senior figures like Milosevic of Yugoslavia, who may give oral orders or nothing more than winks and nods and leave no paper trail, will be difficult unless courts shift the burden of proof to them, at least on the issue of intent, where their forces have perpetrated atrocities. This is not mere speculation. The *New York Times,* citing a senior American official as its source, reports that "from the beginning, Mr. Milosevic sought to build a fire wall around himself, to distance himself from indictable criminal acts carried out against Muslims during the war in Bosnia."[9] According to U.S. intelligence, "Mr. Milosevic has been in meetings where brutal operations against civilians were discussed, but he has allowed his underlings to do the talking, apparently fearing that the conversations might be monitored by sophisticated listening devices."[10]

The discussion of Milosevic's efforts to evade indictment occurred in the context of a news report stating that the U.S. State Department had issued warnings about possible prosecution to the named commanders of nine Yugoslavian army units operating in Kosovo. The U.S. spokesperson declared that "commanders can be indicted, prosecuted and, if found guilty, imprisoned not only for crimes they themselves commit, but also for failing to prevent crimes occurring or for failure to prosecute those who commit crimes." He went on to say that "much of the evidence that the United States has against the nine commanders comes from interviews with refugees [who] are often able to identify military units operating in [areas from which they have fled]."

But on the following day, persons connected to the tribunal told another *New York Times* reporter that "prosecutors require more than names of military commanders or even witness accounts about cruelty and killing. To build their case against commanders, they need to link those responsible for crimes directly to the events and to present proof of who gave orders and who knew about the atrocities."[11]

To import wholesale into war crimes prosecutions the prosecution of persons who have been driving the juggernaut of the state, the safeguards developed to protect the poor and defenseless against the juggernaut of the state may fairly be seen as the exercise of an addled will to fail. Once the prosecutor demonstrates that a determinate unit commanded by the defendant had operational responsibility for the territory where atrocities were committed, the burden of proof should shift to the defendant to show that he or she could not reasonably have known of the atrocities or could not have prevented them. Similarly, when the prosecutors demonstrate a pattern of violations by the armed forces (including paramilitaries) of a government or faction, the head of government and all ministers with responsibilities related to the conflict (or repression) and the most senior officers of the armed forces should be required to establish by a preponderance of the evidence that they were unaware of the atrocities or tried and failed to prevent them from occurring.

Civil libertarians in common law countries and lawyers generally in civil law countries may object to plea bargains, a controversial but powerful instrument of prosecutors in the United States, and are almost certain to rail against broad conspiracy counts in the indictment, which are alien to the civil law but have been used effectively against criminal organizations in the United States. They will also resist employing the Nuremberg Charter tool of prosecuting for membership in elite organizations specializing in systematic torture and massacre, organizations like the Nazi SD and Gestapo.

Civil libertarians will also tend to oppose trials in absentia. Yet such trials are the only means of reaching perpetrators who remain in control of or protected by the states in whose names they have slaughtered. Conviction after a trial in absentia is much more than a symbolic exercise. In the first place, it permanently limits the perpetrator's movements. That itself should inflict some modest degree of unpleasantness. In addition, it places the defendants permanently at risk from a change in local power balances. Moreover, if they are functionaries rather than masters of the state, they must live with the oppressive knowledge that those actually in command of the state may find it convenient to trade them for a reciprocal benefit.

A second and possibly more compelling virtue of trial in absentia is its implications for the economic agendas of latent delinquents. Conviction could facilitate worldwide confiscation of the delinquents' assets, assuming confiscation were one of the sanctions at the disposal of an international criminal tribunal, as it should be. National governments would, of course, have to adopt legislation requiring the executive branch to assist in the identification of assets attributable to the convicted person and requiring the judicial one to enforce the tribunal's confiscation orders.

A third source of unease about the extrapolation is the presence in the international sphere of both national and multinational community interests that will often compete powerfully against the interest in enforcing penal sanctions. Economic and environmental interdependence, porous borders, weapons of mass destruction—all are prominent among the contextual feature of the present international system that lend governments and often the insurgents in minor states a sharply higher level of systemically disruptive power than, in general, they have previously enjoyed. They may drive hordes of refugees across borders, destroy great tracts of rain forest, or credibly threaten terrorist attacks on nuclear power plants, dams, or commercial airline systems. Imagine the disruptive effect on economy and society in Europe or the United States (or a host of other places for that matter) if it were believed that a few terrorists with handheld antiaircraft missiles were in position to attack civilian planes. The havoc inflicted on Colombia for half a decade by the Medellin cocaine cartel led by Pablo Escobar, a cartel with no more than a few hundred core operatives, suggests the rising nihilistic power even of relatively small but well-organized criminal groups. In short, potential defendants may neither control a powerful state nor enjoy this support in order to discourage law enforcement by their perceived capacity both to escalate and to expand their delinquencies. In that way they may confront law-supporting states with the grim choice of flinching and thereby undermining the international rule of law or plunging ahead possibly at huge costs to the public interest.

A fourth barrier to easy extrapolation is the inchoate character of the "global community." A legal order is a set of norms and supporting institutions that shape expectations about how one should and how others probably will behave most of the time. Because the international legal order is very decentralized, self-declared "realists" dismiss it as nothing more than a cosmetic thinly concealing the pocked face of power. Their premise, of course, is that law regulates behavior only where it is backed by intimidating force. In the absence of police and troops to execute their orders, courts are impotent, and law is a dangerous illusion.

The evident flaw in the realists' argument is its reliance on a cramped view of legal order and of the means available for its enforcement. They rely on a criminal-law paradigm, a hellish vision of society in which all of us are latent criminals restrained from villainy by fear of punishment alone. And they correspondingly ignore the facilitative dimension of law: law as a means of enabling persons to cooperate over time by embodying their collective goals in a body of rules, principles, and policies. Imagine, for instance, a group of steelworkers who become the joint owners of a bankrupt company in the hope of restoring its viability. Having no bosses, they can—indeed they must—decide on work rules that will express their common interest in producing steel efficiently and safely.

Of course the image is too pretty. Character and energy being distributed unequally, the "free-rider" problem will no doubt insinuate itself into this Elysium. We can anticipate that some workers will be tempted to substitute recreational diversions for work assignments. But particularly where the number of workers is few and cooperation is highly integrated and so clandestine rule evasion is difficult, the threats both of enterprise failure and of the collective exclusion of malingerers from this system of cooperation may suffice to keep cheating to a workable minimum. These are precisely the types of threats or sanctions that operate in the international system of sovereign states, complicated, of course, by the fact that though the number of states is small, unlike the individual steelworkers none of them possess a single consciousness and will. Instead their policies are determined in part by internal concerns and parochial politics that may often take little account of external commitments.

Whether at the international or the village level of social life, the law-as-a-system-of-cooperation paradigm fits when there is in fact a consensus about means and ends. In certain areas of international life—such as ocean navigation and commercial air flight and diplomatic intercourse—consensus is high and compliance with the rules embodying it are predictable. The question relevant to this chapter is whether the same can be said for the rules limiting the power of governments to repress challenges to their authority. Skeptics about the potential influence of international criminal sanctions might argue that consensus is not universal and is particularly weak among elites with a fragile grip on power or running countries with restless minorities. For such elites, treaties may well be little more than scraps of paper.

Dissent from the application of criminal sanctions to hooligan leaders, skeptics might fairly argue, is not limited to hooligan leaders. It can be spied at the very heart of the Western world. One need only recall the recent decision of Great Britain's Law Lords in the Pinochet case. There we had the spectacle of five out of seven successfully straining to so construe the law of extradition as to narrow maximally the basis and hence prospects for extraditing the unrepentant butcher even as they purported to uphold the humanitarian claim that former heads of state are not immune. Similarly, in Spain the government itself sought to insulate Pinochet from prosecution by appealing over the head of the examining magistrate, Baltasar Garzon, for a ruling that Spain had no jurisdiction to try the general for crimes committed outside the country.[12]

The gravity of the interests at stake is a final source of skepticism about the ability of criminal sanctions to influence the behavior of parties in a civil armed conflict. By the time tensions between groups turn violent, they normally have demonized each other and convinced themselves that defeat, unlike the loss of most interstate conflicts, means the utter physical destruction of their respective communities. Moreover, civil conflict is by definition coterminous with the collapse of public order. The remote threat of criminal sanctions, it could be argued, will not resonate in the paranoid world of domestic armed conflict.

The predictive value of these various caveats about reliance on penal sanctions is likely to depend to some degree on the character of the international criminal justice system that gets put in place. Certainly they deserve a place among the concerns of the system's architects and those who assess their work. It is with those caveats in mind that I turn now to the system that is beginning to appear.

The Norms

The authors of the draft treaty submitted in summer 1998 to the diplomatic representatives gathered in Rome to negotiate the terms of an International Criminal Court (ICC) had proposed three categories of crime. They essentially reiterate those contained in the Charter of the post–World War II Nuremberg tribunal, which specified crimes against the humanitarian laws of war (i.e., "war crimes"), crimes against humanity, and crimes against peace.

War Crimes

For the most part codified in the Hague Conventions on Land Warfare, the Geneva Conventions of 1949 and the Two Protocols Additional of 1977, war crimes function primarily to protect civilians and soldiers who have surrendered or been rendered *hors de combat,* broadly speaking, all noncombatants. In addition, through the norm prohibiting gratuitously cruel weapons and the treaties prohibiting use of bacteriological and chemical weapons, they offer limited protection even to combatants.

This corpus of norms comprehensively covers interstate war scenarios and, in that context, commands a broad international consensus. Its application in civil conflicts is more problematic. The almost universally adopted Geneva Conventions contain a common Article Three, which alone applies to such conflicts. It prohibits torture, summary execution, and, more generally, cruel treatment. But under the convention, it applies only in the case of "armed conflicts not of an international character." And it has been the consistent practice of governments struggling with insurgents to deny Article Three's applicability on the grounds that they are merely conducting police operations rather than a true armed conflict, as if the latter could be said to exist only where insurgents control and govern a large swath of territory like the Confederacy in the American Civil War. Protocol Additional II goes well beyond Article Three in detailing humanitarian norms applicable to civil conflicts. But not only does it enjoy less widespread acceptance than the Geneva Conventions, in addition it too is subject to the claim that it applies only in the instance of full-scale civil war.[13]

Without any international tribunal available to assess such claims, governments have, until recently, been far freer to make them with reasonable expectation of acquiescence from the many states whose governing elites can envision themselves someday engaged in a similar sort of struggle and hence inclined to keep their options open. Until recently, rigid conceptions of sovereignty as a high wall blocking external appreciation of a state's internal behavior (conceptions that developed several centuries ago) reinforced a state's freedom to define internal struggles out of the reach of Article Three. Any advantage in so doing has, however, fallen in conjunction with the rise of human rights norms, some of which are generally conceded to be nonderogable; that is, not subject to suspension in time of emergency. In addition, by making effective their core claim that a state's treatment of people within its territory is subject to international standards, human rights norms have transformed ideas about the prerogatives of sovereignty and hence, inevitably, views about the conditions in which the laws of war are applicable.

Crimes Against Humanity

The authors of the Nuremberg tribunal's charter included this category of criminality in order to cover the slaughter of Jews and other targets of the Nazis who were citizens of Germany or its allies, since German troops and paramilitary units operating on the territory of allied states were not *occupiers* within the meaning of the applicable convention.[14] Yet they were sensitive to the anticipatable charge that convicting the senior Nazis for committing this newly defined crime would violate the fundamental principle *sine lege*.[15] Hence they limited its applicability to slaughter that occurred in the course of aggressive war, as if by doing so they might make it almost indistinguishable from traditional war crimes.[16] Moreover, they could argue that during the war, the allied powers had issued warnings that German leaders would be held responsible for all inhuman acts violating the conscience of mankind and therefore they had sufficient notice to satisfy the rationale of the *sine lege* principle. Jordan Paust has enumerated various uses of the term long before Nuremberg, for instance in the 1915 condemnation by Great Britain, France, and Russia of the Armenian massacres in

Turkey.[17] The defendants, and some legal pundits with a presumably more objective perspective, nevertheless insisted that even if the acts charged violated customary international law, responsibility for them had hitherto been attributable to states only. To satisfy the *sine lege* principle, they therefore argued, it would have been necessary to have precedents for individual criminal responsibility. In short, though the defendants might have had full knowledge that they were committing grave violations of international law, they had a right to rely on the historical practice of states to treat each other as the sole subjects of international law. Of course they made the same claim in connection with the charges of conspiring to wage and waging aggressive war.[18] Even today, legal thought is not entirely immune to this sort of formalism.

The Nuremberg convictions and developments since then have, I believe, knocked the struts from under this shaky claim. If Nuremberg were the only precedent for individual criminal responsibility, then one might dismiss it as an aberration. But it is not. The 1948 Genocide Convention, which enjoys virtually universal adherence, envisions criminal liability for perpetrators and makes prosecution an international obligation of countries with specified jurisdiction. So does the much more recent convention prohibiting torture. So even those odd legal positivists who think it unjust to punish mass murderers if there is no penal system in place at the time of their crimes would have to concede that the genocidists of Rwanda and the assorted criminals who rampage through the former Yugoslavia had sufficient notice that they risked criminal punishment.

Waging Aggressive War

The Nuremberg prosecutors and later the tribunal in finding culpability relied primarily on the 1928 Treaty for the Renunciation of War as an Instrument of National Policy, the so-called Kellogg-Briand Pact. In reviewing a book on Nuremberg, Jonathan Bush claims that prior to Nuremberg, "[i]nternational law had long defined and condemned aggression."[19] If so, there is special irony in the fact that for some three decades after Nuremberg and despite or literally because of endless debate, the United Nations failed to discover a definition that summoned broad agreement among its members. Although

conceived until now as a delinquency peculiar to interstate relations, the crime (however defined) is relevant in a number of
ways to our discussion of internal conflict.

In the first place, if, as many governments and scholars
have claimed since the adoption of the UN Charter, force used
for any purpose other than self-defense against an armed attack
by another state is aggression, then humanitarian interventions
to halt genocide and arrest its perpetrators would itself be criminal. Supporters of this confining definition organize the uni-
verse of force into three categories: aggression, self-defense,
and enforcement measures authorized or ordered by the Security Council under Chapter VII of the UN Charter. During the
Cold War, the United States championed a more nuanced set
of categories. It upheld the power of regional and subregional
organizations to legitimize forceful measures without Security
Council approval. And it claimed lawful authority to initiate
reprisals against a state for terrorist attack or sustained "low-
intensity" belligerence.

Governments and scholars remain divided about the conditions for the legitimate employment of force. Some scholars
have claimed there exists legal authority for unilateral intervention as a last recourse to prevent gross violations of human
rights, even to restore democracy.[20] But the stricter view, resting
on the most straightforward reading of the Charter, still enjoys
considerable support and, particularly in light of the World
Court's opinion in the Nicaragua case, that view might prevail
in the opinions of the ICC. Concern about this risk shaped U.S.
opposition to including aggression among the crimes over
which the ICC would exercise jurisdiction.

The concept of aggression might, however, be reconceived
to make it a tool against, rather than a potential shield for,
mass murderers and ethnic cleansers. Rather than being limited to interstate wars, it might be conscripted for service in internal conflicts and used there to criminalize violent repression
and the initiation of armed conflict by one faction, government, or insurgent. This would have to be done, of course, with
due regard for the right of properly constituted authorities to
maintain order and territorial integrity. Otherwise it would be
a license for terrorism and secession.

It is not hard to imagine a set of manageable criteria, manageable in the sense that they could be applied consistently by

courts. On one hand, one might start with the proposition that governments have a right to use force, within the bounds of international humanitarian and human rights law, to maintain territorial integrity. On the other hand, governments have obligations to respect the rights of minorities, rights that are increasingly well defined in international instruments. The sustained failure to respect those rights would, then, lead to forfeiture of the right to employ force against secessionists. Once that right was forfeit, use of force would be "aggression." Aggression could also be found where one party to an internal conflict disregards a call for cease-fire issuing from the Security Council or, perhaps, the General Assembly or a relevant regional organization.

Institutions

For the foreseeable future, national criminal justice systems must serve as the principal executors of international penal law. That was as clear to the architects of the Nuremberg tribunal as it is to their contemporary successors. The former reserved the international tribunal for trial of the senior officials of Nazidom. The tens, indeed hundreds of thousands, who had executed their commands were left to national trials, of which there were many and which continue to this day.[21] Any other course would have required the construction of a huge bureaucratic apparatus at great cost and delay.

Today there are no fewer candidates for indictment. Tens of thousands joined to make the Rwandan holocaust possible. And they are only a small fraction of those who, in purlieus as widely spaced as Chile and the Sudan, have during the past thirty years committed crimes against humanity. Not only would it take years and vast sums to produce a criminal justice apparatus—judges, prosecutors, bailiffs, marshals, investigators—able to cope with the potential catch, in addition the system could not function independently without a broad permission to exercise its functions, including its investigative activities, within states. Such permission would constitute a cession of sovereign rights that is not yet thinkable within the political cultures of many states. After all, one of the oldest and clearest and most fiercely defended rules of international law prohibits one state from exercising any judicial function within the territory of another without its permission. Permission has very rarely been granted, for a monopoly of law enforcement authority is accurately seen as a defining feature of national independence. One need only recall the furious reaction of the Mexican Congress in 1998 to the scam conducted by U.S. agents operating undercover on both sides of the border that exposed the money-laundering activities of Mexican bankers.

In authorizing establishment of the ad hoc tribunals for international crimes committed in former Yugoslavia and in Rwanda, the Security Council took account of these realities in that it made no effort to give the tribunals exclusive jurisdiction. It did, however, give them a superior status in the sense that once they choose to hear a particular case, the national courts are required to defer. The treaty establishing the ICC reverses the order of precedence. The ICC is supposed to "complement" national courts. Its statute "explicitly establishes that a case will, *inter alia,* be inadmissible before the ICC whenever it is being investigated or prosecuted by a state which has jurisdiction, unless the state is 'unwilling or unable genuinely' to carry out the investigation or prosecution."[22] Consistent with the logic of complementarity, a case is inadmissible when it has been investigated by a state with jurisdiction that has decided not to prosecute the accused, unless the international prosecutor can convince the ICC that the state's decision resulted from "unwillingness or inability genuinely" to investigate or prosecute.

The effort to construct an effective system for applying penal law at the international level raises many of the same issues encountered in domestic jurisdictions. All criminal tribunals require means for investigating alleged crimes, compelling the accused's appearance, conducting fair trials (which is normally deemed to include a right of appeal), and executing sentences. Since most UN member states appear unready to concede to any international institution a general authority to arrest and detain persons wanted as defendants or material witnesses or to enter premises and seize pertinent documents, any now imaginable international tribunal must rely on states to perform these functions for it. The ad hoc tribunals for Rwanda and the former Yugoslavia enjoy the formal authority to command cooperation granted to them by the Security Council acting under Chapter VII. In theory, then, where national authorities refuse a request, the tribunals can apply to the Council for sanctions against the obdurate government. The

Council's readiness to enforce the demands of its creation has not yet been tested but could soon be if, for instance, Croatia persistently refuses to deliver to the Yugoslavia tribunal one or another of its nationals who has been indicted for war crimes.

The International Criminal Court, should it actually materialize, will be less well armed, at least in theory. Being a creature of treaty, its legal authority will be limited in most respects to those states that ratify it.[23] And it will have no formal right of appeal to the Security Council in the event of nonperformance by a treaty party. At best, the tribunal's president or prosecutor could persuade a sympathetic state to bring an instance of noncompliance to the Security Council's attention if it could be plausibly associated with a threat to international peace.

Despite the Pinochet case, it is fair to note a growing readiness at least of liberal democratic states to cooperate in punishing violators of international criminal law. The Euro-Canadian push to establish the ICC testifies to a changing political and moral sensibility. In a paradoxical way, so does the Pinochet case taken in all its parts: its initiation within the Spanish judicial system, the ambivalence rather than focused hostility of Spain's executive branch (while its attorney-general was fighting to abort, its foreign minister was claiming that his government would take no action to block extradition), even the House of Lord's judgment to the extent it rejected the view that former heads of state enjoyed immunity for crimes committed by them when in office. One reasonably can, therefore, anticipate a growing measure of compliance by governments with their obligations to cooperate in global law enforcement. How extensive are their extant obligations, particularly their obligations under customary international law that is binding irrespective of applicable treaties? In particular, do their obligations extend to the key task of actively seeking and arresting accused persons and extraditing them for trial (where the arresting state does not itself choose to prosecute)?

A growing number of legal scholars answer the second question affirmatively. They stand on reasonably firm ground. The notion of such an obligation is hardly novel. It is foreshadowed in Common Article 49 of the 1949 Geneva Conventions, which provides that

> Each High Contracting Party shall be under the obligation
> to search for persons alleged to have committed, or to have

ordered to be committed, such grave breaches, and shall bring such persons, regardless of their nationality, before its own courts. It may also, if it prefers, and in accordance with the provisions of its own legislation, hand such persons over for trial to another High Contracting Party concerned, provided such High Contracting Party has made out a *prima facie case*.[24]

The grave breaches to which it refers—including willful killing and torture or inhuman treatment—are unfortunately limited to interstate conflicts; they do not include violations of common Article Three's regulations for civil wars. Nevertheless, in that they impose an obligation on states to seize, detain, and prosecute or extradite persons who may not be their own nationals or who have committed crimes against their nationals, the conventions are a milestone in the development of the procedural side of international criminal law. With respect to internal violence, the almost coincident milestone is the 1948 Genocide Convention. Though it looked primarily to prosecution by the state where a perpetrator was found, it gave the arresting state the future option of transferring the accused to an international tribunal should one be established. Since the late 1940s, conventions criminalizing various acts as threats to the general interest of peoples and states and requiring prosecution or extradition have multiplied.[25] Enumerating some sixty-four of them, at least one scholar concludes that their cumulative evidentiary weight confirms the evolution of a rule of customary law.[26]

Whether acting from a sense of legal or of moral obligation, most states willing to cooperate with the ICC need correspondingly to alter or modify national laws and regulations. This is particularly true for a country like Great Britain—where the courts refuse to apply international norms until they are formally incorporated by Parliamentary Act into domestic law—or the United States, where customary international law is subordinate to congressional acts (and, arguably, executive decrees), even if earlier in time, and treaties are rarely deemed self-executing. Moreover, whatever the actual status of international obligations in domestic law and their theoretical applicability to a given case, the United States experience is that lower court judges and many lawyers lack awareness of international norms and when made aware, may still ignore or misconstrue them on behalf of personal agendas. Elaboration and clarification at the highest level of government of the commitment to collaborate with international tribunals should heighten awareness and inhibit evasion and distortion of international law.

The commitment to cooperation entails at a minimum the following elements. First, effective provision for extradition. Countries with well-developed legal systems generally do not recognize in the executive power a unilateral right to extradite.[27] They require either legislative authorization or a preexisting international agreement. Some standard elements of extradition treaties will require modification. For instance, such agreements often specifically exclude nationals from their reach; that is, most of the people over whom any state has jurisdiction. In addition, they generally contain exceptions for so-called political crimes, which some U.S. judges have defined as crimes of any kind committed by members of organized groups for political reasons.[28] Virtually all of the potential defendants in international criminal trials could obtain shelter under that construction. Furthermore, states would need to eliminate the standard double criminality requirement—the offense charged must be a crime in both countries at the time of the extradition request[29]—if they were unwilling to include international crimes in their own criminal codes.

Second, effective cooperation entails providing international courts with access to witnesses both at the investigative and trial stages of a proceeding. Providing access to those who are willing to meet with international tribunal prosecutors requires nothing more than permission for the latter to enter and exercise judicial functions, permission the executive can doubtless grant. Unwilling witnesses provide a considerably more challenging set of procedural and political problems. Compelling their appearance for interrogation by agents of the ICC's prosecutor within the country and subject to all of its constitutional protections would obviously be less problematic than attempting to compel their presence before the tribunal, where if they remain obdurate they might be found in contempt and imprisoned. The domestic political reverberations of this scenario could be considerable. Whether it raises serious constitutional issues under provisions comparable to the U.S. due process clause is less clear, but surely constitutional issues would be argued in a suit to block coerced removal of a citizen to another jurisdiction without any showing or even claim that the citizen was him- or herself criminally responsible for the acts charged in the foreign trial.

International tribunals will also require assistance in securing documentary evidence whether through judicial compulsion or searches and seizures conducted by the executive. There is both precedent and experience in this area as a result of the mutual legal assistance treaties that have begun to proliferate largely in response to the globalization of organized crime.[30] But the treaties themselves and practice thereunder reveal at least one common defect, namely their frequent failure to secure cooperation in the pursuit of the assets of delinquents or of proof that such assets exist.[31]

Armed conflict—with its murky and repressive ambiance—often provides unusual opportunities and incentives for corruption, indeed wholesale asset stripping by government officials and leaders of armed factions. Its risks encourage export of financial assets (whether acquired during or before the conflict) to one or another venue in the global archipelago of financial safe havens generally located in picturesque and sunny places with good cuisine. Criminal penalties can and should include confiscation of assets. Indeed, the credible threat of confiscation may surpass the threat of imprisonment as an instrument of influence for external actors attempting to promote peaceful settlement and to restrain atrocity. Military victory, howsoever secured, provides the winners with a safe haven from prosecution but cannot by itself protect resources previously shipped to foreign venues.

War crimes prosecutions, whether occurring in national courts or international tribunals, should be able to reach, initially freeze, and ultimately confiscate the assets of delinquents. In prosecuting its war against drug traffickers, the United States has had fair success in pressuring and persuading foreign governments to cooperate with searches for drug-trafficking proceeds. But haven states have resisted lowering the bank secrecy bar with respect to investigations into other crimes.

To be maximally effective, an assault on externally held assets requires all states with jurisdiction over financial havens to adopt a legislative package with the following features: First, it must authorize or, preferably, require the executive and judicial branches to cooperate with investigations conducted by foreign national and international tribunals; second, it must modify laws imposing criminal or civil penalties on employees of financial institutions who reveal information about the transactions of their institutions; third (and perhaps most controversially), it must require financial institutions to make good-faith efforts to identify and thereafter to maintain records concerning the real identity of ultimate parties in interest. The difficulties successor governments have encountered in trying to track the plunderings of notorious dictators underscore the need to increase transparency in global financial centers and tax havens. Obviously the competition among financial centers for "hot money" will inhibit the requisite changes in law and policy unless they are done in concert. The gradual albeit slight lowering of the bars to money-laundering investigations and, more recently, to inquiries into the disposition of assets belonging to persons consumed by the European Holocaust and their survivors attest to the power of the United States in particular, much less the Group of Seven acting together, to pry open the closed windows of other jurisdictions favored by runaway capital.

Cooperation with international tribunals, whether established by a Security Council Resolution or a broadly ratified treaty, is a moral imperative. Does the same imperative apply to the operations of national tribunals seeking assistance purportedly in order to enforce the relevant international norms? Is there not much greater danger there of inadvertently helping to advance illicit essays in revenge or sheer predation marching under the banner of humanitarianism?

Rooted in a political order of sovereign states, designed by those states to express, define, and defend sovereignty, international law has served rather to separate than to universalize the sum of global authority to make and apply law. The authority of each state's duly constituted authorities to decide what behavior shall be tolerated or required on its territory or on the part of its nationals and to enforce such decisions has been a defining feature of national sovereignty. Within the tolerances of international law, states have also authorized themselves to prohibit and punish acts albeit committed by aliens in foreign venues where such acts are directed against them, as in the case of a conspiracy to counterfeit their currency. And, though not without dissent, states have occasionally asserted the authority to outlaw assaults on their nationals abroad, although in doing so they in effect extend their legislative jurisdiction into the sovereign space of other states. But until very recently, they have rarely recognized a general right to legislate against and punish acts, regardless of where they occur and who is the victim, simply on the grounds that the acts in question threaten universally shared interests.

Piracy was one of the rare exceptions. Now there are, at least arguably, quite a few more. Widely ratified treaties impose "extradite or prosecute" obligations primarily in connection with terrorist acts (attacks on airlines and on diplomatic personnel, for instance) and gross violations of human rights (such as torture).[32] Wide ratification, repetition (torture, for instance, is prohibited in, among other texts, the Geneva Conventions and the International Covenant on Civil and Political Rights, and by regional human rights instruments and the torture convention itself), the clandestine character of violations, and the absence of official defenders collectively evidence the incorporation into customary international law of certain prohibitions initially established by treaty. In the face of this development, states now have discretion to prosecute transient aliens for various crimes against human rights and humanitarian law, crimes committed abroad against other aliens, even where the state is not obligated to do so by virtue of being a party to a prosecute-or-extradite treaty.

A world swarming with police and prosecutors on the lookout for those who have killed, maimed, raped, tortured, and ethnically cleansed and with courts ready to try the villains might well seem rather more intimidating to prospective Pinochets and Idi Amins than one marked by a solitary tribunal in the Hague or wherever. How might this happy prospect come about in a world where past or present high-ranking villains have become accustomed to traveling or even settling here or there without great difficulty, much less fear of incarceration? Perhaps the first few instances of vigorous national enforcement of international criminal law might generate powerful pressures on other governments to follow suit or, at the very least, to deny safe havens to murderous former heads of state like the ones provided for Idi Amin in Saudi Arabia and Mengistu Haile Mariam in Zimbabwe. There could be a general ripping aside of the veil of immunity for government officials.

Quite apart from the plausibility of this scenario, does it provide grounds for concern no less than for anticipatory jubilation?

One ground for concern is possible abuse of loosened restraints on national jurisdiction. The risk of contestable use and incontestable abuse should grow in rough proportion to the variety of delinquencies seen to justify the assertion of universal jurisdiction. Consider, for instance, the crime of "aggression" conditionally included in the Statute for the new International Criminal Court.[33] Its position buttressed by the Statute's recognition that such a crime exists, a state might include the crime in its penal code, exclude statutes of limitations, make jurisdiction limitless, and adopt the view that any use of force for purposes other than defense against an armed attack or execution of a Security Council mandate or license under Chapter VII of the Charter constitutes the crime. Since that definition would embrace the current NATO operation against Milosevic and his colleagues, senior civilian and military officials in all nineteen NATO countries would be liable to prosecution in country X as long as they live. Moreover, as notions about the legitimacy of universal jurisdictional assertions by national courts gain currency, in future years country X might be able to secure their arrest and extradition by third countries.

A second ground for concern is the slight measure of due process that is obtained in many countries. Even someone prosecuting in good faith may do so by means that could easily lead to miscarriages of justice.

Populist reactions to the prosecution of fellow citizens in far-off countries with unfamiliar legal codes will push governments to protest or take strong measures even in cases where, in the eyes of neutral observers, the prosecuting state appears to be acting in good faith. It seems fair to suspect that the proliferation of international criminal trials by national courts will add to the sum total of acrimony among states. One way of reducing the risk of abuse and the certainty of acrimony would be to achieve an international consensus that judgments in national trials must be appealable to the International Criminal Court. That would, of course, require an amendment to the ICC's statute and probably an expansion in its numbers. Achieving consensus is not likely to prove easy, particularly since what I am proposing constitutes ceding ultimate power away from national judiciaries, a concession that could raise constitutional and political issues in many states.

Individual Criminal Responsibility,
Peace Processes, and Transitions to Democracy

One ground for concern that applies to international as well as national enforcement of international criminal law is the impact of threatened criminal prosecutions on efforts to negotiate the settlement of civil armed conflicts and transitions from authoritarian to democratic regimes. In recent years, immunity from prosecution has been a prominent and contentious issue particularly in democratic transitions.[34] Among scholars and activists, debate has swirled around the ethical and legal propriety of blanket amnesties. Exposure without punishment, once championed as a means of reconciling antagonists without derailing peaceful settlement or transition, has disappointed, at least in the former respect. Still, in some cases, impunity (with or without exposure) has probably been essential to democratic transitions and peace.

One might argue that the combination of an international criminal tribunal and national tribunals with jurisdiction to punish humanitarian crimes committed abroad allows a necessary measure of flexibility in managing transitions or peace negotiations without sacrificing all the imagined—and probably to some degree, real—virtues of criminal sanctions. Negotiators, after all, can give no more than they have. They can guarantee Pinochet's ilk impunity at home but cannot assure their freedom to take tea abroad with honorable persons or to exercise their human right to shop at Gucci in Miami. If the ICC stood alone as a threat to the pleasures of retirement, sociopathic leaders in states that had become parties (presumably during some earlier democratic interlude) could simply withdraw from the treaty establishing the court prior to relinquishing power or agreeing to autonomy for or power sharing with some insurgent group. The beauty of national tribunals enforcing international criminal law is their immunity to such ploys. They would not be providing merely a forum to enforce foreign law, civil or criminal. For in that event, normally they would apply the substantive law of the foreign jurisdiction, hence the law granting immunity.[35] No, they would be applying international law, and it would not be affected by arrangements between the contending parties.

To me it seems implausible that the risk of prosecution in a foreign jurisdiction or an international tribunal would weigh heavily on the issue of democratic transition or domestic peace. Moreover, if national and international law conspires to treat state terrorists no better than the private sort, then it should not weigh at all since, in terms of the opportunities to cavort abroad, state killers would gain nothing of formal value. To be sure, they might conceivably calculate that by retaining power, they retain ways to extract concessions, including de facto immunity, from states that need to deal with them concerning one or another of the many issues (from global warming to transnational crime) that crowd the contemporary diplomatic agenda. Still, conceding the other and far larger stakes on the table in negotiations to end a conflict or effect a transition, it is hard to believe that this one could matter very much.

An obligation to punish is most likely to conflict with strategic and humanitarian interest in the early termination of civil conflicts where powerful external actors—possibly acting at the behest of the United Nations or a regional organization—are employing armed mediation on behalf of peace. That was Bosnia and in a sense Haiti as well. Political and military leaders who feel themselves vulnerable to prosecution will then be demanding impunity from the very countries with the means to grant it de facto by refusing to deliver the miscreants to an international tribunal or to prosecute them in their national courts. Western governments with troops in Bosnia have felt the flail of public opinion for failing to arrest notorious war criminals. Even negotiating with them has been a problem.

Making Security Council permission a condition for an international court initiating investigations, much less seeking the arrest of persons where investigation has led to indictment, would reduce the risk of collision between the commitment to punish and the goal of peaceful settlement. It would also tend to emasculate the court at birth and assure that in such future cases as it did try to act, it would do so subject to the accusation of doing justice unequally. During the negotiations in Rome over the statute of the International Criminal Court, the United States failed in its efforts to secure such a limit on the court's authority. The statute as approved by the great majority requires an affirmative vote of the Security Council adopted under Chapter VII of the Charter to block the initiation or continuation of an investigation or trial.

Despite all the deductive grounds for skepticism I sketched at the outset, the reported efforts of Milosevic to conceal his responsibility for atrocities in the former Yugoslavia suggest that the risk of criminal responsibility could weigh on the decisions of the principals to internal armed conflict. How much it will weigh in the short term will be affected, I would guess, by the success of the extant ad hoc tribunals for Yugoslavia and Rwanda in trying, convicting, and punishing severely a number, if not a majority, of the principal organizers respectively of war crimes and genocide. In the Yugoslavian case, success may require a decision by the United States and its allies to demonstrate to the Serbian officer corps and related civilian elites that they must choose between, on the one hand, losing Kosovo altogether and also the Serbian rump in Bosnia (which would then be divided between Croats and Muslims) and remaining a pariah state, or on the other hand, to deliver at least Milosevic and his wife and certain paramilitary leaders like Arkan to the tribunal. The will to impose those alternatives is not visible, in some measure, perhaps because the moral and strategic prudence of their imposition is debatable.[36] It would, moreover, require impunity for most of the officer corps. In the longer term, the weight of criminal sanctions will be a function largely of what one cannot yet foresee, namely a robust commitment to deploy national criminal justice systems on behalf of international criminal law.

Notes

1. Jonathan A. Bush, reviewing Telford Taylor's *The Anatomy of the Nuremberg Trials: A Personal Memoir,* 93 Columbia L. Rev. 2022 (1993), at 270.

2. Jelena Pejic, *Creating a Permanent International Criminal Court: The Obstacles to Independence and Effectiveness,* 29 Columbia Human Rights L. Rev. 291 (1998), at 292.

3. Ibid.

4. See the Statute of the International Criminal Tribunal for Rwanda, Art. 23, Annex, U.N. Doc S/RES/955 (1994), and Int. Crim. Trib. For Rwanda, Rules of Procedure and Evidence, Rule 101(A), stating: "A convicted persons may be sentenced to imprisonment for a term up to and including the termination of his life." U.N. Doc. ITR/3/Rev.1 (1995) entered into force June 29, 1995. Rwanda authorities initially opposed the creation of the the tribunal over the issue of capital punishment. They believed that it would result in unfairness because the leaders of the genocide, who were found guilty of the most egregious crimes, would be given prison sentences whereas their subordinates who were tried before local courts faced the death penalty if convicted. See "Kigali Agrees to Cooperate with the Genocide Tribunal," *Irish Times,* November 10, 1994, p. 10.

5. Though Yugoslavia has a death penalty, it does not have a life imprisonment sentence. Yugoslav lawmakers view life imprisonment as cruel

punishment. Other European states, such as Norway, Spain, and Portugal, have done away with life imprisonment and established maximum prison terms of twenty to twenty-five years. See William A. Schabas, *Sentencing by International Tribunals: A Human Rights Approach*, 7 Duke J. Comp. & Int'l L. 461, 494, Spring 1997.

6. William A. Schabas, *Sentencing by International Tribunals: A Human Rights Approach*, 7 Duke J. Comp. & Int'l L. 461, 481, footnote 90, Spring 1997.

7. S.C. Res. 827, 25 May 1993, U.N. SCOR, reprinted in 32 I.L.M. 1203 (1993).

8. See Monroe Leigh, *Witness Anonymity Is Inconsistent with Due Process*, 91 Am. J. Int'l Law 80 (1997).

9. Raymond Bonner, "9 Yugoslavs Are Warned of Liability for Atrocities," *New York Times*, April 8, 1999, p. A10.

10. Ibid.

11. Marlise Simons, "Court Calls for Evidence Not Politics," *New York Times*, April 9, 1999, p. A11.

12. Marlise Simons (for the New York Times News Service), "Spanish Officials Quietly Fight Pinochet Extradition," *Denver Post*, October 21, 1998, p. 8A.

13. Protocol II does not apply to "situations of internal disturbances and tensions, such as riots, isolated and sporadic acts of violence and other acts of a similar nature, as not being armed conflicts." Protocol II (Relating to the Protection of Victims of Non-International Armed Conflicts) opened for signature December 12, 1977, U.N. Doc. A/32/144, Annex I, II (1977).

14. The charter of the International Military Tribunal (IMT or Nuremberg tribunal) referred to "murder, extermination, enslavement, deportation, and other inhumane acts committed against any civilian population, before or during the war, or persecution on political, racial or religious grounds in execution of or in connection with any crime within the jurisdiction of the Tribunal." The Charter of the IMT, August 8, 1945, Art. 6(c), 59 Stat. 1544, 82 UNTS 279. Hence, persecution had to be connected by the prosecution to the defendants waging or conspiring to wage aggressive war or violating the laws of war. Following the IMT, the Allies held a number of additional war crimes trials in their respective zones of occupation. These military tribunals were based on Allied Control Council Law No. 10 (Law No. 10), which omitted the nexus requirement between the crime and the waging of war. Subsequent developments in international law appeared to do away with the nexus-to-war requirement. See *Fourth Report on the Draft Law Code of Offenses Against the Peace and Security of Mankind* by Doudou Thiam, Special Code Rapporteur, 38 U.N. GAOR C.4 at 56, U.N. Doc A/CN.4 398 (1986); and Diane F. Orentlicher, *Yugoslavia War Crimes Tribunal*, Focus, American Society of International Law (Summer 1993), at 3, where she asserts that the accepted view is that crimes against humanity do not require a nexus to war. Read literally, the statute of the war crimes tribunal for former Yugoslavia appears to revive the nexus requirement by stating that the tribunal shall have the power to prosecute persons responsible for certain enumerated crimes "when committed in armed conflict, whether national or international in character" (Secretary General's report, U.N. Doc S/25704, May 1993). Nevertheless, the distinguished authority on international criminal law, Theodore Meron, argues that the statute for Yugoslavia affirms that crimes against humanity do not require a nexus with international wars.

15. The principle of *nullum crimen sine lege* is "the principle that conduct does not constitute crime unless it has previously been declared to be so by

the law"; Virginia Morris and M. Christine Bourloyannis-Vrailas, *The Work of the Sixth Committee at the Forty-Eighth Session of the U.N. General Assembly*, 88 Am J. Int'l L. 343, 351 n. 43 (1994), citing *A Concise Dictionary of Law* 246 (1983). Justice Robert H. Jackson, the Nuremberg tribunal's chief prosecutor, does not appear to have shared the doubts of the Charter's authors. Referring to "crimes against humanity" in a 1945 report to the president of the United States, Jackson stated that "atrocities and persecutions on racial or religious grounds" were already outlawed under general principles of domestic law of civilized states and that [these principles] have been assimilated as a part of International Law at least since 1907." Report of Justice Robert H. Jackson to the President of the United States, released June 7, 1945, reprinted in Dep't State Bull. 1071, 1076 (June 10, 1945). Jordan Paust notes that "Jackson found support for the latter part of his statement in the de Martens clause of the 1907 Hague Convention No. IV Respecting the Laws and Customs of War on Land [Oct. 18, 1907, 36 Stat. 2277, T.S. 539] which affirmed the existence of 'principles of the law of nations' resulting 'from the laws of humanity.'" Paust, *Threats to Accountability After Nuremberg: Crimes Against Humanity, Leader Responsibility and National Fora*, 12 N.Y.L. Sch. J. Hum. Rts 5, at 6 (1995).

16. The English translation of the relevant text of the original Charter seems to require that connection only if persecution is alleged. The broader construction narrowing the use of crimes against humanity (which in the event were virtually pushed offstage) stems from the later Berlin Protocol. For the text of the Protocol see 1 IMT 17–18.

17. Ibid. at 5.

18. This controversial charge was omitted from the statutes of the international criminal tribunals for Rwanda and the former Yugoslavia.

19. Bush, supra, note 1 at 2031.

20. See, e.g., Anthony D'Amato, *The Invasion of Panama Was a Lawful Response to Tyranny*, 84 Am. J. Int'l L. 516, at 520 n.16 (1990); and Anthony D'Amato, "Foreword" to Fernando R. Teson, *Humanitarian Intervention: An Inquiry into Law and Morality*, at viii (1988). But compare Tom J. Farer, *Human Rights in Law's Empire: The Jurisprudence War*, 85 Am. J. Int'l L. 117, at 121 (1991) (explaining that an interpretation of the Charter that considers any nondefensive use of force, humanitarian or otherwise, illegal is consistent with the intent of the Charter's framers); see also Tom J. Farer, "A Paradigm of Legitimate Intervention," in L. Damrosch (ed.), *Enforcing Restraint, Collective Intervention in Internal Conflicts* (N.Y.: Council on Foreign Relations, 1993), 326 (noting "the danger to minimum world order of competitive interventions carried out by states acting in good faith").

21. See, e.g., Sarah Lyall, "Nazi Crimes Bring Man 2 Life Terms in Britain," *New York Times*, April 2, 1999, p. A5, describing case of first person in Britain to be tried under the country's 1991 War Crimes Act. The defendant, a 78-year-old emigré from Poland, was convicted for presiding over the 1942 extermination of the Jewish population of Domachevo (now in Belarus).

22. Pejic, supra note 2, at 309.

23. One exception to that limit: On the complaint of a state party on whose territory crimes subject to the court's jurisdiction have occurred, it may try nationals of a nonparty state. Rome Statute of the International Criminal Court U.N. Doc A/con.183/97 Part 2, Art. 12.

24. Art. 49, First Geneva Convention for the Amelioration of the Condition of the Wounded and Sick in Armed Forces in the Field, Aug. 12, 1949, 6 U.S.T. 3114, 75 U.N.T.S. 31; Art. 39, Second Geneva Convention for the Amelioration of the Condition of the Wounded and Sick and Shipwrecked

Members of Armed Forces at Sea, Aug. 12, 1949, 6 U.S.T. 3217, 75 U.N.T.S. 85; Art. 49, Third Geneva Convention Relative to the Treatment of Prisoners of War, Aug. 12, 1949, 6 U.S.T. 3316, 75 U.N.T.S. 135; Art. 49, Fourth Geneva Convention Relative to the Protection of Civilian Persons in Time of War, Aug. 12, 1949, 6 U.S.T. 3516, 75 U.N.T.S. 287.

25. See, e.g., *The Convention Against Torture and Other Cruel, Inhuman, or Degrading Treatment or Punishment*, in 23 Int'l Legal Materials 1027 (1984), Articles 4–8.

26. Michael P. Scharf, *Swapping Amnesty for Peace: Was There a Duty to Prosecute International Crimes in Haiti?* 31 Tex. Int'l L. J. 1, 28 (1996).

27. "[T]he constitution creates no executive prerogative to dispose of the liberty of the individual." *Valentine v. United States*, 299 U.S. 5, 7 (1936).

28. See, e.g., *In the Matter of the Requested Extradition of James Joseph Smyth*, No. CR 92152 MISC BAC United States District Court for the Northern District of California, 863 F. Supp. 1137; 1994 U.S. Dist. LEXIS 13087; 94 Daily Journal DAR 15821 September 15, 1994, Decided September 15, 1994, Filed.

29. Under the precedent-shattering opinion of the majority in the Pinochet appeal, the acts charged apparently would have to have been crimes in both parties to the agreement at the time the crime was allegedly committed.

30. See generally Tom Farer (ed.), *Transnational Crime in the Americas* (New York and London: Routledge, 1999).

31. See Jack, "Offshore Money," Blum, in Farer, *Transnational Crime in the Americas.*

32. See article 9 of the Convention Against Torture and Other Cruel, Inhuman or Degrading Treatment or Punishment, in 23 Int'l Legal Materials 1027 (1984).

33. 37 Int'l Legal Materials 999 (1998). Article 5(2) states that the "Court shall exercise jurisdiction over the crime of aggression once a provision is adopted in accordance with articles 121 and 123 defining the crime and setting out the conditions under which the Court shall exercise jurisdiction with respect to the crime," p. 1004.

34. The volume of writing on this subject should raise serious concerns for forest preservationists. A representative sampling of work might include the following: Jaime Malamud-Goti, *Transitional Governments in the Breach: Why Punish State Criminals?* 12 Hum. Rts. Q. 1 (1990); John L. Moore Jr., *Problems with Forgiveness: Granting Amnesty Under the Arias Plan in Nicaragua and El Salvador*, 43 Stan L. Rev. 733 (1991); Aryeh Neier, *What Should Be Done About the Guilty?* N.Y. Rev. of Books, Feb. 1 1990, at 32; Diane F. Orentlicher, *Settling Accounts, the Duty to Prosecute Human Rights Violations of a Prior Regime*, 100 Yale L. J. 2537 (1991); Naomi Roht-Arriaza, *State Responsibility to Investigate and Prosecute Grave Human Rights Violations in International Law*, 78 Cal. L. Rev. 451 (1990).

35. Of course with an exception to this normality in cases where the foreign law offends what the courts regard as forum state public policy.

36. One might plausibly argue that Milosevic commands greatest support when the country is most isolated, and therefore the best strategy for effecting his ultimate removal is one of reincorporating Serbia into European society, eliminating sanctions, and generally seeking to make Serbians feel that they live in an ordinary European country. In such a country, Milosevic should appear as an anomalous malignancy requiring excision.

Acronyms

AFDL	Alliance of the Democratic Forces for the Liberation of Congo
ASADHO	African Association for Human Rights
DRC	Democratic Republic of the Congo
ECACP	Environmental Change and Acute Conflicts Project
ELN	National Liberation Army (Colombia)
EU	European Union
FARC	Revolutionary Armed Forces of Colombia
FINCEN	Financial Crimes Enforcement Network
FNLA	National Front for the Liberation of Angola
ICC	International Criminal Court
ICRC	International Committee of the Red Cross
IFIs	international financial institutions
IMF	International Monetary Fund
IMT	International Military Tribunal
LRA	Lord's Resistance Army (Uganda)
MLC	Mouvement de Libération du Congo; Movement for the Liberation of Congo
MPLA	Popular Movement for the Liberation of Angola
NGOs	nongovernmental organizations
NPFL	National Patriotic Front of Liberia
NPRC	National Provisional Ruling Council (Sierra Leone)
OECD	Organization for Economic Cooperation and Development
OFAC	Office of Foreign Assets Control
OPC	Oodua People's Congress (Nigeria)
RCD	Rassemblement Congolais pour la Démocratie; Congolese Rally for Democracy

RENAMO	Mozambique National Resistance Movement
RPF	Rwandan Patriotic Front
RUF	Revolutionary United Front (Sierra Leone)
SAMs	sanctions assistance missions
SDNTs	specially designated narcotics traffickers
UNITA	National Union for the Total Independence of Angola
WTO	World Trade Organization

Selected Bibliography

Anstee, Margaret. *Orphan of the Cold War: The Inside Story of the Collapse of the Angolan Peace Process.* New York: St. Martin's Press, 1996.

Askin, Steve, and Carole Collins. "External Collusion with Kleptocracy: Can Zaire Recapture Its Stolen Wealth?" *Review of African Political Economy* 57 (1993).

Ayres, R. L. *Crime and Violence as Development Issues in Latin America and the Carribbean.* Washington D.C.: World Bank, 1998.

Becker, G. S. "Crime and Punishment: An Economic Approach." *Journal of Political Economy* 78 (1968): 169–217.

Berdal, Mats. "Disarmament and Demobilisation After Civil Wars." *Adelphi Paper* 303. Oxford: Oxford University Press for the International Institute for Strategic Studies, 1996.

Berdal, Mats, and David Keen. "Violence and Economic Agendas in Civil Wars: Some Policy Implications." *Millennium* 26, no. 3 (1997): 795–818.

Bradbury, Mark. *Rebels Without a Cause? An Exploratory Report on the Conflict in Sierra Leone.* London: Care, 1995.

Chabal, P., and J.-P. Daloz. *Africa Works: Disorder as Political Instrument.* Oxford: James Currey, 1999.

Cilliers, Jackie, and Peggy Mason (eds.). *Peace, Profit, or Plunder: The Privatization of Security in War-Torn African Societies.* Halfway House: Institute for Security Studies, 1999.

Ciment, James. *Angola and Mozambique: Postcolonial Wars in Southern Africa.* New York: Facts on File, 1997.

Clapham, Christopher. *Africa and the International System.* Cambridge: Cambridge University Press, 1996.

Collier, Paul. "Demobilisation and Insecurity: A Study in the Economics of the Transition from War to Peace." *Journal of International Development* 6, no. 3 (1994).

———. "The Economics of Civil Wars." Mimeo, Development Research Group. Washington, D.C.: World Bank, 1998.

———. "Ethnicity, Politics and Economic Performance." Mimeo, Development Research Group. Washington, D.C.: World Bank, 1998.

Collier, Paul, and Anke Hoeffler. "On Economic Causes of Civil War." *Oxford Economic Papers* 50 (1998): 563–573.

235

de Soto, Alvaro, and Graciana del Castillo. "Implementation of Comprehensive Peace Agreements: Staying the Course in El Salvador." *Global Governance* 1, no. 2 (1995).

DiIulio, J. J., Jr. "Help Wanted: Economists, Crime and Public Policy." *Journal of Economic Perspectives* 10 (1996).

Doyle, Michael, Ian Johnstone, and Robert Orr (eds.). *Keeping the Peace: Multidimensional UN Operations in Cambodia and El Salvador.* Cambridge: Cambridge University Press, 1997.

Duffield, Mark. "The Political Economy of Internal War: Asset Transfer, Complex Emergencies and International Aid." In *War and Hunger: Rethinking International Responses*, by Joanna McRae and Anthony Zwi (eds.). London: Zed, 1994.

———. "Post-Modern Conflict: Warlords, Post-Adjustment States and Private Protection." *Civil Wars* 1, no. 1 (1998).

Ehrlich, I. "Participation in Illegitimate Activities: A Theoretical and Empirical Investigation." *Journal of Political Economy* 81 (1971): 521–565.

Ellis, Stephen. "Analysing Africa's Wars." *Anthropology in Action* 3, no.3 (Winter 1996).

———. *The Mask of Anarchy: The Roots of Liberia's War.* New York: New York University Press, 1999.

Global Witness. *Corruption, War and Forest Policy: The Unsustainable Exploitation of Cambodia's Forests.* London: Global Witness Ltd., 1996.

———. *A Rough Trade: The Role of Companies and Governments in the Angolan Conflict.* London: Global Witness Ltd., 1998.

Gurr, T. R. *Minorities at Risk: A Global View of Ethnopolitical Conflicts.* Washington, D.C.: United States Institute for Peace, 1993.

———. "Why Minorities Rebel: A Global Analysis of Communal Mobilisation and Conflict Since 1945." *International Political Science Review* 14 (1993): 161–201.

Harding, Jeremy. "The Mercenary Business: 'Executive Outcomes.'" *Review of African Political Economy*, no. 71 (1997): 87–97.

Howe, Herbert. "Global Order and the Privatization of Security." *Fletcher Forum of World Affairs* 22 (Summer/Fall 1998): 1–9.

Human Rights Watch. *Angola Between War and Peace: Arms Trade and Human Rights Abuses Since the Lusaka Protocol.* New York: Human Rights Watch, 1996.

Hutchinson, Sharon E. *Neur Dilemmas: Coping with Money, War, and the State.* Berkeley: University of California Press, 1996.

Isenberg, David. *Soldiers of Fortune Ltd.: A Profile of Today's Private Sector Corporate Mercenary Firms.* Washington, D.C.: Center for Defense Information, 1997.

Kaldor, Mary. *New and Old Wars: Organized Violence in a Global Era.* Oxford: Polity Press, 1999.

Karim, Ataul, Mark Duffield, et. al. *OLS (Operation Lifeline Sudan): A Review.* Report to the United Nations Department of Humanitarian Assistance, Geneva. Birmingham, Ala.: University of Birmingham, 1996.

Karl, Terry Lynn. *The Paradox of Plenty.* Berkeley: University of California Press, 1998.

Keen, David. *The Benefits of Famine: A Political-Economy of Famine and Relief in Southwestern Sudan, 1983–1989.* Princeton: Princeton University Press, 1994.

———. "The Economic Functions of Violence in Civil Wars." *Adelphi Paper* 303. Oxford: Oxford University Press for the International Institute for Strategic Studies, 1996.

———. "Organised Chaos: Not the New World Order We Ordered." *The World Today* 52, no. 1 (1996).

King, Charles. "Ending Civil Wars." *Adelphi Paper* 308. Oxford: Oxford University Press for the International Institute for Strategic Studies, 1997.

Knack, S., and P. Keefer. "Does Social Capital Have an Economic Payoff? A Cross-Country Investigation." *Quarterly Journal of Economics* 112 (1997): 1251–1288.

Krain, Mathew W. "State-Sponsored Mass Murder: The Onset and Severity of Genocides and Policides." *Journal of Conflict Resolution* 41 (1997).

MacCrae, Joanna, and Anthony Zwi (eds.). *War and Hunger: Rethinking International Responses to Complex Emergencies.* London: Zed, 1994.

Menkhaus, Ken, and John Prendergast. *Political Economy of Post-intervention Somalia.* Issue Paper No. 3, April 1995 (Washington, D.C.: Somalia Task Force, April 1995).

Mohammed, N. "Economic Implications of Civil Wars in SSA and Economic Policies for Successful Transition from War to Peace." Paper presented at the AERC Bi-Annual Research Workshop, Harare, Zimbabwe, December 6–11, 1997.

Naylor, R. T. *Patriots and Profiteers: On Economic Warfare, Embargo Busting and State-Sponsored Crime.* Toronto: McClelland & Stewart, 1999.

Reno, William. *Corruption and State Politics in Sierra Leone.* New York: Cambridge University Press, 1995.

———. "War, Markets, and the Reconfiguration of West Africa's Weak States." *Comparative Politics* (July 1997): 493–507.

———. *Warlord Politics and African States.* Boulder, Colo.: Lynne Rienner, 1998.

Richards, Paul. *Fighting for the Rainforest: War, Youth and Resources in Sierra Leone.* London: James Currey, 1996.

Rufin, Jean-Christophe, and François Jean (eds.). *Economie des guerres civiles.* Paris: Hachette, 1996.

Shawcross, William. *Cambodia's New Deal.* Washington, D.C.: Carnegie Endowment for International Peace, 1994.

Shearer, David. "Outsourcing War," *Foreign Policy* (Fall 1998): 68–81.

———. *Private Armies and Military Intervention.* New York: Oxford University Press, 1998.

Tilly, Charles. *Coercion, Capital and European States, A.D. 990–1990.* New York: Basil Blackwell, 1990.

———. "War Making and State Making as Organized Crime." In *Bringing the State Back In,* by Peter Evans, Dietrich Rueschemeyer, and Theda Skocpol (eds.). New York: Cambridge University Press, 1985.

Turton, David (ed.). *War and Ethnicity: Global Connections and Local Violence.* New York: University of Rochester Press, 1997.

United Nations. "The Causes of Conflict and the Promotion of Durable Peace and Sustainable Development in Africa." Report of the United Nations Secretary-General to the Security Council, April 1998.

Varese, Federico. "Is Sicily the Future of Russia? Private Protection and the Rise of the Russian Mafia." *Archives Européenes de Sociologie* 35, no. 2 (1994).

Vines, Alex. *Angola and Mozambique: The Aftermath of Conflict.* London: Research Institute for the Study of Conflict and Terrorism, May/June 1995.

Wallensteen, Peter (ed.). *International Intervention: New Norms in the Post–Cold War Era?* Uppsala, Sweden: Uppsala University in Sweden, 1997.

———. *Preventing Violent Conflicts: Past Records and Future Challenges.* Uppsala, Sweden: Uppsala University in Sweden, 1998.

Wallensteen, Peter, and Margerita Sollenberg. "Armed Conflict and Regional Conflict Complexes, 1989–1997." *Journal of Peace Research* 35 (1998): 621–634.

———. "Armed Conflicts, Conflict Termination and Peace Agreements, 1986–1996." *Journal of Peace Research* 34 (1997): 339–358.

World Bank. *Post Conflict Reconstruction: The Role of the World Bank.* Washington, D.C.: World Bank, 1998.

Zartman, William I. *The Elusive Peace.* Washington, D.C.: Brookings Institute, 1995.

The Contributors

Mats Berdal is director of studies at the International Institute for Strategic Studies. Between 1997 and 2000 he was a research fellow at the Center for International Studies, Oxford University. He has published extensively in the area of international security, focusing in particular on issues related to internal conflict and the use of force in international relations after the Cold War.

Paul Collier is director of the Development Research Group of the World Bank. He is on leave from the University of Oxford, where he is professor of economics and director of the Centre for the Study of African Economies. He has published about eighty articles and books, with a predominant focus on Africa.

Richard Cornwell studied at the School for Oriental and African Studies. He emigrated to South Africa in 1974 and worked variously as a military historian, editor, researcher, and lecturer on African affairs and development studies before taking up his present position at the Institute for Security Studies as head of the Africa Early Warning Programme in 1997.

Indra de Soysa has a Ph.D. in political science from the University of Alabama and is a senior research associate at the International Peace Research Institute in Oslo, Norway. He is currently editing a bibliography on disarmament and conversion. He has published recently in the *Journal of Conflict Resolution, American Sociological Review,* and the *Environmental Change and Security Project Report.*

Mark Duffield is professor of development, democratization, and conflict at the Institute for Politics and International Studies, University of

Leeds, U.K. His fields of interest include the political economy of internal war, the organization and management of systemwide humanitarian operations, conflict resolution, and social reconstruction. He has worked in both Africa and the Balkans.

Tom Farer is professor and dean of the Graduate School of International Studies at Denver University; former president of the Inter-American Commission on Human rights and the University of New Mexico; legal consultant to UNOSOM II; and former fellow of the Carnegie Endowment for International Peace, the Council on Foreign Relations, and the Smithsonian's Wilson Center. His latest book is *Transnational Crime in the Americas.*

Virginia Gamba is the head of the Arms Management Programme at the Institute for Security Studies in South Africa. Past postings included director of the Disarmament and Conflict Resolution Project at the United Nations Institute for Disarmament Research in Geneva and program officer for arms control, disarmament, and demobilization at the John D. and Catherine T. MacArthur Foundation of Chicago. She is an Argentine national.

David Keen is the author of *The Benefits of Famine: A Political Economy of Famine and Relief in Southwestern Sudan, 1983–89; The Economic Functions of Violence in Civil Wars; The Kurds in Iraq: How Safe Is Their Haven Now?;* and *Refugees—Rationing the Right to Life.* He is a lecturer in development studies at the London School of Economics and Political Science. He has completed a doctorate in sociology at Oxford University.

David M. Malone has been president of the International Peace Academy since 1998. He has served as Canada's deputy permanent representative at the UN and as director general of the Policy, International Organizations, and Global Issues Bureaus in the Canadian Foreign and Trade Ministry. He is an adjunct professor of law at New York University.

Musifiky Mwanasali specializes in political, economic, and security issues in Central Africa. A faculty member at Sarah Lawrence College, he served as a consultant to the UN Standing Advisory Committee on Security Questions in Central Africa. He is currently an information analyst at the Conflict Management Center at the Organization of African Unity.

Samuel D. Porteous is the director of the Business Intelligence Services Group of Kroll Associates Canada, headquartered in Toronto. A former member of the Canadian Foreign Service and the Canadian Security Intelligence Service, he has published widely on intelligence, organized crime, and international business issues, including a major study on the impact of organized crime on Canada and the 1998 book *Economic Intelligence and National Security,* which he coauthored.

William Reno is an associate professor of political science at Northwestern University. He is the author of *Corruption and State Politics in Sierra Leone* and *Warlord Politics and African States* (1998, Lynne Rienner). His current research considers why some violent commercial organizations become businesses and others become mafias, and if some become states.

David Shearer is a research associate at the International Institute for Strategic Studies. He was recently a senior humanitarian advisor to the United Nations stationed in Yugoslavia and Albania during the Kosovo crisis. Previously he has worked in Rwanda and Liberia for the UN humanitarian office and has headed the Save the Children Fund (U.K.) operations in Rwanda, Somalia, Iraq, and Sri Lanka.

Index

AFDL. *See* Alliance of the Democratic Forces for the Liberation of Congo
Africa: lack of personal security, 53–54; post-colonial fractionalization of, 164; transborder trade, 77, 79. *See also individual countries*
African Association for Human Rights (ASADHO), 142
Aid, humanitarian, 86, 127; absorptive capacity for, 107; effect of transborder trade on, 76–77; impact on course of conflict, 189–190, 194–198, 201–202; mobilization of populations, 191–192; the politicization of, 199–201; positive potential of, 37–38; as short-term economic function of conflict, 30; theft and extortion of, 36, 132(n8), 192–193, 196; as Western intervention, 197–199
Albania, private use of state assets, 46
Algeria, aggression against civilians, 33–34
Alliance of the Democratic Forces for the Liberation of Congo (AFDL), 141, 153(nn2, 5), 193
American Mineral Fields, 148
Amnesties, 227
Angola: commercial complicity in war economy, 84–85; government

structure of, 167–168; homogeneity of warring groups, 147–148; income from diamond trade, 195; industrial security, 57; natural resources as cause of conflict, 115; sanctions against, 16(n15); transborder economic linkages, 74; UNITA control of resources, 5. *See also* Arms, Angola; Diamond industry
Annan, Kofi, 15(n12), 168
Arafat, Yassir, 39
Arkan, 13, 34, 229
Armenia, control by paramilitaries, 52
Arms: difficulty in controlling, 160–164; targeted economic sanctions, 187(n9)
Arms, Angola: control of, 160–164, 171(n4); funding for, 166–167; internal and external movement of, 159–160; sources and quantities of, 157–159
ASADHO. *See* African Association for Human Rights
Asia, controlling clandestine finance, 183
Assets: private use of, 46–47
Assets, personal and national, 179–181, 188(n13); electronic tracking of, 177–179; freezing or blocking, 174–175; major financial institutions, 182–184; war crimes prosecutions and, 223–224

243

244   *Index*

About the Book

Current scholarship on civil wars and transitions from war to peace have made significant progress in understanding the political dimensions of internal conflict, but the economic motivations spurring political violence have been comparatively neglected. This path-breaking volume identifies the economic and social factors underlying the perpetuation of civil wars, exploring as well the economic incentives and disincentives available to international actors seeking to restore peace to war-torn societies.

The authors consider the economic rationality of conflict for belligerents, the economic strategies that elites use to sustain their positions, and in what situations elites find war to be more profitable than peace. They strive consistently for policy relevance in both their analysis and their prescriptions.

Mats Berdal is director of studies at the International Institute for Strategic Studies. **David M. Malone** is president of the International Peace Academy.